A Chanticleer Press Edition

Taylor's Guide to Bulbs

Houghton Mifflin Company Boston 1986

Contributors

Gordon P. DeWolf, Jr., Ph.D.
Coordinator of the Horticulture Program at Massachusetts Bay Community College in Wellesley Hills, Massachusetts, Gordon P. DeWolf revised and edited the fifth edition of *Taylor's Encyclopedia of Gardening,* upon which this guide is based. He also prepared most of the essays in this guide, and edited the flower descriptions. DeWolf previously served as Horticulturist at the Arnold Arboretum at Harvard University and is a frequent contributor to *Horticulture* magazine.

George Harmon Scott
Consultant for this book, George Harmon Scott has been writing about gardening for the *Los Angeles Times Home Magazine* for more than ten years. He is also the author of *Bulbs: How to Select, Grow, and Enjoy* (HP Books, 1982). Scott lives in southern California, where he is an avid gardener.

Barbara Damrosch
A landscape designer, Barbara Damrosch has written extensively on the subject for *Horticulture* and other magazines. She wrote the essays on garden design and cut flowers in this guide. She is also the author of *Theme Gardens* (Workman, 1982).

Mary Ann McGourty
Author of the essay on buying bulbs, Mary Ann McGourty is the proprietor of Hillside Gardens, a nursery in Norfolk, Connecticut, that specializes in uncommon perennials and perennial-garden design. She and her husband, Fred, grow some 700 kinds of perennials in their garden.

Katharine D. Widin
Author of the essay on pests and diseases, Katharine D. Widin holds an M.S. and Ph.D. in plant pathology from the University of Minnesota. Currently Widin operates a private consulting firm, Plant Health Associates, in Stillwater, Minnesota.

William Aplin

A photographer specializing in horticulture, William Aplin is a frequent contributor to *Sunset* magazine and to HP and Ortho books.

Gillian Beckett

Contributor Gillian Beckett is a well-known British horticultural photographer.

Derek Fell

A widely published garden writer, Derek Fell has also photographed thousands of plants. His publications include *Annuals,* an HP Book.

Charles Marden Fitch

Media specialist, horticulturist, and photographer, Charles Marden Fitch lives in Westchester County, New York. Most of his plant and flower pictures are taken in his own garden.

Pamela J. Harper

A well-known horticultural writer and lecturer, Pamela J. Harper has also taken more than 80,000 photographs of plants and gardens.

Walter H. Hodge

A leading botanist, Walter H. Hodge has photographed plants and animals throughout the world. He is the author of *The Audubon Society Book of Wildflowers.*

Joy Spurr

A nature photographer for more than 30 years, Joy Spurr manages a photographic agency in Seattle, Washington. Her photographs have been published in numerous books and magazines.

Steven M. Still

A contributor to *Taylor's Guide to Perennials,* Steven M. Still is a professor of horticulture at The Ohio State University in Columbus. He is a prolific photographer.

George Taloumis

A horticultural writer and photographer, George Taloumis has written a gardening column in *The Boston Globe* for more than 30 years. He is a frequent contributor to *The New York Times* and *Flower and Garden.*

Library of Congress
Cataloguing-in-Publication Data
Main entry under title:
Taylor's guide to bulbs.
(Taylor's guides to gardening)
Based on: Taylor's encyclopedia of gardening.
4th edition. 1961.
Includes index.
1. Bulbs. I. Taylor's encyclopedia of
gardening. II. Title: Guide to bulbs.
III. Series.
SB425.T38   1986   635.9'44   85-30508
ISBN 0-395-40449-5 (pbk.)

Prepared and produced by Chanticleer Press,
Inc., New York
Cover photograph: *Hyacinthus* hybrid
'Wedgewood' by Charles Marden Fitch

Designed by Massimo Vignelli

Color reproductions by Reprocolor
International, s.r.l., Milan, Italy
Printed and bound by Dai Nippon, Tokyo, Japan
Typeset by American–Stratford Graphic Services, Inc.

First Edition.

00   10   9   8   7   6   5   4   3   2   1

Contents

Preface

There are few sights as lovely as the first crocus of the year, peeking up out of the frozen landscape of winter—and few surprises as happy as the sight of a bowl of 'Paper-white' Narcissus blooming indoors on a winter's day. The flowers that we know as bulbs—tulips, daffodils, crocuses, irises, lilies, and many others—contain a hidden world of color, lying beneath the ground, waiting to be realized. Fortunately for us, bulbs are not only beautiful, but also easy to grow, lending themselves to a wide variety of terrains and performing well for anyone—from the novice to the most expert of gardeners.

In this guide you will find everything you need to know to bring these hidden worlds to life, with a bounty of blooms that will take you, if you plan correctly, through the entire year.

Bulbs in History

The origin of flowers grown from bulbs is part of world history, for the individual species, cultivars, and hybrids that are so popular today are native to countries and regions throughout the globe. Thus, a garden planned with a variety of bulbs will represent a sampler of world cultures.

For example, the crocus originated in the Mediterranean region, and many thousand years ago it was a flower greatly valued by the Minoans, the aesthetically advanced people who lived on the island of Crete before the Golden Age of Greece.

The iris had a place in the ancient history of Syria and Egypt, as well as in the French crusades. And the lily has long been the artist's symbol for purity; its history suggests an origin in ancient Sumeria. From other parts of the world come other bulb plants: Narcissus, or the common daffodil, come from Southern Europe, while gladiolus and amaryllis come from South Africa, and still other bulbs are native to the Americas, Eastern Europe, and Asia.

Perhaps the flower we most often think of as a bulb is the tulip. Although native to Turkey, it was brought back to Europe and quickly took the fancy of Holland. Tulips were at first considered great rarities and sold at extravagant prices; but the Dutch soon became tulip growers and suppliers to the world—a tradition that continues today.

The spread of bulbs through the world parallels the history of travel itself. The crusaders and explorers carried bulbs as precious cargo back to Europe, as the pharaohs did to Egypt. And when the Mennonites came to America, they brought tulip bulbs with them. For good luck, tulips were represented in the hex signs of the Pennsylvania Dutch, finding a place in the folk art of this country.

Gardening with Bulbs

The long history of bulbs should not intimidate the inexperienced gardener. By following a few simple rules, even a beginner will have a garden to be proud of.

First, remember never to let your bulbs stand in water, or they will rot. Make sure that you plant them in rich, well-drained soil, in a place where they will have full sun while their leaves are green. While the bulbs are growing, be sure they have plenty of water; even when they are dormant, they should not be allowed to dry out entirely. Mulch your bulbs in winter and allow the mulch to decompose in place; this will improve the soil. If you have problem visitors—mice, moles, or chipmunks—plant your bulbs in wire cages in the ground to keep the creatures out. And above all, remember that a bulb is a magnificent energy machine, producing and storing this year all the food it needs to grow and bloom next year. So never remove the leaves from your bulbs until they have yellowed and died naturally.

With these few rules in mind, you are now ready to enter the world of bulbs. This guide will take you there in high style—with lavish color photographs, full descriptive information, and comprehensive advice from the experts on how to make the most of your gardening experience.

How to Use

Growing bulbs is one of the most exciting and delightful of gardening experiences. Bulbs come in an almost endless array of shapes and colors, with enough varieties to please anyone, and every year nurseries introduce still more stunning cultivars to the market. Bulbs are versatile: Not only do they beautify an outdoor garden, but also, planted in pots, they add color and life to an indoor landscape as well.

Whether you live in northern Oregon or southern Florida there are countless bulbs just right for your garden. And there is no mystery to growing them. Designed to answer the needs of both amateurs and seasoned gardeners, this book makes it easy to cultivate a garden that suits your individual needs and tastes. It can also help you identify plants that you see when you visit gardens and nurseries.

If you have never planted bulbs before, you will find all the information you need to grow them in this guide. If you have been growing bulbs for years, you will discover new varieties and fresh ways to use old favorites.

How This Book Is Organized

This guide contains three types of material: color plates, flower descriptions, and expert articles that guide you through every aspect of growing bulbs.

The Color Plates

More than 400 of the most popular and interesting bulbs in cultivation today are illustrated in the color plates. The color section begins with the Visual Key, which shows at a glance how the color section is arranged; the Color Key then sets forth the variations in hue that occur within each group of bulbs. For example, the group called "white flowers" includes some flowers that appear white but may, in fact, be cream-colored, pale yellow, or pale blue.

The illustrations begin with a brief introductory section that will acquaint you with some of the various kinds of structures—true bulbs, corms, and tuberous roots—found in the guide. The color plates illustrating the flowers follow. These are arranged in four convenient groups: Narcissus, Tulips, True Lilies and Daylilies, and Other Bulbs. Within these groups, the illustrations are arranged by color and shape, to help you select the right plants for the visual effect you want to achieve in your garden.

If you are a novice, browse through the color plates looking for plants that appeal to you. Even if you are unfamiliar with their common and scientific names, you will no doubt encounter many that you have seen before. To find out more about these familiar plants, turn to the page numbers provided in the captions.

Captions

The captions that accompany the color plates provide essential

This Guide

nformation at a glance: whether the plants are hardy or tender, how much sunshine they need, and when they bloom. The captions also give the scientific name of the plant, its height, and the length or width of individual flowers or flower clusters. Finally, a page reference directs you to the description of your plant in the Encyclopedia of Bulbs.

Encyclopedia of Bulbs

Here you will find a full description of each flower shown in the color plates. These flower descriptions are based on the authoritative *Taylor's Encyclopedia of Gardening,* revised and updated for this guide. The descriptions are arranged alphabetically by genus and cross-referenced by page number to the color plates. (If you are unfamiliar with scientific names, you can easily find a plant by looking up its common name in the comprehensive index, which begins on page 456.)

Each description begins with a heading indicating the genus name, followed by the common and scientific family names. Pronunciation of the scientific name precedes a brief overview of the genus.

Genus

This section presents the overall characteristics of the garden plants in the genus and tells you the origin of the genus name. The How to Grow section outlines broad growing requirements for the genus.

Species, Hybrids, Cultivars, and Classes

After the genus description, you will find detailed information on each of the flowers included in the color plates and additional information about popular cultivars.

Each species description includes the plant's country of origin and the zone to which it is hardy. (You can find what zone you live in by referring to the map on page 28.) A black-and-white illustration next to a species description depicts the mature plant, and is also representative of other plants in the genus. For three of the major groups—the true lilies, narcissus, and tulips—hybrids are divided by horticulture societies and nursery professionals into various classes based on similarities in the flowers' shape, size, geographical or botanical origin, or other characteristics. Within each of these three groups, descriptions of the hybrid classes follow the species descriptions.

Gardening Articles

Written by experts, these articles explain every aspect of gardening with bulbs—how to prepare the soil, when to plant, how to force bulbs, and other important cultivation information, as well as tips on designing your garden.

In the section on botany, beginners will learn how plants reproduce and the importance of scientific names; the pages devoted to

How to Use This Guide

anatomy describe how to identify the parts of a flower and explain how bulbs mature and grow. The article on keeping a garden diary offers practical advice on keeping track of what you plant and when and where you plant it. Tips on working with cut flowers provide instruction in flower arranging. The gardening calendar provides a practical schedule for monthly maintenance activities geared to the area in which you live. Should you run into difficulty, the pest and disease chart will help you identify your problem, then cure it. Common-sense advice on buying bulbs includes a list of bulb sources. Finally, all the technical terms you may encounter are defined in the glossary.

Using the Flower Chart
A special chart provides you with instant information about 130 of the most popular and interesting plants included in the guide. This chart is designed to help you solve gardening problems at a glance. Say, for example, that you live in Virginia, and are looking for some small, spring-blooming bulbs to use as a border along your sunny front walk. Turn to the chart and look for flowers that bloom in the spring. By then reading across to the height section, you will quickly see that several types of anemones, crocuses, and irises are small, growing to less than 12 inches, and that they like plenty of sun. Now read the zone information, and you will see that several varieties will do nicely in your part of the country. The chart also gives you the page number of the flower description; you then turn quickly to the text to read about which of these plants you may want to grow, and from there to the color illustration.

Using the Color Plates to Plan Your Garden
Bulbs come in a wide array of colors, and today it is almost impossible to learn about every new hybrid or cultivar that is introduced. In this guide, the most popular varieties are illustrated. As you plan your garden, you can narrow your choices by referring to these typical garden plants.
First, decide what colors you want in your garden and when you want them to come up. You may, for example, design an island bed composed of alternating yellow and blue flowers. In each of the sections in the color plates, turn to the photographs of blue flowers, and choose those that appeal to you. Check the caption to see when they bloom and how tall they are. Follow the same procedure for your yellow flowers. Finally, turn to the flower descriptions and make sure that the plants you have chosen are hardy in your zone.

Basic Botany

Certain plants have the ability to store all the food they need for growth in a compact package. For simplicity's sake, these plants are commonly lumped together under the heading of "bulbs," although this group actually includes several different kinds of plants: true bulbs, corms, tubers, tuber-corms, tuberous roots, and rhizomes. All of these kinds are represented in this book, with the exception of the tubers. The ability to store food makes these plants well suited to horticulture, for bulbs and bulblike structures are durable, easy to handle, and sure to produce flowers unless they are badly mistreated.

Cycles of Growth
Most of the bulbs and bulblike plants in this book are perennials: Their periods of growth and flowering are followed by periods of dormancy; they die back to ground level at the end of each growing season, but produce new shoots and flowers in succeeding seasons.

Origins
Many of the plants included in this book are native to the Mediterranean region, where winters are moist but too cold for active growth, while summers are very hot and dry. For these plants, growth is possible for only a few weeks or months in spring and fall. Other plants are woodland species of the temperate zone that bloom and grow only in spring, when temperatures are warm enough to inspire the activity of pollinating insects, but before the forest canopy leafs out and closes overhead, blocking out sunlight.

Bulbs and bulblike structures are a perfect adaptation to cope with such demanding annual cycles. These plants can thus endure periods of unfavorable weather, when growth and flowering are impossible; during the short season available to them, these plants—with their package of growing materials at the ready—can bloom and grow quickly.

Bulbs and Bulblike Structures
Before setting out to plant your garden, it is wise to learn to distinguish among the various bulblike forms that these plants take. Doing this will help you to plan your garden better and to maintain it well.

A true bulb is an enlarged and modified bud. It contains a vertical, foreshortened stem and has leaves crowded so closely together along the length of the stem that they form a dense, almost spherical mass. The leaves are scalelike and swollen with stored food material. Lilies, narcissus, alliums, and tulips have bulbs that are produced below the surface of the soil, while the bulbs of *Hippeastrum* and *Crinum* develop at or above the soil surface.

Corms are solid, vertical, swollen stems. At the top is a bud that produces the flowers and leaves, while on the sides are lateral buds that may form small offsets, or cormels. A corm is an annual structure; all of its stored food is used to produce flowers and fruit

Basic Botany

True Bulbs	A true bulb is an enlarged, modified bud containing a vertical stem surrounded by a dense mass of scale-like leaves. The leaves are swollen with stored food.	Shown from left to right are bulbs of lily, narcissus, and tulip.
Corms	A corm is a solid, vertical stem resembling a bulb, with a bud at the top that produces the flowers and leaves, and lateral buds that form small offsets.	Shown from left to right are corms of crocus, gladiolus, and freesia.
Tuberous Roots	A tuberous root is a swollen root used for food storage. They usually lie just beneath the soil's surface. During growth, plants take in nutrients from fibrous feeder roots.	The tuberous roots of dahlia are shown.
Rhizomes	A rhizome is a swollen horizontal stem at or just below the soil's surface. Roots grow downward from its underside, while the apex produces stems, leaves, and flowers.	Shown is a canna rhizome.
Tuber-Corms	A tuber-corm is a disk- or top-shaped structure with one or more buds on the upper surface and roots below. Tuber-corms are perennial, increasing in size from year to year.	From left to right are tuber-corms of tuberous begonia, ranunculus, and anemone.

These drawings show
representative examples
of the different kinds of
structures collectively
known as bulbs.

Basic Botany

Tuberous Root

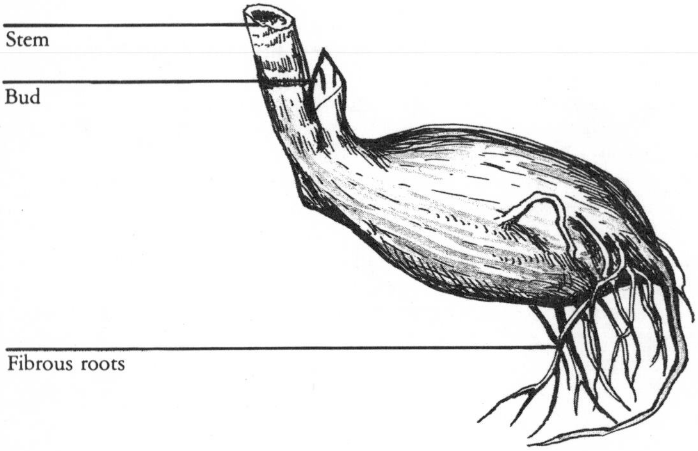

Stem

Bud

Fibrous roots

Bulb

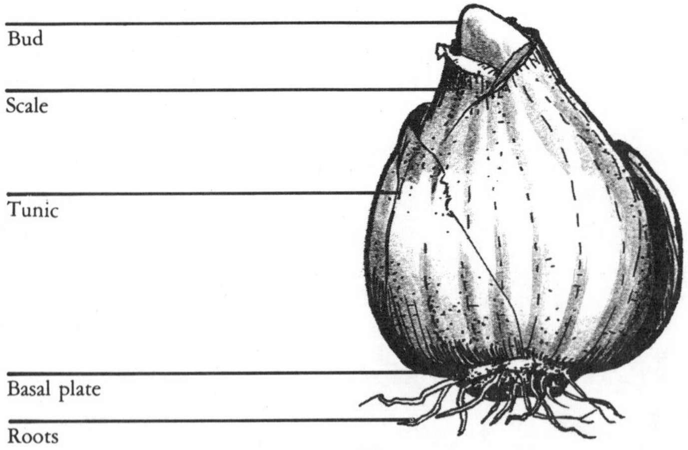

Bud

Scale

Tunic

Basal plate

Roots

nd to begin the growth of a new replacement corm. Replacement orms develop from lateral buds, and have roots that pull the new orms down into the soil as the old one decays. Plants with corms nclude *Crocus, Erythronium,* and *Gladiolus.*

A rhizome is also a modified stem, but it is horizontal rather than ertical, and may lie in the soil or at the surface. Roots grow ownward from the underside of a rhizome, while the apex roduces stems, leaves, and flowers. *Agapanthus* and *Canna* ave rhizomes.

Another kind of food-storage arrangement is provided by tuberous oots, such as those of dahlias. Tuberous roots lie just beneath the urface of the soil and bear a portion of an old stem at one end. Around the base of this stem are buds that will develop into new lants; new tuberous roots also form at this spot. During the rowing season, these plants take in nutrients through fibrous eeder roots.

Tuber-corms are disk-shaped or top-shaped structures bearing one or more buds on the upper surface and usually with an annual crop of oots on the lower surface. Unlike corms, they are perennial ructures, gradually increasing in size with the passing years. Cyclamens and tuberous begonias have tuber-corms.

Not all bulblike structures are formed underground. A few plants, uch as the Tiger Lily (*Lilium lancifolium*), have bulbils—food-orage structures borne in the angles of leaves. Bulbils fall to the round and germinate, like seeds, to produce new plants.

The Parts of a Flower

A typical flower is composed of sepals, petals, stamens, and one or more pistils. The sepals, collectively termed the calyx, are the utermost parts of a flower. In many plants, such as the wood orrels (*Oxalis*), the sepals are green and leaflike, but in most plants n this book they are brightly colored like the petals. The petals lie ust inside the sepals, and are collectively known as the corolla. In a ew plants, like *Anemone* and *Eranthis,* the petals are missing, and the epals take their place as the colorful part of the flower.

The sepals and petals together are known as the perianth, and the arts of the perianth are called perianth segments. When both the epals and petals are present and are alike, they are often called epals. In daffodils and a few other plants there is a crownlike xtension of the perianth; this is called the corona.

The male reproductive organs of a flower are the stamens, each one onsisting of a slender filament bearing a pollen-containing anther. The stamens are found inside the ring of petals. The pistil is the emale reproductive organ, and is located at the center of the flower. A pistil is composed of three parts—the ovary, containing one or more undeveloped seeds, a columnar style, and the stigma, a sticky urface to which pollen grains adhere during pollination.

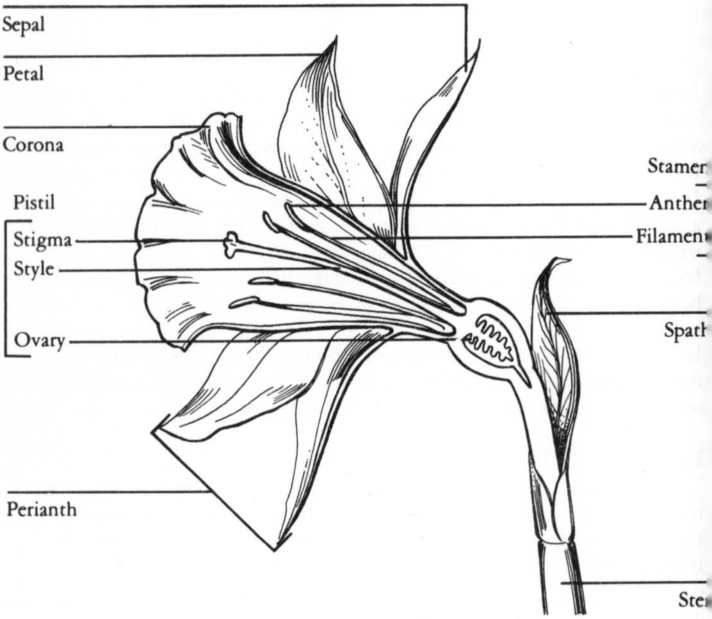

Sepal
Petal
Corona
Pistil
Stigma
Style
Ovary
Perianth

Stamen
Anther
Filament
Spath
Ste

Symmetry

When the petals and sepals of a flower are evenly spaced, like the spokes of a wheel, around the center, the flower is said to be radially symmetrical, or regular. But if the perianth segments are differently shaped, so that the flower is not radially symmetrical, the flower is then termed bilaterally symmetrical.

A good example of a regular flower is that of a crocus; the flowers of *Gladiolus* and *Sprekelia* are bilaterally symmetrical. In a few genera, such as *Canna,* no perianth segment is exactly like another; these flowers are truly irregular.

Flower Clusters

Many flowers, like those of tulips, are solitary, borne alone at the end of a stalk. Others, however, are found in clusters of varying arrangements. Among the most common kinds of arrangements are the umbel, the spike, and the raceme.

In an umbel, the stalks of all the flowers arise from a central stalk at a single point; the flower clusters of *Allium* and *Hippeastrum* are umbels.

In a spike, the flowers are borne along a central stalk and do not have smaller stalks of their own; the flowers of *Gladiolus* are borne in spikes.

In a raceme—seen in *Hyacinthus* and *Lilium,* among others—the flowers grow along a single stalk, but each one has a smaller stalk, or pedicel, of its own.

Leaves

The leaves of most plants in this book are basal—appearing at or near soil level from the base of the central stalk or from the top of the bulb or corm. Leaves that are borne along a stalk—as in *Lilium* and *Fritillaria*—may be arranged in one of three different ways.

Two leaves that form a pair, located opposite each other at the same point on the stalk, are termed opposite. If more than two leaves are attached at the same point, then the leaves are said to be whorled. If the leaves are attached singly along the stalk, each one at a different level and none opposite another, the leaves are considered alternate.

English and Scientific Names

Most of the more familiar garden plants have English names. These names are easy to remember, and the average gardener maintains a vocabulary of scores or hundreds of them, from African Lily to Zephyr Lily. But English names are not standardized; a single species or cultivar may be known by different names in different areas, or a single English name may be applied to more than one plant. For example, the name Turk's-Cap Lily is given to *Lilium superbum* in the northeastern states, to *Lilium Michauxii* in the Southeast, and to *Lilium Martagon* in Britain.

Basic Botany

Umbel	A flower cluster in which the individual flower stalks grow from the same point	

Raceme	A long, tall cluster in which individual flowers are borne on short stalks	
Spike	An elongated flower cluster that bears individual flowers without stalks	
Solitary	Borne singly or alone on a stalk, and not in clusters	

Scientific names avoid this confusion by providing a universal system of nomenclature, accepted and understood throughout the world. While there may be some uncertainty about what a "Turk's-Cap Lily" is, there is no doubt which plant is meant by the name *Lilium superbum.*

According to this system (devised in the 18th century by the Swedish botanist Carolus Linnaeus), every plant is assigned to a species, and every species to a genus. The name of the plant consists of two words, the first one (the generic name) being that of the genus, the second (the specific epithet) that of the species. A generic name can be used for only one group of species in the Plant Kingdom, and a specific epithet only once in a particular genus. Both the generic name and the specific epithet are italicized, and the generic name always begins with a capital letter. The specific epithet begins with a small letter unless it is based on a generic name, as in *Narcissus Bulbocodium;* or the name of a person, as in *Erythronium Hendersonii;* or when it is derived from a name in a modern language, as in *Camassia Quamash,* where both *Camassia* and *Quamash* come from the Chinook Indian name for this plant. Scientific names may seem formidable at first, but they are not difficult to learn and are worth knowing, because only by using scientific names can one be absolutely sure what plant one is talking about or buying. In fact most of us are already using scientific names. When we speak of chrysanthemums, irises, begonias, cyclamens, or dahlias, we are using generic names as comfortably as if they were long-established English words. And the words "lily" and "tulip" are not far removed from *Lilium* and *Tulipa,* the scientific names of these two groups of plants.

Variety, Form, Cultivar, or Hybrid?

Many beginning gardeners—and indeed many who can claim a score of seasons in their backyards—are not clear in their minds about what the differences are between a variety, a cultivar, a form, and a hybrid. Here again, learning a few basics will help you to know what to expect from your garden plants.

Varieties

A variety is a naturally occurring variant of a species, usually with a different geographical origin from that of the typical species plant. These variants are often called subspecies by some botanists. The scientific name of a variety contains the abbreviation "var." An example is *Allium cyathophorum* var. *Farreri,* which is found in the wild in Kansu Province of China. The typical *Allium cyathophorum* is found in central Asia. Some botanists omit the abbreviation "var.," and the plant will then have a three-part name: *Allium cyathophorum Farreri.*

Growth Cycles

True Bulb: Narcissus

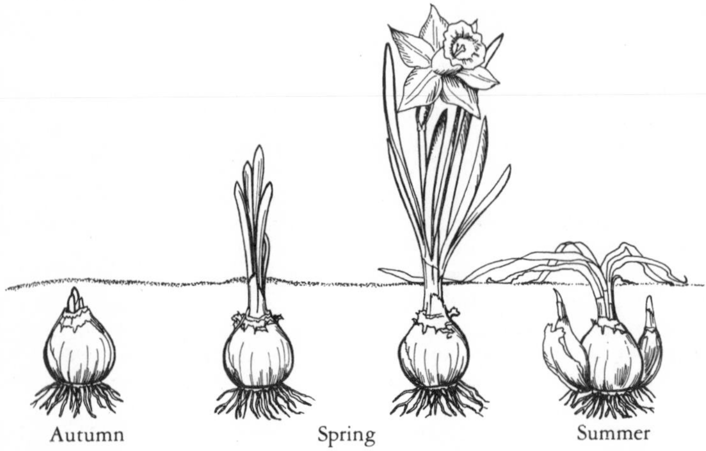

Autumn   Spring   Summer

Corm: Gladiolus

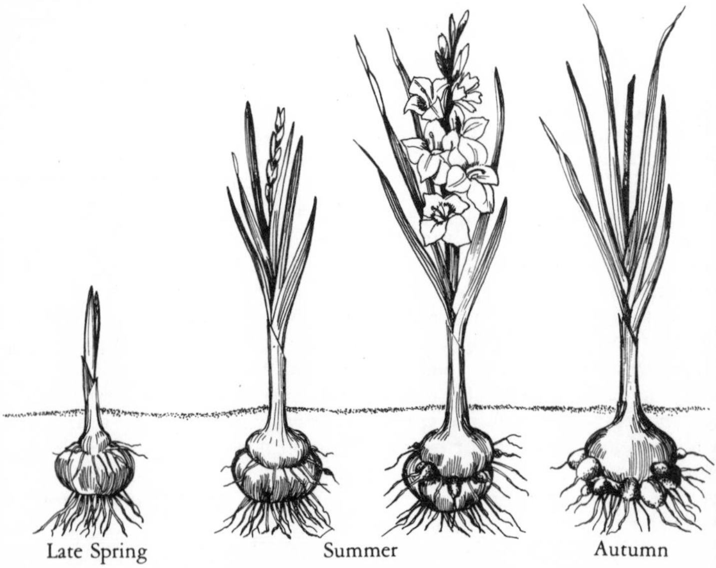

Late Spring   Summer   Autumn

Bulbs and bulblike structures have distinct stages of growth, bloom, and dormancy in their annual life cycles; cycles vary according to bulb type, species, climate, and planting time. These drawings represent growth habits of four different structures: a true bulb, a corm, a tuberous root, and a rhizome.

Tuberous Root: Dahlia

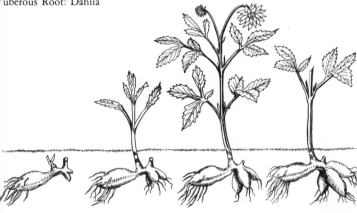

Spring   Summer   Autumn

Rhizome: Canna

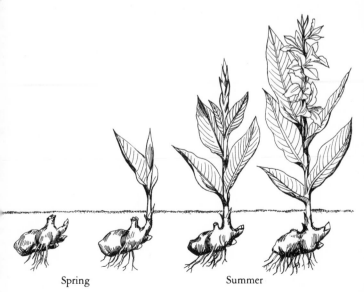

Spring   Summer

Forms
A form is a variant of a species that is not separated geographically from the typical plant. For example, if a species normally has red flowers, a white-flowered form found in the same region would be designated *forma alba*.

Cultivars
Plants in cultivation are often bred with the intention, on the part of the breeder, of enhancing or minimizing certain inherited traits, such as color, fragrance, hardiness, size, or habit of growth. These selected plants or groups of plants are known as cultivars, because they develop under cultivation. (They are also commonly but incorrectly called varieties.)

Cultivars are preserved through vegetative propagation; in some instances, especially in the case of many garden annuals and vegetables, they may be an inbred line of plants that now invariably reproduce from seed.

The name of a cultivar is added to the end of the scientific name of a plant and set off by single quotation marks; the cultivar name is not italicized. An example is *Gloriosa superba* 'Lutea', a cultivar of *Gloriosa superba*.

Hybrids
A hybrid is the result of a cross between two plants belonging to different species, cultivars, varieties, or even—very occasionally—different genera. Modern hybrids are often more disease-resistant than the parent plants, or may have larger or more colorful blooms. The symbol × in a scientific name indicates that the plant is a hybrid. An example is *Crinum × Powellii,* a cross between *Crinum bulbispermum* and *C. Moorei.* Many hybrid plants are sterile; others are fertile but produce offspring that differ from their parents. In most cases it is thus necessary to reproduce hybrids by vegetative means.

Getting Started

Few gardening experiences match the magic and ease of planting bulbs. Whether you have a large garden or a small one, or even just a sunny windowsill, there are countless bulbs that you can grow successfully. Follow a few simple rules, and you can have spectacular displays of color any season of the year—cheerful narcissus to brighten a dreary winter or stately lilies to grace the summertime.

Tender and Hardy Bulbs

All the structures known collectively as bulbs—true bulbs, corms, tuberous roots, and tuber-corms—are either tender or hardy, designations that determine their use in the garden. Tender bulbs are those that cannot stand cold temperatures at any time of year and therefore cannot be left in the ground during winter except in tropical or subtropical climates. In the North, some summer-flowering bulbs, like gladiolus or dahlias, are grown in the garden like annuals: planted in spring and dug up in fall. Other tender bulbs are grown in the house or in a greenhouse so they will flower indoors in winter.

Hardy bulbs are those that need a period of cold during their dormancy. In the North, most are grown in the garden like perennials—left in the ground all winter. In climates where winters are warm, however, hardy bulbs cannot be left outdoors year round, since temperatures may never drop low enough to induce the dormancy the plant requires. When a plant is dormant it can survive considerable cold, the exact amount depending on the specific plant, but none in active growth can survive temperatures that regularly go below freezing.

Hardiness Zones

Since hardiness is a measure of the amount of cold a plant can stand, a plant hardiness map is based only on average minimum temperatures. The United States and Canada have been divided into ten hardiness zones, starting at the far north (Zone 1), where the average minimum temperature falls below $-50°$ F, to the southern tips of Florida and California, where the average minimum temperature range is 30 to $40°$ F. To find the hardiness zone for your own area, consult the map on page 28.

Hardiness is a relative thing. Since it is based on average minimum temperatures, a winter much colder than normal could kill a plant that is otherwise hardy in your zone. But there is usually a fair amount of leeway. An individual species will survive and flower at least one hardiness zone farther north than its indicated zone if you plant it in a sheltered, sunny spot with a southern exposure in humus-rich, well-drained soil and give it a good organic mulch. But only the hardiest will survive in the least desirable conditions: an unprotected area, heavy shade, poor drainage, and no mulch.

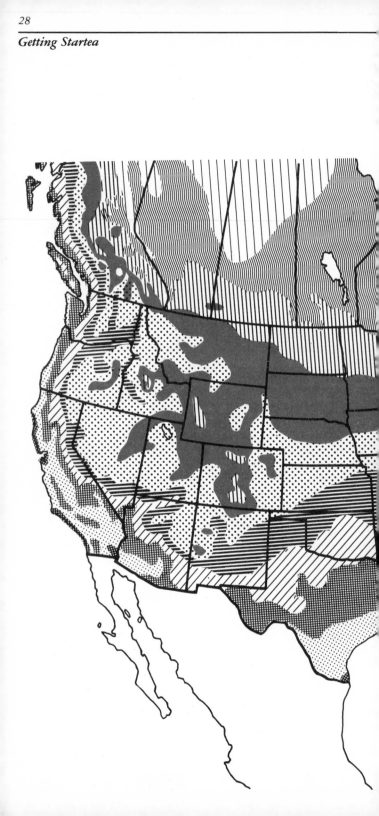

This map was compiled by the United States Department of Agriculture as a broad guideline to temperature extremes in your area.

The key below gives you the average minimum temperatures of the ten zones. Determine if your area corresponds to its zone allocation by comparing your coldest temperatures with those given in the key.

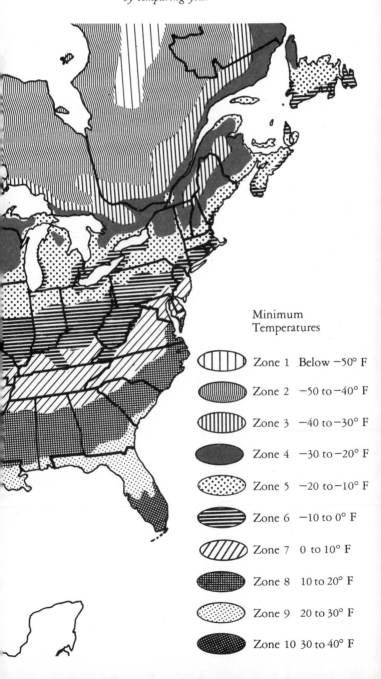

Minimum Temperatures

Zone 1 Below −50° F

Zone 2 −50 to −40° F

Zone 3 −40 to −30° F

Zone 4 −30 to −20° F

Zone 5 −20 to −10° F

Zone 6 −10 to 0° F

Zone 7 0 to 10° F

Zone 8 10 to 20° F

Zone 9 20 to 30° F

Zone 10 30 to 40° F

Choosing a Site

When choosing a site to plant bulbs, keep in mind their needs for warmth and sunlight. You should also provide protection from north and west winds and a humus-rich, well-drained soil.

Heat and Cold

Heat radiates from a warm area to a colder area. Cold air is heavier than warm air and behaves like water—it flows down a slope, is deflected by obstructions, and accumulates like a puddle in a depression. In the spring an exposed garden is slow to warm up because the heat in the soil radiates upward to the atmosphere at night. A garden in a depression is covered each night by a puddle of cold air that absorbs heat from the ground and prevents the soil from retaining warmth.

Sunlight Requirements

Bulbs need the warmth of sunlight to trigger their growth cycle. And after flowering, they need sun on their leaves to manufacture food so they can develop buds for next year's flowers. Once the blossoms have faded, never cut off the leaves, but allow them to mature and die back naturally. If you let bulbs naturalize in your lawn, don't mow the grass until the leaves of the bulbs have turned yellow.

A Spring Bulb Planting

An ideal location for a bed of spring bulbs is an area next to a south-facing house foundation, at the top of a slope. The house protects the plants from north and west winds, the foundation radiates heat and helps the sun to warm the soil, and the slope ensures that cold air will drain away from the area. These optimal conditions will hasten a bulb's growth.

You can grow hardy, spring-flowering bulbs in perennial flower borders, but they do much better when planted in areas close to the house—especially near frequently used doors—where they can be seen from a living room or kitchen window, or when you allow them to naturalize under a stand of trees. Once they are in bloom, spring bulbs usually are not harmed by low air temperatures, although a late snowstorm may flatten the stems of tall species.

A Summer Bulb Planting

Summer bulbs are most often planted in among perennials. Some, such as lilies, *Lycoris squamigera,* and *Galtonia candicans,* are hardy perennials. Others, like gladiolus, dahlias, and tuberous begonias, must be treated like annuals in the North and dug up in the fall, then replanted in the spring.

Preparing the Bed

Hardy bulbs are perennials, usually planted in flower beds or shrub orders to provide an important piece of the total flowering picture. Since a perennial bed or a border is a major, permanent feature of the garden, it pays to prepare the ground thoroughly in the beginning. The two most important qualities are good drainage and soil that contains an abundance of organic matter, or humus—compost, manure, peat moss, or other finely chopped, decayed vegetable matter.

Testing the Soil

To test your own soil for these qualities, take a handful of moist soil and squeeze it tightly. If water is forced from the soil, it is too wet for plant growth. Consider installing drains or building a raised bed. If the soil retains the shape of your clenched fist when you open your hand, it probably has a high proportion of clay. You need to add organic matter. If the mass crumbles, it probably has a high proportion of sand. You need to add organic matter. If the soil retains the shape of your fist but also crumbles a bit, it is probably all right, but add organic matter to keep it that way. Obviously, you can never go wrong by adding organic matter!

Working the Soil

If your planting area is naturally well drained, the actual soil preparation need involve only the top 6 to 12 inches of the bed. First, pull out tree and shrub stumps and roots, either with a shovel or a tractor. Remove the crowns and roots of other plants as well as perennial weeds. If the area is covered with grass, strip off the sod and add it to the compost pile. Cover the bed area with 4 to 6 inches of compost, manure, or other finely chopped and composted organic matter. Apply commercial fertilizer of the general formula 5-10-5 at the rate of 2 pounds per 100 square feet. Using a spade, dig this organic matter and fertilizer into the top 6 to 12 inches of the soil, or use a rotary tiller. Rake the soil smooth and allow it to settle.

If the soil is poorly drained—that is, if water stands on the surface at any time of the year—you will have to take more drastic action. You can either install drains (if there is any place to which the water can be drained) or raise the planting bed.

Raised Beds

A raised bed should be 6 to 12 inches above the existing ground level. Edge it with brick, stone, or timbers, or simply slope the sides down to ground level. The formula for the planting medium is two parts of good topsoil to one part of compost, manure, or any other finely chopped and decayed organic material. To this, add 2 pounds of 5-10-5 fertilizer per 75 cubic feet.

Improving the Soil

Even if you are not digging a new bed for your planting, you can

Getting Started

improve the soil easily by adding a good supply of organic material (humus) and a modest amount of nitrogen, phosphorus, and potassium. The latter is best supplied by a "complete" fertilizer such as 5-10-5 or 10-10-10. In these formulas, the first number refers to the percentage of nitrogen, the second to the percentage of phosphorus, and the third to the percentage of potassium. Either mixture is good for bulbs and other flowering plants. Use the amount recommended on the package. It makes no difference whether the fertilizer is organic or inorganic. Bone meal is often recommended for bulbs, but it is expensive, and doesn't do anything a complete fertilizer won't do better.

A rich soil is one that contains a high proportion of humus. It has a pleasant texture that retains water and air and provides the best conditions for the growth of plant roots.

Compost, the Key to Garden Success

You can improve most garden soils by adding decayed organic matter. More important than the nutritive value of this material is that it improves the physical characteristics of the soil.

In nature, soil is constantly being improved by the decay of leaves, twigs, stems, and roots of the plants growing in it. When you "tidy up" an area by removing plant debris—leaves, grass clippings, and the like—you remove the natural source of humus. If the soil is not to deteriorate in quality, this material must be returned to the soil in some fashion. You can buy manure, spread it on the soil, dig it in, and let it decompose to form humus. You can also make a compost pile from any available organic waste and manufacture a free, natural, well-rotted manure.

Making compost and using it is one of the great satisfactions of gardening. You can use it in the garden as a top-dressing, mix it with soil when you plant trees, shrubs, or flowers, or mix it with soil and other materials to form potting formulas.

Except for fungus- or insect-infested vegetation, any organic matter can be composted—manure, hay, sawdust, weeds, plants, fallen leaves, and even kitchen scraps. Be aware, however, that meat scraps, bones, and fat may attract unwanted animals. Newspapers should be shredded or torn up and well distributed through the layer of the pile so that they will not form a soggy mat.

Building a Compost Heap

Although compost heaps can be free standing, it is easy to build an enclosed one. For a small garden, you need two adjacent areas, each approximately four square feet. Enclose the two areas on three sides with boards, concrete blocks, or wire fencing. Leave the fourth side open to make it easier to work with the material you are composting.

In the first bin, alternate 6 inches of vegetable material with 1 inch of soil until the pile is 3 to 7 feet high. The center of the pile should be slightly depressed to catch the rain; during dry periods, water the pile. An inorganic fertilizer may be sprinkled over each layer of organic material; you can also dust it with powdered agricultural lime.

Decomposition

Once you have collected a respectable mass of material, vigorous decomposition will begin. As it gets underway, the temperature of the material in the center will rise to 150 to 175° F. At this point, start to fork the compost into the adjacent area in layers. Try to move material that was on the outside of the first pile to the center of the second. Forking the material does more than move it; it also ensures that the original layers of soil and vegetable matter are thoroughly mixed.

If the compost is dry, sprinkle each new layer with water. If there is a putrid odor, the pile is too wet; add more dry material. If there is an odor of ammonia, the nitrogen concentration in the pile is too high; to lower it, incorporate more organic material. After you have moved the compost to the second area, wait a month, then turn it again.

During cold weather, decomposition becomes slower. If the pile does not begin to heat within a month or by the time it reaches 4 feet, turn it again and add either fertilizer or manure. To speed up the composting process, cut or chop the organic material into small pieces. For this, a garden grinder is a useful tool. If you prefer, you can chop the material with a sharp spade. Once you have chopped the material, decomposition will begin rapidly, within one or two weeks. When the pile is warm, turn it again, then continue to turn it once a week. When the material becomes black and crumbly, it is ready to use. If decomposition is rapid, this may take only a month.

Some gardeners prepare compost for use by putting it through a one-half-inch sieve. The coarse, undecomposed material that accumulates in the sieve should be returned to the pile.

Buying Bulbs

When you buy bulbs at a garden center or store, look for large, firm bulbs free of any mold. Hardy, spring-flowering bulbs, such as daffodils and crocus, and tender bulbs that flower indoors in winter, such as Dutch amaryllis and freesias, are usually available from August until stocks run out in late fall or early winter. Non-hardy, summer-flowering bulbs, such as gladiolus, dahlias, and tuberous begonias, are available from January to June. 'Paper-white' Narcissus and other tender bulbs commonly grown in pots are available year round. To learn more about purchasing bulbs, see the essay on page 38 and a list of suppliers on page 441.

Getting Started

Planting Bulbs
Ideally, you should plant bulbs as soon as you purchase them.
Planting bulbs immediately is easy enough in autumn, but difficult
in winter if you live in a cold climate. If it is too cold to plant the
summer-flowering bulbs you buy in January or February, store them
in a cool place—never warmer than 70° F—until spring. Start
tuberous begonias in pots when you buy them and you'll have
healthy, husky plants to set in the garden later.
Plant spring-flowering bulbs in late summer or early fall. Although
you can plant them as long as the ground can be worked, it's best to
give them enough time to develop roots and establish themselves
before winter arrives.

How Deep to Plant Bulbs
The rule of thumb for planting bulbs outdoors is to set them two
and a half times deeper than their diameter. A crocus corm with a
one-inch diameter should be planted with its bottom two and a half
inches deep. A lily bulb with a three-inch diameter should be
planted with its bottom seven inches deep.

Placement
In general, bulbs should be planted in groups or clusters—the larger
the group or cluster, the better the show. If you are planting small
bulbs such as crocus or muscari, group 13 or more together. For
larger bulbs such as daffodils and tulips, plant 5 in a group. Plant
the bulbs in odd-numbered groups; 3, not 2; 5, not 4. If you want a
naturalistic look to the planting, take a few bulbs in your hand, toss
them gently on the ground, then plant them where they have
fallen.
If you are naturalizing large bulbs such as daffodils, dig a hole in the
sod with a trowel for each individual bulb. Special bulb-planting
tools are also available at garden centers; they make it easy to dig
neat, circular holes.

When Bulbs Don't Blossom
If bulbs fail to come up the first spring, they may not be hardy in
your region. It is also possible that they were eaten by rodents or
rotted because the soil was too wet. And if you planted them too
shallowly, they may have frozen.
If bulbs do come up and flower the first year, but become weak or
refuse to flower in subsequent years, they have been unable to
manufacture enough food to store up the energy they need to
support flower buds. Most likely you have removed the leaves from
the bulb before it was ready to become dormant.

Animal Pests
Many bulbs are edible and attract moles, rats, mice, and chipmunks.
There is no point in thinking that you can repel vermin either with

chemicals or with other plants. If bulb-eating animals are a problem in your garden, you have three alternatives: Exterminate the animals; plant only nonpalatable bulbs, such as narcissus; or plant the bulbs in a box made from galvanized hardware cloth. Extermination never works in the long run; new animals will move in to take the place of those you have removed.

Maintenance

Like other perennials, bulbs need moderately fertile soil. To keep them growing and flowering well, fertilize them lightly every year. In early spring, before growth or flowering begins, spread a complete fertilizer over your flower beds, following the instructions on the package. You can spread it directly onto the soil or onto whatever mulch you are using; the spring rains will carry the fertilizer down into the soil.

After your bulbs finish flowering, never remove the leaves. While they continue to grow, the bulb underground is manufacturing food for the following year. Cut back the foliage only when it has turned yellow and can be pulled easily away from the bulb.

Storing Tender Bulbs

In colder regions tender bulbs, corms, tuberous roots, and rhizomes that are commonly planted in the garden for summer display must be dug up and stored over the winter. These plants include gladiolus, canna, dahlia, tuberous begonia, and tuberose. When the tops of the plants have been touched by frost, carefully dig up the bulbs. Shake off the soil that clings to them, then cut off all the growth one to two inches above the tops of the bulbs. Allow the bulbs to dry for two to three days in an airy, shady place. After they have dried, put gladiolus and other similar corms in paper bags or cardboard boxes, then store them in a dry place at 40 to 50° F. All other tender bulbs should be packed in *slightly* moistened peat moss or vermiculite, then stored at the same temperature. Inspect stored bulbs frequently to ensure that they don't dry out or become infested with mold.

Tender bulbs that are grown in containers should be left in their containers. Store them at temperatures between 50 and 65° F until growth commences. Never let them dry out completely.

Mulch and Mulching

Mulching covers the soil surface with a porous layer of material. The mulch acts as insulation and slows down changes in soil temperature. It also retards water loss from evaporation, while permitting water to percolate through the soil. Finally, it helps retard the growth of weeds. If you use an organic mulch, the organic matter, humus, will make it easier for the soil to hold water and, at the same time, add small amounts of nutrients to the soil. When you are gardening with bulbs, mulch the soil after the flowers have bloomed and the leaves have turned yellow, or apply the mulch in the fall.

In a garden, unprotected soil begins to freeze as soon as the nighttime temperatures consistently drop below 32° F. If very little snow falls, the garden may freeze to a depth of about 6 feet. If a garden is mulched, however, the soil does not freeze as quickly or as deeply; the frozen layer may be only a few inches deep.

Mulch makes it much harder for weed seeds to germinate. First, because the mulch covers the soil surface, the soil remains dark and cool—conditions that inhibit germination. Those seeds that do germinate may starve before they can get their leaves up into the light. Finally, the light and airy structure of the mulch and the uncompacted nature of the protected soil combine to make it easy to pull out those weeds that do develop.

An organic mulch adds humus to the soil as it decays into progressively smaller particles. The smaller particles filter down between the coarser particles until they reach the soil surface. There they continue to decay; the smaller particles thus produced become distributed among the mineral particles of the soil. At the same time, nutrients released from the organic matter during its decay are dissolved in the water that percolates through the mulch. Eventually they reach the root zone.

Mulching Materials

Choose a reasonably priced mulch that appeals to you aesthetically. Leaves, rotted horse or cow manure, straw, hay, grass cuttings, peat moss, pine needles, coconut fiber, sugar cane bagasse, ground corn cobs, ground or shredded bark, and wood chips are all acceptable mulches. Polyethylene film, fiberglass, and pea stones or gravel may be desirable under commercial conditions, but in the private garden they are unsightly and unpleasant to work with.

Leaves

Nature's own mulch—leaves—are excellent for mulching evergreens, deciduous shrubs, and all native woodland plants, and they are also effective on perennial and bulb borders and in rock gardens.

Although leaves may blow away easily, you can anchor them in the winter with evergreen branches and the like. Compost them over the winter to make them more suitable as a mulching material. Mulches made of soft leaves such as maple or willow decay rapidly, but oak leaves decay more slowly.

Manure

Composted cow or horse manure makes an excellent mulch for ornamental and fruit trees, shrubs and berry bushes, rose and asparagus beds, perennial and bulb borders, and rock gardens.

Straw and Hay

Plain straw or hay can take the place of leaves or manure when the latter are not available. They are especially suitable for mulching strawberry beds; in addition to protecting the soil from freezing during the winter, they also keep the fruit clean as it develops in the summer.

Salt Hay

This mulching material is little different from straw or hay. It is said to be free of any weed seeds, which may be true. Aside from that, though, it is no better as a mulch than hay or straw, which are generally less expensive.

Sawdust

If it has been composted for at least three months, sawdust makes a fine mulch. However, like peat moss, sawdust has a tendency to form a crust that repels water. This crust must be broken up with a hoe or cultivator as soon as it begins to form. All sawdust has a tendency to withdraw nitrogen from the soil because the organisms that digest cellulose use nitrogen as an energy source. To replenish nitrogen, sprinkle one pound of ammonium nitrate or two pounds of nitrate of soda over every 150 square feet of sawdust mulch.

Grass Cuttings

As a temporary mulch during the summer, grass cuttings are adequate. However, they disappear quickly when the weather is very hot or very moist.

Peat Moss

Like sawdust, peat moss tends to form a waterproof surface layer when it is allowed to dry out. Break up this crust as soon as it starts to form. Unlike sawdust, peat moss is very expensive.

Miscellaneous Mulches

Coconut fiber, ground corn cobs, and sugar cane bagasse are coarse, fibrous materials that decompose slowly. They are attractive and expensive.

Pine Needles

Although pine needles are said to be too acid for general garden use, they can be spread as a mulch. If you have a good supply available without cost, add fertilizer and a little lime now and then to the needles to reduce their acidity.

Composted Bark

Ground, composted bark is currently one of the most readily available mulches. It is water-permeable, decomposes slowly so that it ties up little nitrogen, and is essentially weed free. Nuggets of

Getting Started

To divide a clump of bulbs, dig the bulbs up with a spading fork after the leaves have died. Pull the clump apart, detaching any offsets that separate easily, and replant the individual bulbs immediately. The smaller bulbs will flower within a year or two.

pine, fir, or redwood bark, packaged in bags or bales, are also widely available. They are both extremely effective and extremely expensive. Wood chips (chipped twigs, branches, and brush) are also good mulches.

Increasing Your Stock

You can easily increase your stock of bulbs, corms, and tuberous roots by dividing them, by planting the offsets they produce, and by growing new plants from seeds.

Propagating from Offsets

Most true bulbs, such as narcissus and muscari, produce offsets. A few years after you have planted the individual bulbs, each bulb will have produced a number of similar bulbs called offsets, or bulblets. These lie crowded together around the original bulb. Because there are so many individual bulbs in a small area, they compete with each other for nutrients and water. The offsets grow slowly, and frequently are unable to make enough food to produce flower buds; instead, the bulbs produce only leaves. When a clump of bulbs ceases to flower satisfactorily, dig the bulbs up as soon as the leaves die down in early summer. Separate the individual bulbs and reset them immediately. Obviously you will be able to plant a much larger area than you originally did. Provided the soil is well prepared and there is an annual application of fertilizer, most of the small bulbs will grow to flowering size within a year or two. Alternately, the smaller bulbs can be set in a row at the edge of the vegetable garden for a year or two until they reach flowering size.

Tender bulbs like hippeastrum and clivia produce offsets more slowly. However, when offsets are produced they can be separated from the parent bulbs and grown on to flowering size. The process takes two or three years.

Propagating from Cormels

A corm dies each season, but a replacement corm forms on top of the old one, and tiny cormels that can be used for propagation form around the base of the new corm. When you dig up tender corms like gladiolus from the garden in the fall, or turn others, such as freesias, out of pots at the end of the flowering season, allow the corms to dry, separate the old, shriveled corm from the new one, and collect the cormels. In the following season, you can plant the cormels separately and grow them in a well-fertilized soil. They should reach flowering size in a season or two.

Dividing True Bulbs

You can propagate many of the true bulbs (hippeastrum, hyacinth, narcissus, and scilla, among others) by dividing them lengthwise into 2, 4, or 8 sections. Dip each section in a powdered fungicide to

Propagation

True bulbs such as narcissus produce offsets, or bulblets. Separate offsets from parent bulb and replant.

Pull off individual outer scales, dust with fungicide, and store in moist vermiculite. New bulblets will form on the scales.

True Bulb: Narcissus

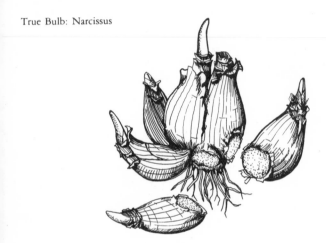

True Bulb: Lily

A corm dies each season but forms a replacement corm and offsets, or cormels. Separate the old corm from the new one, and collect the cormels to plant next season.

Tuberous roots produce new buds, or eyes, around the stem base. With a knife, separate root clump so that each section has a bud and part of the old stem.

Corm: Gladiolus

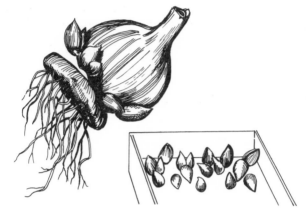

Tuberous Root: Dahlia

discourage decay. Next, place the cut pieces in a plastic bag filled with moist vermiculite. Seal the mouth of the bag with a rubber band, then place the bag in a light place (but not in direct sunlight) at 70° F for 1 to 3 months. Examine the bulbs regularly; when small bulbs and roots have formed they can be planted in a potting mixture made up of one-third soil, one-third compost, and one-third perlite. Hardy bulbs need 12 weeks at 35 to 45° F to satisfy their cold requirements before they can begin to grow.

Dividing Corms
Corms can also be cut up into sections; make sure that each section has at least one growth bud. Propagate them just as you would bulbs.

Dividing Tuberous Roots
You can propagate tuberous-rooted plants such as dahlias by dividing the root clumps. With a knife, separate the clump so that each section has at least one bud and part of the old stem.

Propagating Lilies
Increase your stock of lilies by taking individual scales from a bulb, dipping the broken (bottom) end into fungicide, and then inserting the scales bottom downward in a pot of moist vermiculite or a mixture of equal parts sand and peat moss. Enclose the pot in a plastic bag, then treat the lily scales like true bulbs.

Growing from Seeds
You can buy bulb seeds or collect seed from an existing planting. Many bulbs have somewhat fleshy seed pods that do not dry out and change color at maturity as conspicuously as those of some other plants. Consequently, if you plan to collect seed, you need to watch the development of the pods very closely and collect the seed as soon as the pod cracks open, whether it looks ripe or not.
Sow the seed you collect as soon as it is ripe and the seed you buy as soon as you purchase it. Fill a 6-inch pot with a mixture consisting of one-third garden soil, one-third compost or a commercial potting soil, and one-third perlite. If the seed is small, scatter it thinly over the surface; if it is large enough to handle, space the seeds ¼ inch apart, then cover them with ¼ inch of the soil mixture.

Germination
Set the pot in a larger container filled with water up to the level of the surface of the soil in the pot. When you can see water at the surface of the soil, remove the pot and let it drain overnight. After the pot has drained, enclose it in a clear plastic bag and seal the end with a rubber band. Put the sealed container in a light place (but not in direct sunlight) at a temperature of 65 to 80° F. Germination may occur within a week or two, or it may be delayed for 3 to 4

weeks. If there has been no germination within 8 weeks, place the container in the vegetable compartment of your refrigerator (not the freezer) and leave it there for 12 weeks. Inspect it every week to check for germination. When germination starts, or at the end of 12 weeks, remove the pot from the refrigerator and return it to a warm, light location. If germination does not take place within another 60 days, repeat the cold treatment. If the seeds do not germinate this time, you can assume that they are non-viable.

A few days after germination, open the plastic bag, but do not remove the pot. The bag will help to maintain a moist atmosphere around the developing seedlings. Do not let the pot dry out. After 7 to 10 days, remove the pot from the bag and place it in as light a position as possible. Again, do not let the pot dry out.

When the tiny leaves turn yellow, reduce the amount of water. If you are growing hardy bulbs, begin to treat them as you would adult bulbs: Set them out in the garden at a depth of 1 to 2 inches, mulch them well, then let them grow there until they reach flowering size (approximately 2 to 4 years). At that time, set them in a permanent place in the garden.

If you are growing tender bulbs from seed, reduce the amount of water, providing only enough to keep the pot from drying out. When growth begins, separate the seedlings and pot them singly in 2- or 3-inch pots.

Cold Frames

A cold frame is a bottomless, boxlike structure with a removable top glazed with glass or plastic. It protects marginally hardy plants over the winter, and serves as a place for starting plants early in the spring or extending the growing season in the fall. You can also use a cold frame as a propagating area.

Traditionally garden frames of all kinds, hot or cold, were built to fit a top (called a sash or light) 3 feet wide by 6 feet long. This is an awkward size; a frame 3 feet by 3 feet is much more convenient.

If the frame is to occupy a permanent position, it can be constructed from bricks, concrete blocks, or cast concrete, using the dimensions that follow. If you want the frame to be portable, build it with 2-inch planks. The minimum practical height for the frame is about 16 inches at the back and 10 inches at the front. Although a frame can be any height, the back should always be 6 to 10 inches taller than the front.

If the frame is to be constructed of wood, it should be the most durable wood available; white cedar, western cedar, redwood, or cypress are all excellent. Do not use wood that has been treated with creosote, however, as the fumes will kill the plants.

Building a Cold Frame

A basic frame can be constructed using a 2- by 10-inch plank for the

Getting Started

The lid of a cold frame should prop open securely to three positions: slightly open, half-open, and fully open. Sink the frame into the ground or build a bank of soil part way up the sides. Many cold frames also have rubber insulation around the inner rim.

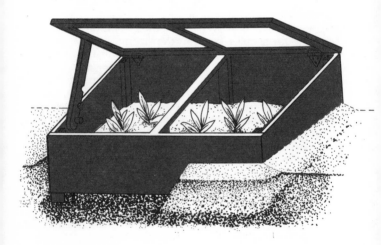

front and two such planks for the back. Use a 2- by 10-inch plank for the bottom portion of each side; cut two more planks diagonally to provide the slope that will connect the top and the bottom. The glazed sash can be laid on the frame or it can be attached to the back of the frame with hinges. This basic frame can be extended to make a larger frame of any desired length.

The removable top of the frame can be a window-sash of suitable size, or a simple wooden frame covered with polyethylene; if you choose to use polyethylene, replace it annually. Rigid, transparent plastic sheets that are available from glass shops or hardware stores are also suitable. The sash itself can be constructed from a 1- by 3-inch plank, reinforced at the corners with right-angle braces.

If you plan to grow plants directly in the soil within the frame, follow the directions on preparing the soil on page 30. If you are going to use the frame to plunge (bury) pots of bulbs, dig up 6 to 12 inches of earth and replace it with sand or mulch.

Location and Uses of the Cold Frame

For maximum use, the cold frame should face toward the south to trap as much sun as possible in the early part of the year. It should also be on ground high enough to prevent surface water from seeping in under normal conditions. It is also a good idea to protect the frame from wind; try to find a sheltered location for the frame near a building, a fence, or a hedge—anything that acts as a wind break.

For the bulb grower, cold frames have two principal uses. They can be used to provide the cool, but not freezing, conditions that potted hardy bulbs need to induce root formation before they are forced into bloom. They also protect pots of seedling bulbs from freezing before they are large enough to be set into the garden.

In the fall, after hardy bulbs have been potted up for forcing, the pots can be plunged—buried up to the rim—into the sand or mulch in the cold frame. Leave the frame open night and day until a hard frost occurs. At that time, cover the pots with at least 6 inches of mulch—damp peat moss, hay, leaves, sawdust, or even pure compost. Close the frame at night but keep it open during the day as long as the daytime temperature is above 32° F. The object is to keep the temperature of the soil in the pots as close to 32 to 41° F as possible. When the daytime temperatures stay below freezing, keep the cold frame shut. You can open it whenever you want to remove pots of bulbs to take indoors for forcing.

In cold areas, additional insulation can be provided by banking the outside of the frame with soil, leaves, or bales of hay, and the top of the frame itself can be covered with bags of leaves or bales of hay.

Tools

To prepare the garden bed you will need a spade, a flat-tined spading

Getting Started

fork, and an iron rake. For planting bulbs, buy a good trowel, one that won't break. There are three types. In one, the entire trowel is made of one piece of cast aluminum. The second type consists of a single piece of curved steel that is attached by screws to a shaped wooden handle. In the third type, the blade is made of a piece of heavy, curved steel; welded to the curved piece is a steel shank, which fits inside a wooden handle. Cheap trowels are made from pressed metal, with or without a wooden handle.

Tubular bulb planters make a neat, round hole. They are particularly useful for planting bulbs in grassy areas.

Growing Bulbs in Containers

Tender summer-flowering bulbs, tender winter-flowering bulbs, and hardy bulbs used for forcing can be grown in pots or other containers. Containers, whatever they may be, must have holes at the bottom to allow water to drain from the soil, and they should be reasonably durable, not subject to rotting or breakage. With these restrictions, containers may be made of pottery, plastic, or wood (redwood is best). Don't use metal containers—they will corrode. If you plan to move containers from place to place, keep in mind that moist garden soil can become quite heavy.

Potting Soil

Potting soil must drain freely, yet it must stay moist for a reasonable period. It should be light and contain plenty of air. Natural garden soil, even when enriched with organic matter, is usually too dense for containers.

A good basic soil mixture for plants growing in pots or other containers consists of one-third natural soil, no matter how good or bad; one-third peat moss put through a ½-inch sieve, or compost, leafmold, soil-less potting mix, or seed-starter mix; and one-third perlite, sand, or calcined clay (kitty litter).

For every gallon of the mixture, add 1 tablespoon each of dolomitic limestone and superphosphate, and ½ tablespoon of a commercial garden fertilizer with a 10-10-10 formula.

While they are actively growing, bulbs need as much light as they can get. When grown indoors, they should have a sunny (east, south, or west) window or be grown under strong fluorescent lights. If you grow plants in a window, turn the pots slightly every day so that the plants do not become one-sided. Supply enough water so that the pots never become completely dry, but not so much that the soil becomes soggy.

Indoor plants benefit from growing outdoors in the summer. Wait for a cloudy day when all danger of frost is past to take the plants outside. This allows a few hours for the plants to acclimate themselves to the stronger light. They should be grown in full sun (except for tuberous begonias, which need light shade), and never be allowed to dry out.

It is frequently said that bulbs must be pot-bound to flower well, but being pot-bound is not essential—having undamaged roots is! Many bulbs produce a great number of thick, fleshy roots, and in the process of dividing crowded pots of bulbs, many of these roots are damaged or shortened or cut away. If this division is done late in the growing season, or while the bulbs are dormant so that the plant does not regenerate the roots immediately, the plant may not flower until a new growing season has allowed it to re-establish itself. This may very well delay flowering for 1½ to 2 years. The same plant, divided just as the growing period begins, may very well flower within 12 months.

Actively growing plants may be fertilized once every two weeks with a liquid fertilizer diluted to one-half the manufacturer's recommended strength. During the winter, when the plants are not actively growing, don't fertilize them.

Forcing Bulbs

Hardy bulbs that are forced for winter flowers are generally treated as "throw-aways." They may be potted in containers with no drainage, or in a potting medium that provides no nutrients (bulb fiber, peat, vermiculite, pebbles, or even plain water), or they may be planted so close together that bulbs touch each other—or all of these.

If you want to save these bulbs for planting in the garden, repot them after the flowers have faded. Put them into a pot 4 inches larger than the original container. Use the potting mixture recommended above. Let the plants grow until the leaves turn yellow—or until there is no danger of frost and they can be set into the garden. Crocuses, hyacinths, lilies, and narcissus do well with this treatment (but remember that Tazetta forms of narcissus such as 'Paper-white', 'Grand Soleil d'Or', and 'Chinese Sacred Lily' are not reliably hardy north of Zone 8). Tulips usually do not do well with this regime, although they occasionally flower in subsequent years. (For more information, see the essay on forcing bulbs in the Appendices.)

The plates on the following pages are divided into five groups, each arranged in a color sequence: Bulbs; Narcissus; Tulips; True Lilies and Daylilies; and Other Bulbs. This last category is subdivided into five groups based on color: white flowers; yellow flowers; red to orange flowers; pink flowers; and blue to purple flowers.

Color Key
The Color Key on pages 54–55 shows the range of hues in the Other Bulbs group. Everyone sees color somewhat differently, and gardening specialists often describe a color in general terms to include numerous variations in intensity and tone. The visual organization of the color plates allows you to select flowers by the colors that you see.

When you purchase bulbs, be aware that the color indicated in the catalogue or on the package may differ from the way you interpret that color. For example, nurseries and horticulturists use the term "blue" to describe colors ranging from lavender to blue to dark purple or even magenta. Moreover, some pink and blue tones are quite similar. Growing conditions, too, may affect flower color.

Visual Key

Bulbs	True bulbs, corms, tubers, tuberous roots, and rhizomes are all commonly referred to as bulbs. A selection of these structures are featured here.	
Narcissus	Daffodils and jonquils, both species plants and popular cultivars, and the rare, daffodil-like *Paramongaia Weberbaueri* are included.	
Tulips	This section features popular garden forms from stately Darwins to flamboyant Parrots, as well as species, or botanical, tulips.	
True Lilies and Daylilies	Here you will find species and cultivars of true lilies (*Lilium*) and daylilies (*Hemerocallis*).	

This chart shows the
range of flower types in
each group of color
plates.

Pages 56–59

Pages 60–87

Pages 88–123

Pages 124–153

Visual Key

White Flowers

Yellow Flowers

Red to Orange Flowers

Pink Flowers

Blue to Purple Flowers

53

Arranged by color, this group encompasses all bulbs other than the named groups and includes such garden favorites as Crocus, Dahlia, and Gladiolus, as well as an array of less familiar plants such as Sprekelia and Streptanthera. The chart indicates the variety of shapes within each color group.

Pages 156–185

Pages 186–199

Pages 200–219

Pages 220–249

Pages 250–271

Color Key

White Flowers

Yellow Flowers

Red to Orange Flowers

Pink Flowers

Blue to Purple Flowers

This chart shows the
range of hues in each
group of color plates.

Bulbs

Narcissus
hybrid bulbs

Planting time: late
summer to autumn
Depth: 1½–2 times
depth of bulb
Spacing: to 6 in.

Hardy
Sun to partial shade
Blooms in spring

Acidanthera
corms

Planting time: early
spring, after last frost
Depth: 3–4 in.
Spacing: to 6 in.
Lift: after foliage dies

Tender
Full sun
Blooms in summer
Store at 60° F in
winter

Dahlia tuberous roots	Planting time: spring Depth: 2–3 in. Spacing: 1–3 ft. Lift: autumn, after first killing frost	Tender Full sun Blooms summer to autumn Store at 35–50° F in winter

Gladiolus corms	Planting time: early spring to midsummer Depth: 3–8 in., depending on corm size Spacing: 3–6 in. Lift: when leaves turn yellow	Half-hardy to tender Full sun Blooms in summer Store at 40–50° F in winter

Narcissus

Narcissus
'Cragford'

Plant height:
14–18 in.
Flower width: 1 in.
Tazetta Narcissus
p. 356

Hardy
Full sun
Blooms in early spring

Narcissus
'Geranium'

Plant height:
12–14 in.
Flower width: ½–1 in.
Tazetta Narcissus
p. 356

Hardy
Full sun
Blooms mid-spring to
late spring

Narcissus Tazetta hybrid

Plant height:
12–14 in.
Flower width: ½–1 in.
Tazetta Narcissus
p. 356

Hardy
Full sun
Blooms in mid-spring

Narcissus poeticus hybrid

Plant height: to 18 in.
Flower width: 3 in.
Poeticus Narcissus
p. 356

Hardy
Full sun
Blooms mid-spring to
late spring

Narcissus
'Actaea'

Plant height: to 18 in.
Flower width: 3 in.
Poeticus Narcissus
p. 356

Hardy
Full sun
Blooms mid-spring to
late spring

Narcissus
'Beryl'

Plant height: 8–10 in.
Flower width: 1 in.
Cyclamineus Narcissus
p. 356

Hardy
Full sun
Blooms in early spring

Narcissus poeticus

Plant height: to 18 in.
Flower width: 2–3 in.
Poet's Narcissus
p. 354

Hardy
Full sun
Blooms in late spring

Narcissus × incomparabilis

Plant height: to 12 in.
Flower width: 3–4 in.
p. 353

Hardy
Full sun
Blooms in early spring

Narcissus
'Foresight'

Plant height:
16–18 in.
Flower width: 3–4 in.
Trumpet Narcissus
p. 356

Hardy
Full sun
Blooms in early spring

Narcissus
'Flower Record'

Plant height:
14–18 in.
Flower width: 4½ in.
Large-cupped Narcissus
p. 355

Hardy
Full sun
Blooms early spring to
mid-spring

Narcissus
'Egard'

Plant height:
16–20 in.
Flower width: 3 in.
Split-corona Narcissus
p. 356

Hardy
Full sun
Blooms mid-spring to
late spring

Narcissus
'Roulette'

Plant height:
14–18 in.
Flower width: 4 in.
Large-cupped Narcissus
p. 355

Hardy
Full sun
Blooms early spring to
mid-spring

Narcissus
'Cheerfulness'

Plant height:
14–16 in.
Flower width: 2 in.
Double Narcissus
p. 355

Hardy
Full sun
Blooms in late spring

Narcissus
'White Lion'

Plant height:
16–18 in.
Flower width: 3 in.
Double Narcissus
p. 355

Hardy
Full sun
Blooms in mid-spring

Narcissus
'Irene Copeland'

Plant height:
14–16 in.
Flower width: 3 in.
Double Narcissus
p. 355

Hardy
Full sun
Blooms in mid-spring

Narcissus
'Paper-white'

Plant height: to 16 in.
Flower width: ½–1 in.
Tazetta Narcissus
p. 356

Tender
Full sun
Blooms in early spring

Narcissus
'Rushlight'

Plant height:
14–16 in.
Flower width: 4½ in.
Large-cupped Narcissus
p. 355

Hardy
Full sun
Blooms early spring to
mid-spring

Narcissus
'Golden Ducat'

Plant height:
14–18 in.
Flower width: 3 in.
Double Narcissus
p. 355

Hardy
Full sun
Blooms in mid-spring

Narcissus
'Angkor'

Plant height:
14–18 in.
Flower width: 3 in.
Double Narcissus
p. 355

Hardy
Full sun
Blooms in mid-spring

Narcissus
'Ascot'

Plant height:
14–18 in.
Flower width: 3 in.
Double Narcissus
p. 355

Hardy
Full sun
Blooms in mid-spring

Narcissus
'Soleil d'Or'

Plant height:
12–16 in.
Flower width:
1–1¼ in.
Tazetta Narcissus
p. 356

Tender
Full sun
Blooms in early spring

Narcissus
'Canary Bird'

Plant height:
12–14 in.
Flower width:
1–1¼ in.
Tazetta Narcissus
p. 356

Half-hardy
Full sun
Blooms in early spring

**Narcissus
'Aranjuez'**

Plant height:
14–18 in.
Flower width: 4 in.
Large-cupped Narcissus
p. 355

Hardy
Full sun
Blooms early spring
to mid-spring

**Narcissus
'Birma'**

Plant height: to 15 in.
Flower width: 2–3 in.
Small-cupped Narcissus
p. 356

Hardy
Full sun
Blooms in early spring

Narcissus
'Suzy'

Plant height:
12–16 in.
Flower width: ½–1 in.
Jonquilla Narcissus
p. 356

Hardy
Full sun
Blooms in early spring

Narcissus rupicola

Plant height: to 6 in.
Flower width:
¾–1¼ in.
p. 355

Hardy
Full sun
Blooms in early spring

Narcissus Jonquilla *Plant height: to 18 in.* Hardy
Flower length: 1 in. Full sun
Common Jonquil Blooms in spring
p. 353

Narcissus juncifolius *Plant height: to 6 in.* Hardy
Flower length: 1 in. Full sun
p. 353 Blooms in early spring

**Narcissus
'Hawera'**

Plant height: to 8 in.
Flower length: 1 in.
Triandrus Narcissus
p. 357

Hardy
Sun to partial shade
Blooms mid-spring to
late spring

**Narcissus
cyclamineus**

Plant height: to 12 in.
Flower length: 1–2 in.
p. 353

Hardy
Full sun
Blooms in early spring

Narcissus triandrus
var. *concolor*

Plant height: to 12 in.
Flower length:
1–1½ in.
p. 355

Hardy
Full sun
Blooms in early spring

Narcissus
Bulbocodium

Plant height: 4–18 in.
Flower length: 1–2 in.
Hoop-Petticoat
Daffodil
p. 352

Hardy
Full sun
Blooms in early spring

Narcissus × odorus

Plant height: to 12 in.
Flower length: 1–2 in.
Campernelle Jonquil
p. 354

Hardy
Full sun
Blooms in early spring

Narcissus minor

Plant height: to 6 in.
Flower length: 1¼ in.
p. 353

Hardy
Full sun
Blooms in early spring

Paramongaia
Weberbaueri

Plant height: to 2 ft.
Flower length: 7 in.
p. 365

Tender
Full sun
Blooms in spring

Narcissus
Pseudonarcissus

Plant height:
12–18 in.
Flower length: 2 in.
Common Daffodil
p. 354

Hardy
Full sun
Blooms in early spring

Narcissus
'Tête-à-Tête'

Plant height: 6–8 in.
Flower width:
½ – ¾ in.
Cyclamineus Narcissus
p. 356

Hardy
Full sun
Blooms in early spring

Narcissus
'Unsurpassable'

Plant height:
16–20 in.
Flower width: 3–4 in.
Trumpet Narcissus
p. 356

Hardy
Full sun
Blooms in mid-spring

**Narcissus
'Peeping Tom'**

Plant height: 6–8 in.
Flower width: ½–1 in.
Cyclamineus Narcissus
p. 356

Hardy
Full sun
Blooms in early spring

**Narcissus
'King Alfred'**

Plant height:
16–18 in.
Flower width: 3–4 in.
Trumpet Narcissus
p. 356

Hardy
Full sun
Blooms in early spring

Narcissus obvallaris   *Plant height: to 12 in.*   *Hardy*
Flower length: *Full sun*
1–2½ in.   *Blooms in early spring*
Tenby Daffodil
p. 354

Narcissus   *Plant height:*   *Hardy*
'Binkie'   *14–18 in.*   *Full sun*
Flower width: 4½ in.   *Blooms early spring to*
Large-cupped Narcissus   *mid-spring*
p. 355

**Narcissus
'Sweetness'**

Plant height: to 12 in.   Hardy
Flower width: ½–1 in.   Full sun
Jonquilla Narcissus   Blooms in early spring
p. 356

**Narcissus ×
Johnstonii**

Plant height: to 10 in.   Hardy
Flower length: 2 in.   Full sun
p. 353   Blooms in early spring

Narcissus **'Carlton'**

Plant height: to 18 in.
Flower width: 4½ in.
Large-cupped Narcissus
p. 355

Hardy
Full sun
Blooms early spring to
mid-spring

Narcissus **'February Gold'**

Plant height: 8–10 in.
Flower width: 1–2 in.
Cyclamineus Narcissus
p. 356

Hardy
Full sun
Blooms in early spring

Narcissus asturiensis
Plant height: 4–5 in.
Flower length: ½–1 in.
p. 352

Hardy
Full sun
Blooms in early spring

Narcissus 'Lemon Tarts'
Plant height: to 12 in.
Flower width: ½–1 in.
Jonquilla Narcissus
p. 356

Hardy
Full sun
Blooms in late spring

Narcissus
'Ice Follies'

Plant height:
14–20 in.
Flower width: 4½ in.
Large-cupped Narcissus
p. 355

Hardy
Full sun
Blooms early spring to
mid-spring

Narcissus moschatus

Plant height: to 18 in.
Flower length: 2–3 in.
White Trumpet
Narcissus
p. 354

Hardy
Full sun
Blooms in early spring

Narcissus
'February Silver'

Plant height: 6–10 in.
Flower width: 1–2 in.
Cyclamineus Narcissus
p. 356

Hardy
Full sun
Blooms in early spring

Narcissus
'Thalia'

Plant height: to 16 in.
Flower width: 2 in.
Triandrus Narcissus
p. 357

Hardy
Full sun
Blooms mid-spring to
late spring

Tulips

Tulipa
'Mount Tacoma'

Plant height: 1½–2 ft.
Flower width: 6 in.
Double Late Tulip
p. 378

Hardy
Sun to partial shade
Blooms in late spring

Tulipa
'Duke of
Wellington'

Plant height:
1½–2½ ft.
Flower length: 3–4 in.
Darwin Tulip
p. 378

Hardy
Full sun
Blooms in late spring

Tulipa 'Purissima'

Plant height: 12–18 in.
Flower length: 4 in.
Fosteriana Tulip
p. 378

Hardy
Full sun
Blooms in early spring

Tulipa 'White Emperor'

Plant height: 12–18 in.
Flower length: 4 in.
Fosteriana Tulip
p. 378

Hardy
Sun to partial shade
Blooms in early spring

Tulipa Kaufmanniana hybrid

Plant height: 4–8 in.
Flower width: 3½ in.
Kaufmanniana Tulip
Water Lily Tulip
p. 379

Hardy
Full sun
Blooms in early spring

Tulipa tarda

Plant height: to 5 in.
Flower length: 2 in.
p. 377

Hardy
Full sun
Blooms in early spring

Tulipa 'Honorose'

Plant height: 4–8 in.
Flower width: 3½ in.
Kaufmanniana Tulip
p. 379

Hardy
Full sun
Blooms in early spring

Tulipa turkestanica

Plant height: to 8 in.
Flower length: 1¼ in.
p. 377

Hardy
Full sun
Blooms in early spring

Tulipa
hybrid

Plant height: 1½–3 ft.
Flower length: 3–4 in.
Cottage Tulip
Viridiflora type
p. 377

Hardy
Full sun
Blooms in late spring

Tulipa
'Giuseppe Verdi'

Plant height: 4–8 in.
Flower width: 3½ in.
Kaufmanniana Tulip
p. 379

Hardy
Full sun
Blooms in early spring

Tulipa
'West Point'

Plant height: 1½–2 *ft.*   Hardy
Flower length: 2–4 *in.*   Full sun
Lily-flowered Tulip   Blooms in late spring
p. 379

Tulipa
'Yellow Parrot'

Plant height: Hardy
18–20 *in.*   Full sun
Flower width: 6–7 *in.*   Blooms in late spring
Parrot Tulip
p. 379

Tulipa sylvestris
Plant height: 8–12 in.
Flower length: 2 in.
p. 377
Hardy
Full sun
Blooms in late spring

**Tulipa
Kolpakowskiana**
Plant height: to 6 in.
Flower length: 2 in.
p. 376
Hardy
Full sun
Blooms in early spring

Tulipa Batalinii Plant height: 5–6 in. Hardy
Flower length: 2 in. Full sun
p. 375 Blooms in early spring

Tulipa australis Plant height: 6–10 in. Hardy
Flower length: 2 in. Full sun
p. 375 Blooms in late spring

Tulipa
'Golden Emperor'

Plant height:
12–18 in.
Flower length: 4 in.
Fosteriana Tulip
p. 378

Hardy
Full sun
Blooms in early spring

Tulipa
'Yellow Emperor'

Plant height:
12–18 in.
Flower length: 4 in.
Fosteriana Tulip
p. 378

Hardy
Full sun
Blooms in early spring

Tulipa
Golden Age'

Plant height:
1½–2½ ft.
Flower length: 3–4 in.
Darwin Tulip
p. 378

Hardy
Full sun
Blooms in late spring

Tulipa
Golden Harvest'

Plant height: 1½–3 ft.
Flower length: 3–4 in.
Cottage Tulip
p. 377

Hardy
Full sun
Blooms in late spring

Tulipa
'Bellona'

Plant height:
14–16 in.
Flower length: 2–4 in.
Single Early Tulip
p. 379

Hardy
Sun to partial shade
Blooms in early spring

Tulipa
'Flaming Parrot'

Plant height: 1½–2 ft.
Flower width: 7 in.
Parrot Tulip
p. 379

Hardy
Sun to partial shade
Blooms in late spring

Tulipa
'Georgette'

Plant height:
1½–2½ ft.
Flower length: 3–4 in.
Cottage Tulip
Multiflowering type
p. 377

Hardy
Full sun
Blooms in late spring

Tulipa
'Johann Strauss'

Plant height: 8–10 in.
Flower width: 3½ in.
Kaufmanniana Tulip
p. 379

Hardy
Full sun
Blooms in early spring

Tulipa
'Golden Oxford'

Plant height:
1½–2½ ft.
Flower length: 3–4 in.
Darwin Hybrid Tulip
p. 378

Hardy
Full sun
Blooms in late spring

Tulipa
'Orange Emperor'

Plant height:
12–18 in.
Flower length: 4 in.
Fosteriana Tulip
p. 378

Hardy
Full sun
Blooms in early spring

Tulipa
'Gudoshnik'

Plant height:
1½–2½ ft.
Flower length: 3–4 in.
Darwin Hybrid Tulip
p. 378

Hardy
Full sun
Blooms in late spring

Tulipa
'Olympic Flame'

Plant height:
1½–2½ ft.
Flower length: 3–4 in.
Darwin Hybrid Tulip
p. 378

Hardy
Full sun
Blooms in late spring

Tulipa
'Flaming Star'

Plant height: 8–12 in.
Flower width: 6 in.
Greigii Tulip
p. 378

Hardy
Full sun
Blooms in mid-spring

Tulipa
'Oriental Splendor'

Plant height: 8–12 in.
Flower width: 6 in.
Greigii Tulip
p. 378

Hardy
Full sun
Blooms in mid-spring

**Tulipa
'Cape Cod'**

Plant height: 8–12 in.
Flower width: 6 in.
Greigii Tulip
p. 378

Hardy
Full sun
Blooms in mid-spring

**Tulipa Clusiana
var. *chrysantha***

Plant height: to 15 in.
Flower length: 2 in.
p. 375

Hardy
Full sun
Blooms in late spring

Tulipa
'Shakespeare'

Plant height: 4–8 in.
Flower width: 3½ in.
Kaufmanniana Tulip
p. 379

Hardy
Full sun
Blooms in early spring

Tulipa
'Kees Nelis'

Plant height: 1½–2 ft.
Flower length: 2–4 in.
Triumph Tulip
p. 379

Hardy
Sun to partial shade
Blooms in mid-spring

Tulipa
'Texas'

Plant height: 18–20 in.   Hardy
Flower width: 6–7 in.   Full sun
Parrot Tulip   Blooms in late spring
p. 379

Tulipa
'Fringed Beauty'

Plant height: 8–12 in.   Hardy
Flower width: 3–4 in.   Full sun
Double Early Tulip   Blooms in early spring
p. 378

Tulipa
'Queen of Sheba'

Plant height: 1½–2 ft.
Flower length: 2–4 in.
Lily-flowered Tulip
p. 379

Hardy
Full sun
Blooms in late spring

Tulipa
'Scarlet Baby'

Plant height: 4–8 in.
Flower width: 3–4 in.
Kaufmanniana Tulip
p. 379

Hardy
Full sun
Blooms in early spring

Tulipa
'Karel Doorman'

Plant height: 1½–2 ft.
Flower width: 6–7 in.
Parrot Tulip
p. 379

Hardy
Full sun
Blooms in late spring

Tulipa
'Orange Bouquet'

Plant height: 1½–2 ft.
Flower length: 3–4 in.
Cottage Tulip
Multiflowering type
p. 377

Hardy
Sun to partial shade
Blooms in late spring

Tulipa acuminata   *Plant height:*   Hardy
                        12–18 in.   *Full sun*
                        Flower length: 3–4 in.   *Blooms in late spring*
                        Turkish Tulip
                        p. 375

Tulipa Orphanidea   *Plant height: 8–12 in.*   Hardy
                         Flower length: 2 in.   *Full sun*
                         p. 376   *Blooms in early spring*

Tulipa Sprengeri   Plant height: 8–12 in.   Hardy
                           Flower length: 2 in.   Partial shade
                           p. 377   Blooms in late spring

Tulipa Hageri   Plant height: to 6 in.   Hardy
                           Flower length: 2 in.   Full sun
                           p. 376   Blooms in early spring

Tulipa
'Red Riding Hood'

Plant height: 8–12 in.
Flower width: 6 in.
Greigii Tulip
p. 378

Hardy
Sun to partial shade
Blooms in mid-spring

Tulipa
'Red Emperor'

Plant height:
12–18 in.
Flower length: 4 in.
Fosteriana Tulip
p. 378

Hardy
Sun to partial shade
Blooms in early spring

Tulipa montana   Plant height: to 8 in.   Hardy
                          Flower length: 2 in.   Full sun
                          p. 376   Blooms in late spring

Tulipa linifolia   Plant height: 5–10 in.   Hardy
                          Flower length: 2 in.   Full sun
                          p. 376   Blooms in early spring

Tulipa praestans

Plant height: to 12 in.
Flower length: 2 in. `
p. 376

Hardy
Full sun
Blooms in early spring

Tulipa
'Red Shine'

Plant height: 1½–2 ft.
Flower length: 2–4 in.
Lily-flowered Tulip
p. 379

Hardy
Full sun
Blooms in late spring

Tulipa
'Princesse
Charmante'

Plant height: 8–12 in.
Flower width: 6 in.
Greigii Tulip
p. 378

Hardy
Full sun
Blooms in mid-spring

Tulipa
'Oxford'

Plant height:
1½–2½ ft.
Flower length: 3–4 in.
Darwin Hybrid Tulip
p. 378

Hardy
Full sun
Blooms in late spring

Tulipa
'Eros'

Plant height: 1½–2 ft.
Flower width: 6 in.
Double Late Tulip
p. 378

Hardy
Full sun
Blooms in late spring

Tulipa
'Jacqueline'

Plant height: 1½–2 ft.
Flower length: 2–4 in.
Lily-flowered Tulip
p. 379

Hardy
Full sun
Blooms in late spring

Tulipa
'May Wonder'

Plant height: 1½–2 ft.
Flower width: 6 in.
Double Late Tulip
p. 378

Hardy
Full sun
Blooms in late spring

Tulipa
'Rosy Wings'

Plant height:
1½–2½ ft.
Flower width: 3–4 in.
Cottage Tulip
p. 377

Hardy
Full sun
Blooms in late spring

Tulipa
hybrid

Plant height: 1½–2 ft.
Flower width: 6–7 in.
Parrot Tulip
p. 379

Hardy
Full sun
Blooms in late spring

Tulipa
'Garden Party'

Plant height: 1½–2 ft.
Flower length: 2–4 in.
Triumph Tulip
p. 379

Hardy
Full sun
Blooms in mid-spring

Tulipa   *Plant height: 2–2½ ft.*   *Hardy*
'Smiling Queen' *Flower length: 3–4 in.*   *Full sun*
                    Cottage Tulip   *Blooms in late spring*
                    p. 377

Tulipa Clusiana *Plant height: to 15 in.*   *Hardy*
                    Flower length: 2 in.   *Full sun*
                    Candy-Stick Tulip   *Blooms in late spring*
                    p. 375

Tulipa
'China Lady'

Plant height: 8–12 in.
Flower width: 6 in.
Greigii Tulip
p. 378

Hardy
Full sun
Blooms in mid-spring

Tulipa Aucheriana

Plant height: to 8 in.
Flower length:
1–1½ in.
p. 375

Hardy
Full sun
Blooms in early spring

Tulipa
'Ballade'

Plant height: 1½–2 ft.
Flower length: 2–4 in.
Lily-flowered Tulip
p. 379

Hardy
Full sun
Blooms in late spring

Tulipa saxatilis

Plant height: to 12 in.
Flower length: 2 in.
p. 377

Hardy
Full sun
Blooms in mid-spring

Tulipa pulchella

Plant height: 4–6 in.
Flower length: 1½ in.
p. 376

Hardy
Full sun
Blooms in early spring

**Tulipa
'Queen of the
Night'**

Plant height: 2–2½ ft.
Flower length: 3–4 in.
Darwin Tulip
p. 378

Hardy
Sun to partial shade
Blooms in late spring

Tulipa
'Maytime'

Plant height: 1½–2 ft.   Hardy
Flower length: 2–4 in.   Sun to partial shade
Lily-flowered Tulip   Blooms in late spring
p. 379

Tulipa
'Blue Parrot'

Plant height: Hardy
18–20 in.   Sun to partial shade
Flower width: 6–7 in.   Blooms in late spring
Parrot Tulip
p. 379

True Lilies &

Daylilies

Lilium
'Imperial Pink'

Plant height: 4–5 ft.
Flower width: 8 in.
Oriental Hybrid
p. 347

Hardy
Partial shade
Blooms in summer

Lilium
'Pink Perfection'

Plant height: 5–6 ft.
Flower length: 6 in.
Aurelian Hybrid
p. 346

Hardy
Sun to partial shade
Blooms in summer

**Lilium
'Bellingham'**

Plant height: 4–8 ft.
Flower width: 4–6 in.
American Hybrid
p. 346

Hardy
Sun to partial shade
Blooms in summer

Lilium Martagon

Plant height: 4–6 ft.
Flower width: 2 in.
Turk's-Cap Lily
p. 344

Hardy
Sun to partial shade
Blooms in late spring

Lilium speciosum
'Rubrum'

Plant height: 4–5 ft.
Flower width: 4–6 in.
Japanese Lily
p. 345

Hardy
Sun to partial shade
Blooms summer to
autumn

Lilium
'Imperial Crimson'

Plant height: 5–7 ft.
Flower width: 8 in.
Oriental Hybrid
p. 347

Hardy
Sun to partial shade
Blooms in summer

Lilium
'Jamboree'

Plant height: 4–6 ft.
Flower width: 6–8 in.
Oriental Hybrid
p. 347

Hardy
Partial shade
Blooms in summer

Lilium
'Maharajah'

Plant height: 4–5 ft.
Flower width: 8 in.
Oriental Hybrid
p. 347

Hardy
Sun to partial shade
Blooms in summer

Hemerocallis
'Chicago Two-Bits'

Plant height: to 2 ft.
Flower width: 5–6 in.
p. 327

Hardy
Full sun
Blooms in summer

Lilium
'Little Rascal'

Plant height:
to 2½ ft.
Flower width: 3–6 in.
Oriental Hybrid
p. 347

Hardy
Sun to partial shade
Blooms in summer

Lilium
'Tiger Babies'

Plant height: 3–4 ft.
Flower width: 6 in.
Asiatic Hybrid
p. 346

Hardy
Sun to partial shade
Blooms in summer

Lilium speciosum

Plant height: 4–5 ft.
Flower width: 4–6 in.
Japanese Lily
p. 345

Hardy
Sun to partial shade
Blooms summer to
autumn

Lilium japonicum

Plant height: to 3 ft.
Flower length: 4–6 in.
p. 343

Hardy
Partial shade
Blooms in summer

**Lilium
'Black Dragon'**

Plant height: 5–8 ft.
Flower length: 6–8 in.
Aurelian Hybrid
p. 346

Hardy
Sun to partial shade
Blooms in summer

Lilium Washingtonianum

Plant height: 4–6 ft.
Flower width: 4 in.
Washington Lily
p. 346

Hardy
Sun to partial shade
Blooms in summer

Lilium regale

Plant height: 4–6 ft.
Flower length: 6 in.
Regal Lily
p. 345

Hardy
Full sun
Blooms in summer

Lilium
'Heart's Desire'

Plant height: 5–6 ft.
Flower width: 8 in.
Aurelian Hybrid
p. 346

Hardy
Sun to partial shade
Blooms in summer

Lilium
'Green Magic'

Plant height: 3–6 ft.
Flower length: 6–8 in.
Aurelian Hybrid
p. 346

Hardy
Sun to partial shade
Blooms in summer

Lilium formosanum

Plant height: 5–7 ft.
Flower length: 5–8 in.
p. 343

Tender
Full sun
Blooms summer to
autumn

Lilium longiflorum
var. eximium

Plant height: 2–3 ft.
Flower length: 6–8 in.
Easter Lily
p. 344

Tender
Full sun
Blooms in spring

Lilium
'Cascade'

Plant height: 3–4 ft.
Flower width: 4–5 in.
Candidum Hybrid
Madonna Lily
p. 347

Hardy
Sun to partial shade
Blooms in summer

Lilium
'Imperial Silver'

Plant height: 5–6 ft.
Flower width: 8–10 in.
Oriental Hybrid
p. 347

Hardy
Partial shade
Blooms in summer

Lilium Martagon
var. *album*

Plant height: 4–6 ft.
Flower width: 2 in.
Turk's-Cap Lily
p. 344

Hardy
Sun to partial shade
Blooms in late spring

Lilium auratum

Plant height: 3–9 ft.
Flower width:
6–10 in.
p. 342

Hardy
Sun to partial shade
Blooms in summer

**Lilium
monadelphum**

Plant height: to 5 ft.
Flower width: 5 in.
Caucasian Lily
p. 344

Hardy
Sun to partial shade
Blooms in late spring

Lilium canadense

Plant height: to 5 ft.
Flower width: 3 in.
Meadow Lily
p. 342

Hardy
Full sun
Blooms in summer

**Hemerocallis
Lilioasphodelus**

Plant height: to 3 ft.
Flower length: 3–4 in.
Lemon Daylily
p. 327

Hardy
Sun to partial shade
Blooms in late spring

Lilium Parryi

Plant height: 4–6 ft.
Flower length: 4 in.
Lemon Lily
p. 345

Half-hardy
Sun to partial shade
Blooms in summer

Lilium
'Golden Showers'

Plant height: 4–6 ft.
Flower width: 8 in.
Aurelian Hybrid
p. 346

Hardy
Sun to partial shade
Blooms in summer

Lilium
'Connecticut
Lemonglow'

Plant height: 2–3 ft.
Flower width: 4–6 in.
Asiatic Hybrid
p. 346

Hardy
Sun to partial shade
Blooms in summer

Hemerocallis citrina
Plant height: to 4 ft.
Flower length: 6 in.
p. 326

Hardy
Full sun
Blooms in summer

**Hemerocallis
'Stella Di Oro'**
Plant height: to 2 ft.
Flower width: 2¾ in.
p. 327

Hardy
Full sun
Blooms late spring to
summer

Hemerocallis
'Double Gold'

Plant height:
to 2½ ft.
Flower width: 5 in.
p. 327

Hardy
Full sun
Blooms in summer

Lilium
'Golden Splendor'

Plant height: 3–6 ft.
Flower length: 6–8 in.
Aurelian Hybrid
p. 346

Hardy
Sun to partial shade
Blooms in summer

Hemerocallis
'Bonanza'

Plant height: to 2 ft.
Flower width: 3–6 in.
p. 327

Hardy
Full sun
Blooms in summer

Hemerocallis
Dumortieri

Plant height: to 18 in.
Flower length: 2½ in.
p. 326

Hardy
Full sun
Blooms in late spring

Hemerocallis
Middendorfii

Plant height: to 18 in.
Flower length: 2¾ in.
p. 327

Hardy
Full sun
Blooms in late spring

Lilium
columbianum

Plant height: 3–5 ft.
Flower width: 3 in.
p. 342

Hardy
Sun to partial shade
Blooms in summer

Lilium
'Impact'

Plant height: 2–4 ft.
Flower width: 6 in.
Asiatic Hybrid
p. 346

Hardy
Sun to partial shade
Blooms in summer

Lilium Hansonii

Plant height: 4–5 ft.
Flower width: 3 in.
Japanese Turk's-Cap
Lily
p. 343

Hardy
Partial shade
Blooms in late spring

Lilium amabile Plant height: to 3 ft. Hardy
Flower length: 2 in. Full sun
p. 342 Blooms in late spring

Lilium Plant height: 4–5 ft. Hardy
'Connecticut Flower width: 6 in. Sun to partial shade
Yankee' Asiatic Hybrid Blooms in summer
p. 346

Lilium Henryi
Plant height: 7–9 ft.
Flower width: 3 in.
p. 343

Hardy
Partial shade
Blooms in summer

Lilium pyrenaicum
Plant height: 3–4 ft.
Flower width: 2 in.
Yellow Turk's-Cap
Lily
p. 345

Hardy
Full sun
Blooms in late spring

Lilium ×
maculatum

Plant height: to 2 ft.
Flower width: 4 in.
p. 344

Hardy
Full sun
Blooms in summer

Hemerocallis
aurantiaca

Plant height: to 3 ft.
Flower width: 4 in.
p. 326

Half-hardy
Sun to partial shade
Blooms in summer

Lilium 'Enchantment'

Plant height: 2–3 ft.
Flower width: 6 in.
Asiatic Hybrid
p. 346

Hardy
Sun to partial shade
Blooms in summer

Hemerocallis fulva

Plant height: to 5 ft.
Flower length: 5 in.
p. 327

Hardy
Sun to partial shade
Blooms in summer

Lilium superbum

Plant height: 5–8 ft.
Flower width: 3 in.
Turk's-Cap Lily
p. 345

Hardy
Sun to partial shade
Blooms in summer

Lilium michiganense

Plant height: to 5 ft.
Flower width: 3 in.
p. 344

Hardy
Sun to partial shade
Blooms in summer

Lilium lancifolium   *Plant height: 4–6 ft.*   *Hardy*
                          Flower width: 5 in.   *Sun to partial shade*
                          Tiger Lily   *Blooms in summer*
                          p. 343

Lilium canadense   *Plant height: to 5 ft.*   *Hardy*
var. *editorum*   *Flower width: 3 in.*   *Full sun*
                          Meadow Lily   *Blooms in summer*
                          p. 342

***Lilium* ×
*hollandicum***

*Plant height:
to 2½ ft.
Flower width: 4 in.
Candlestick Lily
p. 343*

Hardy
Full sun
Blooms in summer

Lilium concolor

*Plant height: 3–4 ft.
Flower width: 3½ in.
Star Lily
p. 342*

Hardy
Full sun
Blooms in summer

Lilium philadelphicum

Plant height: 2–3 ft.
Flower length: 4 in.
Wood Lily
p. 345

Hardy
Partial shade
Blooms late spring to summer

Hemerocallis 'Red Siren'

Plant height: 2½–3 ft.
Flower width: 6 in.
p. 327

Hardy
Full sun
Blooms in summer

Other Bulbs

Cyclamen × Atkinsii Plant height: 3–6 in. Half-hardy
Flower length: Partial shade
¾–1 in. Blooms in early spring
p. 304

Scilla Tubergeniana Plant height: to 5 in. Hardy
Flower width: 1½ in. Full sun
p. 369 Blooms in early spring

Ledebouria socialis   *Plant height: to 6 in.*   *Tender*
     Flower width: ¼ in.   *Full sun*
     p. 339   *Blooms in late spring*

Puschkinia scilloides   *Plant height: to 6 in.*   *Hardy*
     Flower length: ½ in.   *Full sun*
     Striped Squill   *Blooms in early spring*
     p. 366

Hyacinthoides
hispanicus

Plant height: to 20 in.
Flower width: ¾ in.
Spanish Bluebells
p. 330

Hardy
Sun to partial shade
Blooms in late spring

Leucojum aestivum

Plant height: 9–12 in.
Flower length: ¾ in.
Giant Snowflake
p. 339

Hardy
Full sun
Blooms in spring

Leucojum vernum

Plant height: to 14 in.
Flower length: 1 in.
Spring Snowflake
p. 340

Hardy
Full sun
Blooms in early spring

Galanthus Elwesii

Plant height:
4–11 in.
Flower length:
1–1½ in.
Giant Snowdrop
p. 317

Hardy
Full sun
Blooms in early spring

Galanthus byzantinus

Plant height: 3–9 in.
Flower length: ½–1 in.
p. 317

Hardy
Full sun
Blooms in early spring

Calochortus albus

Plant height: to 2 ft.
Flower length: 1½ in.
White Globe Lily
p. 290

Hardy
Full sun
Blooms in early spring

Fritillaria Meleagris

Plant height:
12–18 in.
Flower length: 1½ in.
Guinea-Hen Flower
p. 316

Hardy
Sun to partial shade
Blooms in early spring

**Leucojum
autumnale**

Plant height: 3–6 in.
Flower length: ½ in.
p. 340

Hardy
Full sun
Blooms summer to
autumn

**Erythronium
californicum**

Plant height: to 12 in.
Flower length: 1½ in.
Fawn Lily
p. 311

Hardy
Partial shade
Blooms in early spring

**Erythronium
citrinum**

Plant height:
10–12 in.
Flower length: 1½ in.
p. 311

Hardy
Partial shade
Blooms in early spring

Erythronium montanum

Plant height: to 12 in.
Flower length: 1½ in.
Alpine Fawn Lily
p. 312

Hardy
Sun to partial shade
Blooms in early spring

Anemone blanda

Plant height: to 6 in.
Flower width: 1–2 in.
p. 284

Hardy
Partial shade
Blooms in early spring

Crocus versicolor
'Picturatus'

Plant height: to 5 ½ in.
Flower length:
3 ½ – 5 ½ in.
p. 302

Hardy
Sun to partial shade
Blooms in early spring

Crocus chrysanthus
'Snow Bunting'

Plant height: to 4 in.
Flower length: 4 in.
p. 301

Hardy
Full sun
Blooms in early spring

Crocus chrysanthus 'Blue Pearl'

Plant height: to 4 in.
Flower length: 4 in.
p. 301

Hardy
Full sun
Blooms in early spring

Crocus biflorus

Plant height: to 4 in.
Flower length: 4 in.
Scotch Crocus
p. 300

Hardy
Full sun
Blooms in early spring

Crocus niveus

Plant height: to 9½ in.
Flower length:
4½–9½ in.
p. 302

Half-hardy
Full sun
Blooms in autumn

Zephyranthes candida

Plant height: to 12 in.
Flower length: 2 in.
p. 384

Half-hardy
Full sun
Blooms summer to autumn

Ornithogalum
umbellatum

Plant height: 6–8 in.
Flower width: 1 in.
Star-of-Bethlehem
p. 361

Hardy
Full sun
Blooms in early spring

Lloydia serotina

Plant height: 2–6 in.
Flower length: ½ in.
p. 347

Hardy
Sun to partial shade
Blooms in spring

***Nothoscordum
bivalve***

Plant height: to 16 in.
Flower length: ½ in.
p. 360

Half-hardy
Full sun
Blooms in early spring

***Crinum
americanum***

Plant height: 1½–2 ft.
Flower width: 3 in.
Swamp Lily
p. 298

Tender
Partial shade
Blooms late spring to
summer

Milla biflora

Plant height: 6–12 in.
Flower width: 2½ in.
Mexican Star
p. 349

Tender
Full sun
Blooms in summer

Allium ursinum

Plant height: to 18 in.
Flowers: in clusters
2½ in. wide
Rampions
p. 280

Hardy
Partial shade
Blooms in spring

***Allium
neapolitanum***

Plant height: to 18 in.
Flowers: in clusters
2–3 in. wide
Daffodil Garlic
p. 278

Half-hardy
Full sun
Blooms in spring

***Triteleia
hyacinthina***

Plant height: to 20 in.
Flower length: ½ in.
Wild Hyacinth
p. 373

Hardy
Full sun
Blooms in summer

Allium tuberosum

Plant height:
15–20 in.
Flower length:
3/16 in.
Chinese Chive
p. 280

Hardy
Full sun
Blooms in summer

Allium roseum

Plant height: to 2 ft.
Flowers: in clusters
3 in. wide
p. 279

Hardy
Full sun
Blooms in late spring

Acidanthera bicolor | Plant height: to 2 ft. | Tender
| Flower width: 3 in. | Full sun
| p. 274 | Blooms in summer

Gladiolus × | Plant height: to 2 ft. | Half-hardy
Colvillei | Flower length: 2 in. | Full sun
'**The Bride**' | p. 321 | Blooms late spring to
| | summer

| ***Gladiolus carneus*** | Plant height: to 2 ft.
Flower width: 2–3 in.
p. 321 | Tender
Full sun
Blooms in summer |

| ***Ornithogalum***
thyrsoides | Plant height: 6–18 in.
Flower length: ¾ in.
Wonder Flower
p. 361 | Half-hardy
Full sun
Blooms late spring to
summer |

Allium pulchellum

Plant height: 1½–2 ft.
Flower length:
3/16 in.
p. 278

Hardy
Full sun
Blooms in summer

**Hymenocallis
caribaea**

Plant height: to 3 ft.
Flower length: 6 in.
p. 333

Tender
Sun to partial shade
Blooms late spring to
summer

Calochortus
Gunnisonii

Plant height: to 18 in.   Hardy
Flower length: 1¾ in.   Full sun
  Mariposa Lily   Blooms in late spring
  p. 290

Hymenocallis
narcissiflora

Plant height: to 2 ft.   Tender
Flower length: 8 in.   Full sun
  Basket-Flower   Blooms in summer
  p. 333

Pamianthe
peruviana

Plant height: to 2 ft.
Flower length: 5 in.
p. 364

Tender
Sun to partial shade
Blooms in early spring

Crinum Moorei

Plant height: to 5 ft.
Flower width: 4 in.
p. 299

Tender
Partial shade
Blooms in summer

Zephyranthes
Atamasco

Plant height: to 12 in.
Flower length: 3 in.
  Atamasco Lily
  p. 384

Half-hardy
Full sun
Blooms in early spring

Eucharis
grandiflora

Plant height: 1–2 ft.
Flower width: 4 in.
  Amazon Lily
  p. 312

Tender
Partial shade
Blossom season varies

Freesia × hybrida   *Plant height: 1½–2 ft.*   *Tender*
Flower length: 2 in.   *Full sun*
p. 315   *Blossom season varies*

Polianthes tuberosa   *Plant height: to 3 ft.*   *Tender*
Flower length: 2½ in.   *Full sun*
Tuberose   *Blooms summer to*
p. 366   *autumn*

Ornithogalum nutans

Plant height: 8–12 in.
Flower width: 2 in.
Star-of-Bethlehem
p. 361

Hardy
Partial shade
Blooms in early spring

Albuca Nelsonii

Plant height: to 5 ft.
Flower length: 1 in.
p. 276

Tender
Full sun
Blooms in spring

Crinum latifolium
Plant height: to 2 ft.
Flower length: 4 in.
Milk-and-Wine Lily
p. 299

Tender
Partial shade
Blooms in late spring

Ornithogalum Saundersiae
Plant height: to 4 ft.
Flower width: 1 in.
Giant Chincherinchee
p. 361

Tender
Full sun
Blooms in summer

Galtonia candicans   Plant height: 2–4 ft.   Hardy
                          Flower length: 1½ in.   Full sun
                          Summer Hyacinth   Blooms in summer
                          p. 318

Ornithogalum   Plant height: 1–2 ft.   Tender
arabicum   Flower length: 1 in.   Full sun
                          Star-of-Bethlehem   Blooms in summer
                          p. 361

Ixia viridiflora   *Plant height: to 20 in.*   Tender
                       Flower length: 1 in.   Full sun
                       p. 336   Blooms late spring to
                                                    summer

Gladiolus tristis   *Plant height: to 2 ft.*   Half-hardy
                       Flower length: 2 in.   Full sun
                       p. 322   Blooms in summer

Ixia maculata

Plant height: 6–12 in.
Flower length: 1 in.
p. 336

Tender
Full sun
Blooms late spring to summer

Watsonia
pyramidata
hybrid

Plant height: 3–6 ft.
Flower length: 3 in.
p. 383

Tender
Full sun
Blooms in summer

**Hesperocallis
undulata**

Plant height: to 2½ ft.   Half-hardy
Flower length: 2½ in.   Full sun
Desert Lily   Blooms in spring
p. 328

**Amianthium
muscitoxicum**

Plant height: to 3 ft.   Hardy
Flower width: ½ in.   Full sun
Fly-Poison   Blooms in summer
p. 282

Cardiocrinum
giganteum

Plant height: to 12 ft.
Flower length: 6 in.
p. 294

Hardy
Partial shade
Blooms in summer

Urginea maritima

Plant height: to 5 ft.
Flower length: ½ in.
Sea Onion
p. 381

Tender
Full sun
Blooms in autumn

Eucomis comosa

Plant height: 1–2 ft.
Flower length: ½ in.
Pineapple Flower
p. 313

Tender
Full sun
Blooms in summer

Hermodactylus
tuberosus

Plant height: to 18 in.
Flower length: 2 in.
Snake's Head Iris
p. 328

Hardy
Full sun
Blooms in early spring

Gladiolus ×
hortulanus
'Lucky Shamrock'

Plant height: to 3 ft.
Flower length: 3–4 in.
p. 321

Tender to half-hardy
Full sun
Blooms in summer

Moraea ramosissima

Plant height: 2–3 ft.
Flower length: 1¼ in.
p. 349

Half-hardy
Full sun
Blooms in spring

Ixia maculata *Plant height: 6–12 in.* *Tender*
Flower length: 1 in. *Full sun*
p. 336 *Blooms late spring to summer*

Freesia × hybrida *Plant height: 1½–2 ft.* *Tender*
Flower length: 2 in. *Full sun*
p. 315 *Blossom season varies*

Cypella Herbertii
Plant height: to 18 in.
Flower width: 3 in.
p. 306

Tender
Full sun
Blooms late spring to
summer

Gloriosa superba
'Lutea'
Plant height:
vine to 12 ft.
Flower length: 2–3 in.
p. 323

Tender
Full sun
Blooms in summer

Erythronium grandiflorum

Plant height: 1–2 ft.
Flower length: 1–2 in..
Avalanche Lily
p. 311

Hardy
Partial shade
Blooms in early spring

Erythronium americanum

Plant height: to 12 in.
Flower length: 1½ in.
Yellow Adder's-
Tongue
p. 311

Hardy
Partial shade
Blooms in early spring

| **Erythronium** **tuolumnense** | Plant height: to 12 in.
Flower length: 1¼ in.
p. 312 | Hardy
Partial shade
Blooms in early spring |

| **Fritillaria** **lanceolata** | Plant height: to 2 ft.
Flower length: 1½ in.
Checker Lily
p. 316 | Half-hardy
Full sun
Blooms in early spring |

Fritillaria pallidiflora

Plant height: 6–14 in.
Flower length: 1½ in. .
p. 316

Hardy
Sun to partial shade
Blooms in early spring

Lachenalia aloides 'Luteola'

Plant height: to 12 in.
Flower length: 1 in.
Cape Cowslip
p. 337

Tender
Full sun
Blooms in early spring

Fritillaria pudica   Plant height: to 9 in.   Hardy
                         Flower length: ¾ in.   Sun to partial shade
                         Yellow Fritillary   Blooms in early spring
                         p. 316

Haemanthus albiflos   Plant height: to 12 in.   Tender
                          Flowers: in clusters   Full sun
                          2 in. wide   Blooms in summer
                          p. 325

Allium Moly

Plant height: to 14 in.
Flowers: in clusters
3 in. wide
Lily Leek
p. 278

Hardy
Full sun
Blooms in late spring

Dahlia pinnata
hybrid

Plant height: to 6 ft.
Flower width: 2–4 in.
p. 308

Tender
Full sun
Blooms summer to
autumn

Allium flavum

Plant height: 12–18 in.

Flower length: ⅛ in.

p. 277

Hardy

Full sun

Blooms in summer

Anemone palmata

Plant height: 4–12 in.

Flower width:

1–1½ in.

p. 285

Tender

Sun to partial shade

Blooms in early spring

Oxalis Pes-caprae
Plant height: to 12 in.
Flower width: 1½ in.
Bermuda Buttercup
p. 363

Tender
Full sun
Blooms in early spring

Calochortus luteus
Plant height: 1–2½ ft.
Flower length:
1½–2 in.
Yellow Mariposa
p. 290

Hardy
Full sun
Blooms in late spring

Eranthis hyemalis

Plant height: 3–8 in.
Flower width: 1 in.
Winter Aconite
p. 310

Hardy
Sun to partial shade
Blooms in early spring

Iris Danfordiae

Plant height: to 4 in.
Flower length: 2–3 in.
p. 334

Hardy
Full sun
Blooms in early spring

Zephyranthes citrina   *Plant height: 8–12 in.*   Tender
Flower length: 1½ in.   *Full sun*
p. 384   *Blooms summer to*
autumn

Sternbergia lutea   *Plant height: 4–7 in.*   Hardy
Flower length: 1½ in.   *Full sun*
Winter Daffodil   *Blooms in autumn*
p. 371

Crocus chrysanthus | Plant height: to 4 in. | Hardy
'E. P. Bowles' | Flower length: 4 in. | Full sun
| p. 301 | Blooms in early spring

Crocus flavus | Plant height: to 7 in. | Hardy
| Flower length: | Full sun
| 2½–7 in. | Blooms in early spring
| p. 301 |

***Ranunculus
asiaticus***

*Plant height: 6–18 in.
Flower width: 1–4 in.
Persian Buttercup
p. 367*

Half-hardy
Full sun
Blooms in early spring

Begonia × hiemalis

*Plant height: to 12 in.
Flower width: 1 in.
p. 287*

Tender
Partial shade
Blooms autumn to
winter

Anemone × fulgens

Plant height:
10–12 in.
Flower width:
2–2½ in.
Scarlet Windflower
p. 284

Hardy
Sun to partial shade
Blooms in early spring

Dahlia pinnata
hybrid

Plant height: to 6 ft.
Flower width: 2–4 in.
p. 308

Tender
Full sun
Blooms summer to
autumn

Dahlia pinnata
hybrid

Plant height: to 6 ft.
Flower width: 2–4 in.
p. 308

Tender
Full sun
Blooms summer to
autumn

Dahlia pinnata
hybrid

Plant height: to 6 ft.
Flower width: 2–4 in.
p. 308

Tender
Full sun
Blooms summer to
autumn

| *Dahlia pinnata* 'Biddenham Fairy' | Plant height: to 6 ft. Flower width: 2–4 in. p. 308 | Tender Full sun Blooms summer to autumn |

| *Anemone coronaria* | Plant height: 6–18 in. Flower width: 1½–2½ in. Poppy Anemone p. 284 | Tender Partial shade Blooms in early spring |

Lycoris radiata

Plant height: to 16 in. Half-hardy
Flower length: 1½ in. Full sun
Red Spider-Lily Blooms in autumn
p. 348

Romulea sabulosa

Plant height: to 4 in. Tender
Flower length: Full sun
1–1½ in. Blooms in late spring
p. 368

Tigridia Pavonia
Plant height: 1–2 ft.
Flower width: 3–6 in.
Tiger Flower
p. 372

Tender
Full sun
Blooms in summer

Sparaxis tricolor
Plant height: to 18 in.
Flower length: 1 in.
Harlequin Flower
p. 370

Tender
Full sun
Blooms in late spring

Streptanthera cuprea

Plant height: to 9 in.
Flower width: 2 in.
p. 372

Tender
Full sun
Blooms in late spring

Lapeirousia laxa

Plant height: 6–10 in.
Flower length: 1½ in.
p. 338

Half-hardy
Full sun
Blooms in summer

Oxalis Deppei

Plant height: 4–12 in.
Flower length:
½–1 in.
Good-Luck Plant
p. 363

Tender
Full sun
Blooms in summer

Homeria Breyniana
'Aurantiaca'

Plant height: to 18 in.
Flower length: 1½ in.
p. 330

Tender
Full sun
Blooms in late spring

Watsonia Beatricis
Plant height: to 4 ft.
Flower length: 3 in.
p. 383

Tender
Full sun
Blooms in autumn

Crocosmia ×
crocosmiiflora
Plant height: to 4 ft.
Flower width: 2 in.
Common Montbretia
p. 299

Half-hardy
Full sun
Blooms summer to
autumn

Crocosmia
Masoniorum

Plant height: 2–4 ft.
Flower length: 1 in.
p. 300

Half-hardy
Full sun
Blooms in summer

Curtonus
paniculatus

Plant height: to 4 ft.
Flower length: 2 in.
p. 302

Tender
Full sun
Blooms in summer

**Gloriosa
Rothschildiana**

Plant height:
vine to 8 ft.
Flower length: 3 in.
p. 323

Tender
Full sun
Blooms late spring to
summer

Urceolina peruviana

Plant height: to 18 in.
Flower length: 1½ in.
p. 380

Tender
Full sun
Blooms in summer

Sprekelia *Plant height: to 12 in.* *Tender*
formosissima *Flower length: 4 in.* *Full sun*
Aztec Lily *Blooms in summer*
p. 370

Fritillaria *Plant height: 2-4 ft.* *Hardy*
imperialis *Flower length: 2 in.* *Full sun*
Crown Imperial *Blooms in early spring*
p. 316

Vallota speciosa

Plant height: to 3 ft.
Flower width: 3 in.
Scarborough Lily
p. 381

Tender
Full sun
Blooms in summer

Clivia
hybrid

Plant height:
1½–2 ft.
Flower length: 2–3 in.
p. 296

Tender
Sun to partial shade
Blooms in spring

Clivia miniata   Plant height: 1½–2 ft.   Tender
Flower length: 2–3 in.   Sun to partial shade
p. 296   Blooms in early spring

Begonia ×   Plant height: to 18 in.   Tender
tuberhybrida   Flower width: 4 in.   Partial shade
p. 287   Blooms in summer

Canna × generalis
Plant height: 3–6 ft.
Flower width: 4 in.
Common Garden Canna
p. 293

Tender
Full sun
Blooms in summer

**Veltheimia
viridifolia**
Plant height: to 2 ft.
Flower length: 1 in.
Unicorn Root
p. 382

Tender
Full sun
Blooms in early spring

Canna × generalis   Plant height: 3–6 ft.   Tender
                          Flower width: 4 in.   Full sun
                          Common Garden Canna   Blooms in summer
                          p. 293

Boophone disticha   Plant height: to 12 in.   Tender
                          Flowers: in clusters   Full sun
                          12 in. wide   Blooms summer to
                          Gifbol   autumn
                          p. 288

**Haemanthus
Katherinae**

Plant height:
12–18 in.
Flowers: in clusters
9 in. wide
Catherine-Wheel
p. 325

Tender
Full sun
Blooms in summer

Tritonia crocata

Plant height: to 18 in.
Flower width: 2 in.
Montbretia
p. 373

Tender
Full sun
Blooms late spring to
summer

Haemanthus coccineus

Plant height: to 12 in.
Flowers: in clusters
3 in. wide
Blood Lily
p. 325

Tender
Full sun
Blooms in summer

Gladiolus × gandavensis

Plant height: to 3 ft.
Flower length: 2–3 in.
p. 321

Tender
Full sun
Blooms in summer

Gladiolus ×
hortulanus

Plant height: to 3 ft.
Flower length: 3–4 in.
p. 321

Tender to half-hardy
Full sun
Blooms in summer

Hippeastrum
hybrid

Plant height: to 2 ft.
Flower length: 6 in.
Dutch Amaryllis
p. 329

Tender
Full sun
Blooms in early spring

Gladiolus ×
hortulanus

Plant height: to 3 ft.
Flower length: 3–4 in.
p. 321

Tender to half-hardy
Full sun
Blooms in summer

Hippeastrum
hybrid

Plant height: to 2 ft.
Flower length: 6 in.
Dutch Amaryllis
p. 329

Tender
Full sun
Blooms in early spring

Habranthus
tubispathus

Plant height: to 9 in.
Flower length: 3 in.
p. 324

Tender
Full sun
Blooms summer to
autumn

Colchicum
autumnale

Plant height: 8–10 in.
Flower width: 3–4 in.
Autumn Crocus
p. 297

Hardy
Full sun
Blooms in autumn

Colchicum speciosum   Plant height: to 12 in.   Hardy
Flower width: 4 in.   Full sun
Autumn Crocus   Blooms in autumn
p. 297

Crocus Goulimyi   Plant height: to 10 in.   Half-hardy
Flower length: Sun to partial shade
4–10 in.   Blooms in autumn
p. 301

Calochortus
macrocarpus

Plant height: to 2 ft.
Flower length: 2 in.
Green-banded
Mariposa
p. 290

Hardy
Full sun
Blooms in summer

Habranthus
brachyandrus

Plant height: to 12 in.
Flower width: 3 in.
p. 324

Tender
Full sun
Blooms in summer

Calochortus splendens

Plant height:
1¼–2 ft.
Flower length: 2 in.
p. 291

Hardy
Full sun
Blooms in late spring

Habranthus Andersonii

Plant height: to 6 in.
Flower length: 1½ in.
p. 324

Tender
Full sun
Blooms in late spring

Erythronium
Hendersonii

Plant height: to 12 in.
Flower length: 1½ in.
p. 311

Hardy
Partial shade
Blooms in early spring

Erythronium
Dens-canis

Plant height: 6–12 in.
Flower width: 2 in.
Dogtooth Violet
p. 311

Hardy
Partial shade
Blooms in early spring

Erythronium revolutum

Plant height: to 16 in.
Flower length: 1¾ in.
Coast Fawn Lily
p. 312

Hardy
Partial shade
Blooms in early spring

Cyclamen hederifolium

Plant height: 3–6 in.
Flower length: 1 in.
Sowbread
p. 304

Half-hardy
Partial shade
Blooms summer to
autumn

Cyclamen coum

Plant height: 3–6 in.
Flower length: ¾ in.
p. 304

Half-hardy
Partial shade
Blooms in early spring

***Cyclamen
purpurascens***

Plant height: 3–6 in.
Flower length: ¾ in.
p. 305

Half-hardy
Partial shade
Blooms summer to
autumn

Cyclamen persicum   Plant height: 6–12 in.   Tender
                        Flower length: 2 in.   Partial shade
                        Common Cyclamen   Blooms in early spring
                        p. 305

Cyclamen repandum   Plant height: 3–6 in.   Half-hardy
                        Flower length: 1¼ in.   Partial shade
                        p. 305   Blooms in early spring

Begonia grandis

Plant height: 1–2 ft.
Flower width: 1½ in.
Hardy Begonia
p. 286

Tender
Partial shade
Blooms in summer

Oxalis Bowiei

Plant height: to 12 in.
Flower width:
1–1½ in.
p. 362

Tender
Full sun
Blooms in summer

Oxalis violacea Plant height: to 10 in. Hardy
 Flower length: ¾ in. Partial shade
 Purple Wood Sorrel Blooms in late spring
 p. 364

Oxalis adenophylla Plant height: to 6 in. Half-hardy
 Flower width: 1 in. Full sun
 p. 362 Blooms in summer

Oxalis corymbosa

Plant height: to 12 in.
Flower width: ¾ in.
p. 363

Tender
Full sun
Blooms in summer

Oxalis rubra

Plant height: 6–12 in.
Flower length: ¾ in.
p. 364

Tender
Full sun
Blooms in winter

Oxalis purpurea   *Plant height: to 6 in.*   *Tender*
                        Flower width: 2 in.   *Full sun*
                        p. 363   *Blooms in autumn*

Oxalis lasiandra   *Plant height: to 12 in.*   *Tender*
                        Flower width: ½ in.   *Full sun*
                        p. 363   *Blooms in summer*

Oxalis braziliensis

Plant height: 5–10 in.
Flower width: 1 in.
p. 363

Tender
Full sun
Blooms in summer

Dahlia pinnata
hybrid

Plant height: to 6 ft.
Flower width: 2–4 in.
p. 308

Tender
Full sun
Blooms summer to
autumn

Anemone hortensis   Plant height: to 10 in.   Hardy
                            Flower width: 3 in.   Sun to partial shade
                            Garden Anemone   Blooms in early spring
                            p. 285

Allium pulchellum   Plant height: 1½–2 ft.   Hardy
                            Flower length: 3/16 in.   Full sun
                            p. 278   Blooms in summer

**Allium
sphaerocephalum**

Plant height: to 3 ft.
Flowers: in clusters
⅜–2 in. wide
p. 279

Hardy
Full sun
Blooms in summer

**Allium
Rosenbachianum**

Plant height: 2–2½ ft.
Flower width:
½–¾ in.
p. 279

Hardy
Full sun
Blooms in late spring

Allium
Schoenoprasum

Plant height: to 12 in.
Flower length:
¼ – ½ in.
Chive
p. 279

Hardy
Full sun
Blooms in late spring

Allium giganteum

Plant height: 3–4 ft.
Flowers: in clusters
4–6 in. wide
Giant Garlic
p. 277

Hardy
Sun to partial shade
Blooms late spring to
summer

Allium karataviense   *Plant height: 6–10 in.*   *Hardy*
                            Flowers: in clusters   *Full sun*
                            3–4 in. wide   *Blooms in late spring*
                            p. 278

Nerine sarniensis   *Plant height: 18 in.*   *Tender*
                          Flower length: 1½ in.   *Full sun*
                          Guernsey Lily   *Blooms in autumn*
                          p. 358

Allium Christophii

Plant height:
1½–2½ ft.
Flowers: in clusters
8–12 in. wide
Star of Persia
p. 277

Hardy
Full sun
Blooms in late spring

Allium senescens

Plant height: to 2 ft.
Flower width: ⅜ in.
p. 279

Hardy
Full sun
Blooms in summer

Allium tibeticum	*Plant height: to 12 in.*	*Hardy*
	Flower length: ¼ in.	*Full sun*
	p. 280	*Blooms in summer*

Dichelostemma	*Plant height: to 2 ft.*	*Half-hardy*
pulchellum	*Flower length: ¾ in.*	*Full sun*
	Blue Dicks	*Blooms in early spring*
	p. 309	

Allium stellatum	*Plant height: to 18 in.*	*Hardy*
	Flower width: ⅜ *in.*	*Full sun*
	Prairie Onion	*Blooms summer to*
	p. 279	*autumn*

Allium	*Plant height:*	*Hardy*
cyathophorum	*10–15 in.*	*Full sun*
var. *Farreri*	*Flower length:* ⅓ *in.*	*Blooms in late spring*
	p. 277	

Fritillaria
verticillata

Plant height: to 2 ft.
Flower length: 1¼ in.
p. 317

Hardy
Sun to partial shade
Blooms in early spring

Dierama pendulum

Plant height: to 5 ft.
Flower length: 1 in.
p. 309

Tender
Full sun
Blooms in summer

Fritillaria Meleagris   *Plant height:*   *Hardy*
                            12–18 in.   *Sun to partial shade*
                            Flower length: 1½ in. *Blooms in early spring*
                            Guinea-Hen Flower
                            p. 316

Allium   *Plant height: 4–10 in.* *Half-hardy*
narcissiflorum   *Flower length: ½ in.*   *Full sun*
                            p. 278   *Blooms in summer*

Crinum × Powellii

Plant height: to 2 ft.
Flower length: 3 in.
p. 299

Tender
Partial shade
Blooms in summer

Nectaroscordum siculum

Plant height: to 4 ft.
Flower length: ½ in.
p. 357

Hardy
Full sun
Blooms in early spring

Crinum
bulbispermum

Plant height: to 3 ft.
Flower width: 4 in.
p. 298

Tender
Partial shade
Blooms in late spring

Nectaroscordum
bulgaricum

Plant height: to 4 ft.
Flower length: ½ in.
p. 357

Hardy
Full sun
Blooms in early spring

Notholirion
Thomsonianum

Plant height: 3–4 ft.
Flower length: 2 in.
p. 359

Tender
Partial shade
Blooms in early spring

Gladiolus
byzantinus

Plant height: to 3 ft.
Flower length: 1¼ in.
p. 321

Half-hardy
Full sun
Blooms in summer

Gladiolus illyricus   Plant height: 1–3 ft.   Half-hardy
                            Flower width: 1½ in.   Full sun
                            p. 322   Blooms late spring to
                                                       summer

Gladiolus segetum   Plant height: 1½–2 ft.   Half-hardy
                           Flower length: 1½ in.   Full sun
                           Cornflag   Blooms in summer
                           p. 322

Allium oreophilum   Plant height: to 4 in.   Hardy
                        Flower length: ⅜ in.   Full sun
                        p. 278   Blooms in late spring

Nerine Bowdenii   Plant height: 1–2 ft.   Tender
                       Flower length: 3 in.   Full sun
                       p. 358   Blooms in autumn

Allium acuminatum   Plant height: to 12 in.   Hardy
Flower length: ½ in.   Full sun
p. 276   Blooms in late spring

Lycoris squamigera   Plant height: to 2 ft.   Hardy
Flower length: 3 in.   Full sun
Magic Lily   Blooms in summer
p. 348

× **Amarcrinum**
memoria-Corsii

Plant height: to 4 ft.
Flower length: 3 in.
p. 281

Tender
Full sun
Blooms in summer

Zephyranthes
grandiflora

Plant height: to 12 in.
Flower length: 3 in.
Zephyr Lily
p. 384

Tender
Full sun
Blooms late spring to
summer

Amaryllis Belladonna
Plant height: to 18 in.
Flower length: 3½ in.
Belladonna Lily
p. 282

Tender
Full sun
Blooms in summer

Zephyranthes rosea
Plant height: to 12 in.
Flower length: 1 in.
p. 384

Tender
Full sun
Blooms in autumn

Iris reticulata
'Harmony'

Plant height: 6–18 in.
Flower length: 3–6 in.
p. 335

Hardy
Full sun
Blooms in early spring

Iris xiphioides

Plant height: 8–15 in.
Flower length: 3 in.
English Iris
p. 335

Hardy
Full sun
Blooms late spring to
summer

Iris histrioides
'Major'

Plant height: 4–9 in.
Flower width: 3 in.
p. 335

Hardy
Full sun
Blooms in early spring

Iris reticulata
'Violet Beauty'

Plant height: 6–18 in.
Flower length: 3–6 in.
p. 335

Hardy
Full sun
Blooms in early spring

Iris Xiphium Plant height: to 2 ft. Hardy
Flower length: 4 in. Full sun
Spanish Iris Blooms in late spring
p. 335

Ferraria crispa Plant height: to 18 in. Tender
Flower width: 3–4 in. Full sun
p. 314 Blooms late spring to
summer

Iris Histrio   Plant height: to 6 in.   Hardy
var. *aintabensis*   Flower width: 3 in.   Full sun
                        p. 335   Blooms in early spring

Romulea   Plant height: 2–3 in.   Tender
Bulbocodium   Flower length: Full sun
                       1–1½ in.   Blooms in early spring
                       p. 368

Crocus vernus   Plant height: to 8 in.   Hardy
Flower length: Sun to partial shade
1½–8 in.   Blooms in spring
Common Crocus
p. 302

Crocus longiflorus   Plant height: to 5½ in.   Hardy
Flower length: Sun to partial shade
2¾–5½ in.   Blooms in autumn
p. 301

Crocus Imperati
Plant height: to 5½ in.
Flower length:
2½–5½ in.
p. 301

Half-hardy
Sun to partial shade
Blooms in early spring

Crocus etruscus
Plant height: to 4 in.
Flower length: 4 in.
p. 301

Hardy
Sun to partial shade
Blooms in early spring

Crocus Tomasinianus

Plant height: to 5½ in.
Flower length:
2½–5½ in.
p. 302

Hardy
Sun to partial shade
Blooms in early spring

Crocus medius

Plant height: to 10 in.
Flower length: 4–10 in.
p. 301

Hardy
Sun to partial shade
Blooms in autumn

Crocus biflorus
var. *Adamii*

Plant height: to 4 in.
Flower length: 4 in.
Scotch Crocus
p. 300

Hardy
Full sun
Blooms in early spring

Crocus vernus

Plant height: to 8 in.
Flower length:
1½–8 in.
Common Crocus
p. 302

Hardy
Sun to partial shade
Blooms in spring

Anemone apennina
Plant height:
2½–12 in.
Flower width: 1½ in.
p. 284

Half-hardy
Partial shade
Blooms in early spring

Anemone coronaria
Plant height: 6–18 in.
Flower width:
1½–2½ in.
Poppy Anemone
p. 284

Tender
Partial shade
Blooms in early spring

Anemone blanda
Plant height: to 6 in.
Flower width: 1–2 in.
p. 284

Hardy
Partial shade
Blooms in early spring

Ipheion uniflorum
Plant height: to 8 in.
Flower width: 1½ in.
Spring Starflower
p. 334

Half-hardy
Full sun
Blooms in early spring

| Chionodoxa sardensis | Plant height: 3–6 in.
Flower width: 1 in.
Glory-of-the-Snow
p. 295 | Hardy
Full sun
Blooms in early spring |

| Chionodoxa Luciliae | Plant height: 3–6 in.
Flower width: 1 in.
Glory-of-the-Snow
p. 295 | Hardy
Full sun
Blooms in early spring |

Brodiaea coronaria
*Plant height:
12–18 in.
Flower length: 1½ in.
p. 289*

*Tender to half-hardy
Full sun
Blooms in summer*

**Hyacinthus
orientalis**
*Plant height: to 18 in.
Flower length: 1 in.
Common Garden
Hyacinth
p. 332*

*Hardy
Full sun
Blooms in early spring*

Brimeura
amethystina

Plant height: 4–10 in.
Flower length: ⅜ in.
p. 288

Hardy
Full sun
Blooms in early spring

Hyacinthoides
hispanicus

Plant height: to 20 in.
Flower width: ¾ in.
Spanish Bluebells
p. 330

Hardy
Sun to partial shade
Blooms in late spring

**Hyacinthoides
non-scriptus**

Plant height: to 18 in.
Flower length: ¾ in.
Bluebells of England
p. 330

Hardy
Sun to partial shade
Blooms in late spring

Scilla siberica

Plant height: 4–6 in.
Flower width: ½ in.
Siberian Squill
p. 369

Hardy
Sun to partial shade
Blooms in early spring

Muscari botryoides
Plant height: to 12 in.
Flower length: ⅛ in.
Bluebells
p. 350

Hardy
Full sun
Blooms in early spring

Muscari azureum
Plant height: to 8 in.
Flower length: 3/16 in.
Grape-Hyacinth
p. 350

Hardy
Full sun
Blooms in early spring

Muscari armeniacum

Plant height: to 12 in.
Flower length: 5/16 in.
Grape-Hyacinth
p. 350

Hardy
Full sun
Blooms in early spring

Muscari latifolium

Plant height: to 12 in.
Flower length: ¼ in.
Grape-Hyacinth
p. 351

Hardy
Full sun
Blooms in early spring

Allium caeruleum
    Plant height: 2–3 ft.   Hardy
    Flower width: 2/5 in.   Full sun
    p. 277   Blooms in late spring

Agapanthus orientalis
    Plant height: 2–3 ft.   Tender
    Flower length: 2 in.   Full sun
    p. 275   Blooms in summer

Scilla peruviana

Plant height: to 18 in.   Half-hardy
Flower length: ½ in.   Full sun
Cuban Lily   Blooms in early spring
p. 369

Agapanthus africanus

Plant height: Tender
1½–3½ ft.   Full sun
Flower length: 1½ in.   Blooms in summer
African Lily
p. 275

Allium cyaneum

Plant height: 6–12 in.
Flower length: ¼ in.
p. 277

Hardy
Full sun
Blooms in summer

Hyacinthoides italicus

Plant height: to 12 in.
Flower length: ¼ in.
Italian Squill
p. 330

Hardy
Sun to partial shade
Blooms in late spring

Scilla bifolia　　Plant height: to 6 in.　　Hardy
　　　　　　　　　Flower width: ½ in.　　Sun to partial shade
　　　　　　　　　p. 369　　　　　　　　Blooms in early spring

Camassia Quamash　　Plant height: 1–2 ft.　　Hardy
　　　　　　　　　　　Flower length: 1 in.　　Full sun
　　　　　　　　　　　Camas　　　　　　　　Blooms in late spring
　　　　　　　　　　　p. 292

Camassia scilloides
Plant height: to 2½ ft.   Hardy
Flower length: ½ in.   Full sun
Wild Hyacinth   Blooms in late spring
p. 292

Camassia Leichtlinii
Plant height: to 4 ft.   Hardy
Flower length: 1 in.   Full sun
p. 291   Blooms in late spring

Camassia Cusickii   Plant height: to 3½ ft.   Hardy
                          Flower length: 1 in.   Full sun
                          p. 291   Blooms in late spring

Muscari comosum   Plant height: to 18 in.   Hardy
                         Flower length: 5/16 in.   Full sun
                         Tassel-Hyacinth   Blooms in late spring
                         p. 350

Acidanthera
Iris family
Iridaceae

As-i-dan'the-ra. About 25 species of bulbous
herbs native to tropical and South Africa.
Only a single species is much grown here.
Its summer-blooming, long-tubed flowers are
handsome, somewhat resembling gladiolus.
(Named from the Greek for "cusp" and
"anther," in allusion to the cusplike anthers
of some species.)

Description
Leaves sword-shaped. Flowers in a long,
loose, rather leafy spike, the corolla-tube
slightly expanded toward the top. Fruit an
oblong capsule.

How to Grow
Acidanthera is tender; it should be treated
exactly like gladiolus. The many cormels that
start around the old corm can be used for
propagation. Start plants in pots indoors in
spring. Store corms at 60° F (16° C) during
winter.

bicolor p. 172
The brownish corm is 1 in. (2.5 cm) in
diameter. Stem unbranched, to 2 ft. (60 cm)
high. Leaves few, usually only 1 or 2. Spike
few-flowered, its leafy sheaths 3 in. (7.5 cm)
long. Flowers fragrant, cream-white outside,
splashed chocolate-brown inside, 3 in. wide.
Tropical Africa. Summer. *A. Murieliae* is a
trade name for color variants of *A. bicolor*.
Zone 7.

Agapanthus
Amaryllis family
Amaryllidaceae

Ag-a-pan'thus. Rhizomatous herbs of the
amaryllis family, often grown in tubs or pots
for their showy flowers. (From Greek for
"love flower.")

Description
Leaves all at base of stem, numerous, long
and narrow. Flowers numerous, in a terminal
umbel that arises from between 2 sheathlike
bracts. Corolla funnel-shaped, its oblong
segments about as long as the tube. Fruit a
3-celled pod.

How to Grow

Grown in greenhouses in large pots or tubs. The plant flowers in the summer, after which it should be rested over the winter with little water and in a frost-free place. These vigorous growers need a large pot or tub. If kept in the same one, they should be fed liberally with liquid manure.

africanus p. 267

African Lily; Lily-of-the-Nile. Plant 1½–3½ ft. (45–105 cm) high. Leaves 20 in. (50 cm) long, rather thick. Flower-stalk longer than leaves, the cluster consisting of about 12–30 striking blue flowers, 1½ in. (4 cm) long. There are many horticultural varieties, some larger than the species, some very much smaller, others with variegated leaves, and still others with flowers paler blue, or violet, or white. South Africa. It may be grown outdoors in Zones 8 and 9, and flowered outdoors northward as a summer pot specimen. Summer. Zone 9.

orientalis p. 266

Flowering stalk 2–3 ft. (60–90 cm) high. Leaves numerous, thickish, 1–2 ft. (30–60 cm) long and nearly 3 in. (7.5 cm) wide. Flowers numerous (often 40–100) in a dense terminal umbel, blue, 2 in. (5 cm) long. A very showy plant but suited to outdoor culture only in frost-free regions. South Africa. Summer. Zone 9.

Albuca
Lily family
Liliaceae

Al-bu′ka. A genus of about 50 species of bulbous perennial herbs, most native to South Africa. Related to *Ornithogalum* and *Urginea*. (*Albuca* is from the Latin *albicans,* "off-white," or *albus,* "white.")

Description

Leaves flat, linear to lance-shaped, all arising from top of bulb. Flowers white or yellow, the 3 outer perianth segments spreading, the 3 inner segments short, erect, hooded, and enclosing stamens.

How to Grow

Hardy outdoors only in Zone 10; elsewhere grown in pots indoors or in the greenhouse. Pot up in early autumn, in a well-drained,

compost-rich soil. Give just enough water to prevent soil from drying out until growth commences, in late fall or early winter. While growing, provide ample water. After flowering, in spring or early summer, leaves will die down. Reduce water at this time, providing just enough so that soil does not become totally dry.

Nelsonii p. 179
To 5 ft. (1.5 m) high. Leaves bright green, to 3½ ft. (105 cm) long and 2 in. (5 cm) wide. Flowering stalk to 5 ft. (1.5 m) high, the flowers carried in a raceme. Flowers white, to 1 in. (2.5 cm) long. Natal Prov. (South Africa). Spring. Zone 9.

Allium
Amaryllis family
Amaryllidaceae

Al′li-um. A large genus of some 400 species of mostly onion-scented herbs that includes the common onion, the leek, garlic, chive, and shallot, as well as a group of perennial herbs grown for their ornamental flowers. The latter are featured here. Nearly all produce bulbs, often of considerable size, as in the common onion. (*Allium* is the classical name for garlic.)

Description
Leaves mostly at base of stem, typically hollow, but usually flat in the ornamental species. Flowers white, yellow, or pink to purple, few to a great many, always in an umbel, which is usually ball-shaped. Fruit a small 3-celled capsule.

How to Grow
The ornamental alliums are good border plants, and easy to grow in any ordinary garden soil. All need full sun except *A. ursinum,* which needs partial shade. Some of the species produce bulbils in the flower cluster, which provide an easy method of propagation and may even need to be controlled to curb spreading. Plant the bulbs in autumn or spring or sow seeds in spring. Some yield an onion-scented honey.

acuminatum p. 247
An ornamental species from the Rocky Mts., usually less than 12 in. (30 cm) high. Leaves about ½ in. (13 mm) wide. Flowers

numerous, ½ in. (1.3 cm) long, the
umbels profuse, rose-purple. British
Columbia south to Calif. and east to Mont.
and Ariz. Late spring. Zone 4.

caeruleum p. 266
A stout herb, 2–3 ft. (60–90 cm) high,
grown for ornament. Leaves 3-sided. Flowers
deep blue, 2/5 in. (1 cm) wide. Turkestan
and Siberia (U.S.S.R.). Late spring. Zone 4.

Christophii p. 237
Star of Persia. Bulb globular, the flowering
stalk 1½–2½ ft. (45–75 cm) high. Leaves
flat, white-hairy beneath, 12–18 in. (30–
45 cm) long, 1–2 in. (2.5–5.0 cm) wide.
Flowers numerous, lilac, star-shaped, to 1 in.
(2.5 cm) across, borne in an umbel often
8–12 in. (20–30 cm) in diameter. The
flowering heads dry easily and are excellent
for use in dried arrangements. Cen. Asia.
Late spring. Zone 4.

cyaneum p. 268
A perennial, 6–12 in. (15–30 cm) high, the
narrow leaves channeled above, scarcely
1/12 in. (2 mm) wide. Flowers ¼ in. (6 mm)
long, bell-shaped, nodding, blue or purplish,
the bluish stamens protruding. China.
Summer. Zone 5.

cyathophorum var. *Farreri* p. 239
Plant 10–15 in. (25–38 cm) high, the stalk
angled or winged, and red below. Leaves
12–15 in. (30–38 cm) long, keeled and
channeled. Flowers bell-shaped, purplish red,
⅓ in. (8 mm) long, in a loose umbel. Nw.
China. Late spring. Zone 5.

flavum p. 195
Flowering stem 12–18 in. (30–45 cm) high,
the leaves narrow, cylindrical, channeled.
Flowers ⅛ in. (3.2 mm) long, yellow, rather
lustrous, in a loose cluster, below which are
2 long bracts. S. Europe and w. Asia.
Summer. Zone 4.

giganteum p. 235
Giant Garlic; Giant Onion. A huge
ornamental allium, the flowering stalk
3–4 ft. (90–120 cm) high. Leaves bluish gray,
strap-shaped, 2 in. (5 cm) wide and 18 in.
(45 cm) long. Flowers pinkish purple in a
dense, globelike cluster 4–6 in. (10–15 cm)
across. Cen. Asia. Tolerates partial shade.
Late spring to early summer. Zone 5.

karataviense p. 236

A very broad-leaved ornamental onion, 6–10 in. (15–25 cm) high, the leaves as long, and nearly 5 in. (12.5 cm) wide, bluish green, sometimes variegated. Flowers reddish white, ⅝ in. (16 mm) wide, crowded in a dense globelike umbel 3–4 in. (7.5–10.0 cm) in diameter. Turkestan (U.S.S.R.). Late spring. Zone 4.

Moly p. 194

Lily Leek. A decorative species for use in borders or rock gardens, usually not over 14 in. (35 cm) high, the leaves flat. Flowers showy, yellow, ¾–1 in. (2.0–2.5 cm) in diameter, in a small, compact umbel to 3 in. (7.5 cm) across. S. Europe. Late spring. Zone 4.

narcissiflorum p. 241

A striking perennial, 4–10 in. (10–25 cm) high, the flat, narrow leaves about ⅛ in. (3 mm) wide. Flowers to ½ in. (1.3 cm) long, showy, rose-pink, nodding, but ultimately erect, bell-shaped. Italy. Summer. Zone 5.

neapolitanum p. 170

Daffodil Garlic. A decorative plant, 18 in. (45 cm) high. Leaves flat, a little shorter than stalk of flower cluster. Flowers white, fragrant, ¾–1 in. (2.0–2.5 cm) across, in a dense umbel 2–3 in. (5.0–7.5 cm) in diameter. S. Europe. Grown outdoors in Zones 6–9; elsewhere safer to grow in pots with protection in the cold frame. Spring. Zones 6–9.

oreophilum p. 246

Flowering stalk to 4 in. (10 cm) high. Leaves ⅛–¼ in. (3.2–6.0 mm) wide. Flowers purplish pink, to ⅜ in. (9 mm) long. Caucasus, Turkestan (U.S.S.R.), cen. Asia. Late spring. Similar to *A. Ostrowskianum,* a larger species with rose-pink flowers. Zone 4.

pulchellum pp. 174, 233

Plant 1½–2 ft. (45–60 cm) high, the leaves nearly as long but thread-thin and roughish. Flowers 3/16 in. (5 mm) long, in a loose umbel, pink to rose-purple or yellow, nodding; beneath the cluster are 2 long bracts. There is also a white-flowered form. S. Europe, w. Asia. Summer. Zone 6.

Rosenbachianum *p. 234*

A showy onion, the flowering stalk 2–2½ ft. (60–75 cm) high, the 2 or 3 leaves much shorter than the stalk, ½–2 in. (1.2–5.0 cm) wide, and smooth. Flowers ¼ in. (6 mm) long, in a large, rather loose umbel; pinkish purple, often with a dark stripe in the center of each segment of corolla. Turkestan (U.S.S.R.). Late spring. Zone 5.

roseum *p. 171*

Flowering stems to 2 ft. (60 cm) high, with leaves to ½ in. (13 mm) wide, shorter than the flowering stalk. Flowers rose-white, to ½ in. (13 mm) long, in open umbels to 3 in. (7.5 cm) across. Sometimes bears bulbils in the inflorescence. S. Europe, n. Africa, and Asia Minor. Late spring. Zone 5.

Schoenoprasum *p. 235*

Chive. Flowering stems to 12 in. (30 cm) high, as long as the flat, grasslike, hollow leaves. Flowers rose-pink, ¼–½ in. (6–13 mm) long, in a tight head. Eurasia. The leaves are cut and used for flavoring. Though chiefly grown for these leaves, the plant's attractive flowers are suitable in borders. Often forms sods or clumps of stems without much bulb development. Every 2 or 3 years it should be dug up, divided, and replanted, especially if cutting is frequent. Late spring. Zone 4.

senescens *p. 237*

To 2 ft. (60 cm) high, but usually much shorter, with short leaves to ⅓ in. (8 mm) wide. Flowers rose or purple, ⅜ in. (9 mm) wide, in many-flowered clusters, the flowers sometimes replaced by bulbils. The var. *glaucum* has grayish leaves. Europe to Siberia. Summer. Zone 4.

sphaerocephalum *p. 234*

A rather coarse ornamental allium, the flowering stem to 3 ft. (90 cm) high, the leaves channeled, semicylindrical, and hollow, scarcely ½ in. (13 mm) wide. Flowers 1/7–1/5 in. (3.5–5.5 mm) long, in small, dense clusters ⅜–2 in. (0.9–5.0 cm) in diameter, reddish purple. S. and cen. Europe and n. Africa. Summer. Zone 4.

stellatum *p. 239*

Prairie Onion. A native American decorative allium from the plains, the flowering stem to 18 in. (45 cm) high. Leaves flat, to ¼ in. (6 mm) wide. Flowers pinkish rose, to ⅜ in.

(9 mm) across, in stalked umbels. Easily grown in the border. Minn. south to Ill., west to Nebr. and Kans. Summer to autumn. Zone 5.

tibeticum p. 238

A Tibetan herb grown for ornament, the flowering stem not over 12 in. (30 cm) high, the bulbs somewhat fibrous-coated. Leaves linear, shorter than the flowering stalk. Flowers nodding, cup-shaped, to ¼ in. (6 mm) long, deep bluish pink, the stamens included. Summer. *A. cyathophorum* var. *Farreri* is often sold under this name. Zone 4.

tuberosum p. 171

Chinese Chive; Garlic Chive. An Asiatic salad plant grown here as an ornamental, the flowering stalk 15–20 in. (38–50 cm) high. Leaves slightly cylindrical, but not hollow (as in many onions), scarcely ¼ in. (6 mm) wide. Flowers fragrant, 3/16 in. (5 mm) long, white to greenish white, often with dark line in middle of segment. Se. Asia. Summer. Plants offered in the trade as *A. odorum* are often *A. tuberosum.* Zone 5.

ursinum p. 169

Rampions; Ramsons. Leaves narrowly elliptic to egg-shaped, 2½–8 in. (6–20 cm) long. Flowering stalk to 18 in. (45 cm) high, with a flat-topped umbel to 2½ in. (6 cm) in diameter. Flowers white, to ½ in. (13 mm) long. Europe. Spring. Zone 4.

× *Amarcrinum*
Amaryllis family
Amaryllidaceae

Am-ar-cry'num. A cultivated hybrid between *Amaryllis Belladonna* and *Crinum,* produced in Calif. (*Amarcrinum* is a contraction of *Amaryllis* and *Crinum.*) Also called *Crinodonna.*

Description
Leaves strap-shaped. Flowers fragrant, funnel-shaped. Only a single species.

How to Grow
Usually grown as a pot plant, it should be treated the same as *Amaryllis.*

memoria-Corsii p. 248
Amaryllis Belladonna × *Crinum Moorei.*
A garden hybrid resembling *Amaryllis
Belladonna.* Intermediate between the parent
plants. Flowers fragrant, shell-pink, to 3 in.
(7.5 cm) long, the segments recurving, the
cluster dense; on stalks often 4 ft. (120 cm)
high. Summer. Also called × *Amarcrinum
Howardii.* Zone 8.

Amaryllis
Amaryllis family
Amaryllidaceae

Am-a-rill'is. Technically a genus of one
species, a South African bulbous herb. But
by extensive garden usage, plants belonging
to the genera *Crinum, Hippeastrum,
Brunsvigia, Sprekelia, Lycoris,* and *Vallota* are
also often called amaryllis. (*Amaryllis* is
named for a shepherdess in classical Latin
poetry.)

Description
The genus *Amaryllis* has large, showy, lilylike
flowers on a tall, solid stalk (hollow in
Sprekelia and *Hippeastrum*), which are
produced before the leaves appear. Flowers
funnel-shaped, the tube short, its 6 segments
erect and ascending. Fruit a globe-shaped
capsule, its irregular bursting revealing the
large pelletlike seeds.

How to Grow
In Zones 9 and 10, plant *Amaryllis* in the
garden where it will not be disturbed for
several years. In the North, plant in spring
while dormant in pots large enough to allow
4 in. (10 cm) between bulb and wall of pot
on all sides. Neck of bulb should extend
slightly above surface of soil. Place pot in a
sunny location where night temperature does
not go below 65° F (19° C). Keep soil
moist, but not wet, until growth
commences. Neck of bulb will start to swell
with beginning of young flower stalk very
shortly after potting. Increase water and keep
soil moist. Flowers appear in summer. After
flowering, the plant produces its leaves,
which usually last into winter. Encourage
their growth with plenty of water and
regular fertilization. When leaves begin to
wither, reduce water and cease fertilizing;
when they have completely withered (late
autumn to winter), allow soil in pot to dry

out between waterings. Propagate by seed or by offsets; detach offsets from parent bulb at time of repotting.

Belladonna p. 249
Belladonna Lily. Leaves strap-shaped, usually appearing after the plant blooms. Flowers typically rose-pink or white, sweet-scented, 3½ in. (9 cm) long, in dense umbels at the end of a stout, naked stalk that is often 18 in. (45 cm) long. South Africa. Blooms outdoors in summer. Often offered as *Brunsvigia rosea.* Zone 9.

Amianthium
Lily family
Liliaceae

A-mee-an'thee-um. A genus of 2 species of North American rhizomatous herbs, one of which is cultivated in collections of native plants. (*Amianthium* from the Greek, meaning "unspotted flower.")

Description
Flowers small, in a dense raceme, sepals and petals persistent. Stem and leaves arising from a swollen, bulblike base.

How to Grow
Prefers moist, well-drained soil in full sun. Grows naturally in sandy, grassy bogs and open woodlands where soil is acid.

muscitoxicum p. 184
Fly-Poison. Intensely poisonous plant, with a basal cluster of leaves to 1 in. (2.5 cm) wide. Flowers white, to ½ in. (13 mm) across in a dense raceme on a stalk to 3 ft. (1 m) tall. Pa. to Fla. and westward to Mississippi River. Summer. Zone 5.

Anemone
Buttercup family
Ranunculaceae

Correctly, a-nee-moe'nee; usually,— a-nem'o-nee. Windflower or anemone; also the pasque-flowers, *Anemone patens* and *A. Pulsatilla,* not included here. These most popular garden plants comprise a large genus of some 120 species of perennial herbs, mostly confined to the north temperate zone.

(*Anemone* is the classical Greek name for these plants.)

Description
Leaves compound, or if simple, divided or dissected, mostly basal. Flowers usually showy, blooming in spring, summer, and autumn, having not petals, but petal-like sepals.
The sepals are 5 in most species, but often much more numerous in horticultural forms.
Fruit a cluster of short-beaked achenes.

How to Grow
A. coronaria, A. × *fulgens,* and *A. hortensis,* the poppy anemones, and *A. blanda,* are the forms from which most modern hybrids have originated.

Growing from Tuber-corms
The tuber-corms appear dried and shriveled and should be soaked overnight in warm water before planting. In the greenhouse, plant in benches or flats in rich loamy soil in autumn and grow at a temperature of 40–45° F (4.5–7.0° C). To grow outdoors, plant in autumn south of Zone 6 (from Zone 5 southward for *A. blanda*), and in spring from Zone 6 northward. Outdoor species enjoy a humus-rich, loamy soil; adding lime is sometimes recommended. Partial shade at midday keeps the young plants growing vigorously; if slightly shaded as weather becomes warm, seedlings will flower early and keep up continuous succession of bloom for many weeks. After foliage matures, you can leave tubers in ground or lift and dry them and keep in dry sand until replanting. In the greenhouse leave them in benches and keep absolutely dry for a period of rest. Begin watering again in autumn to start them for winter flowering.

Growing from Seed
Anemone is easily raised from seed. Save seed from the largest flowers and the best colors and when mature sow immediately in good rich soil. The very light seed may be difficult to handle. Sow evenly and thinly. When seedlings are large enough, prick off into flats 2 in. (5 cm) apart each way, then transfer to permanent beds in a shady part of the greenhouse. Plant 4 in. (10 cm) apart and allow them to grow undisturbed until they flower. (This may take up to 18 months.) They dislike heat and will respond with better and larger flowers at cooler temperatures, even as low as 35° F (1.5° C).

Pests and Diseases
Anemones are sometimes attacked by aphids
and leafminers. Apply malathion according
to directions. Rusts, smuts, and other fungal
diseases are sometimes a problem. Remove
the diseased plants.

apennina p. 258
A perennial herb with a short, thickened,
tuberlike rhizome, producing 1 or 2 basal
leaves, 3-times divided and hairy on the
lower surface, and an erect flowering stalk
2½–12 in. (6–30 cm) high. Flowers solitary,
1½ in. (4 cm) wide, perianth rays 8–14,
azure-blue or white. S. Europe. Early spring.
Zone 6.

blanda pp. 163, 259
Tuberous-rooted and usually less than 6 in.
(15 cm) high; otherwise resembling
A. apennina, except that lower surfaces of
leaves lack hairs, and flowers are larger and
darker blue. Se. Europe. Early spring. Can be
potted in autumn and forced indoors like
Crocus for late-winter bloom. White, pinkish,
blue and white, and dark blue varieties
commonly offered in the trade. Zone 6.

coronaria pp. 203, 258
Poppy Anemone; the biblical "lily-of-the-
field." This and *A.* × *fulgens* and *A. hortensis*
are the species most often used for pot
culture and are much grown by florists.
Rhizome thick and tuberous. Basal leaves
long-stalked, compound or twice-compound,
the ultimate segments narrowly wedge-
shaped. Flowers 1½–2½ in. (4–6 cm) wide,
on a smooth stalk 6–18 in. (15–45 cm)
high, solitary, poppylike, red, blue, or white,
the dark blue anthers forming a boss in the
center. Many shades exist in horticultural
varieties, the best known of which are
'St. Brigid' and 'De Caen'. Some varieties are
double-flowered. They can be grown
outdoors from Zone 5 southward.
Mediterranean region. Early spring. Zone 5.

× *fulgens* p. 201
Scarlet Windflower. A perennial, tuberous-
rooted, natural hybrid between *A. hortensis*
and *A. pavonina,* 10–12 in. (25–30 cm)
high. Resembles *A. coronaria* except for its
brilliant scarlet or vermilion flowers, 2–2½
in. (5–6 cm) wide, which have 8–15 sepals
and conspicuous black stamens. Leaves

bright green, 3-lobed. S. France. Early spring. Zone 5.

hortensis p. 233

Garden Anemone. Related to *A. coronaria* and grown like it, differing only in having brownish stamens, and in the leaves being only once-compound, or even merely divided. Plant 10 in. (25 cm) high; flowers 3 in. (7.5 cm) wide, rose-purple or red, usually single, with 12–19 sepals. S. Europe. Early spring. Zone 6.

palmata p. 195

Hairy stems 4–12 in. (10–30 cm) high, rising from a tuberlike rhizome. Basal leaves semicircular with 3–5 shallow lobes. Flowers 1–1½ in. (2.5–4.0 cm) in diameter, yellow, with 10–15 perianth segments. Sw. Europe. Early spring. Zone 8.

Begonia
Begonia family
Begoniaceae

Bee-go'ni-a. An immense genus of perhaps 1000 species of tropical foliage and flowering herbs, with soft or succulent stems. *Begonia* is the only horticultural genus of this family. Widely diversified by breeders, it is now found in a multitude of horticultural forms, many of which have been given Latin names as though they were true wild species. Begonias in cultivation are best divided into two groups: those with tuberous roots, and those with fibrous roots. Only tuberous-rooted begonias will be considered here. Modern varieties come in gorgeous colors; many forms, such as "Carnation" Begonia, "Rosebud" Begonia, and "Camellia" Begonia, are named for their resemblance to other flowers. They are superb plants for summer bedding or hanging baskets. (Named for Michel Begon, a French antiquary and patron of botany.)

Description
Leaves alternate, often brightly colored or with colored veins, nearly always oblique in general outline. Flowers red, pink, yellow, or white, slightly irregular, waxlike, single or double, the male and female separate. Male flowers with 2–5 or more parts scarcely distinguishable as petals and sepals. Ovary

inferior, 2-celled, the fruit a many-seeded
capsule.

How to Grow
All begonias, when in active growth, require
plenty of liquid manure, but when growth
stops they need a short resting period,
during which you should cease watering and
stop feeding entirely. Repot after new
growth begins. Start tuberous begonias
indoors in early spring in boxes or pots.
Transplant them to a semi-shaded, partially
moist site only after all danger of frost is
over.

Propagation
Begonias are grown from stem cuttings, leaf
cuttings, division of the tubers, and seeds.
To make a stem cutting, cut below joint
with sharp knife, and insert in moist sand at
room temperature. Some forms may be
propagated by inserting stalk of a leaf in
sand, soil, or water. Another method,
especially for *B. grandis,* is to use bulbils that
sprout at axil of leafstalk where it joins stem.
Spread bulbils over surface of potting
mixture, press down, and cover with glass.
Bulbils will soon produce young plants. To
divide tubers, cut as in potatoes, leaving an
eye on each cut; dust with charcoal and
cover lightly with peat. When sprouted,
plant in potting soil. To grow from seeds,
which are as fine as dust, place in groove of
a bent card and tap lightly over potting
mixture to sow evenly. Do not cover with
soil, but place sheet of glass and paper over
pot or pan. Water from below by dipping
the pot.

Pests and Diseases
Apply malathion to control whiteflies and
mealybugs. Gray mold can cover old dead
flowers and advance from them onto
adjacent leaves and stems. Pick all flowers as
soon as they have passed their prime. If gray
mold or leafspot become problems on
outdoor plants or in humid greenhouses,
destroy infected foliage, provide good
ventilation, and spray with zineb according
to label recommendations.

grandis p. 228
Hardy Begonia. A smooth, branching plant,
1–2 ft. (30–60 cm) high. Leaves red on the
underside, more or less oval, with toothed
lobes. Flowers large, male flowers with 4
tepals of unequal size, the female flowers

with 2 tepals; flesh-pink, 1½ in. (4 cm) wide. China and Japan. The hardiest of all cultivated forms, *B. grandis* will survive winter in the north, withstanding temperatures of 0° F (−18° C), provided the soil is mulched so that the tuberous roots do not freeze. Summer. Zone 6.

× *hiemalis* p. 200
A large group of winter-flowering hybrids, to 12 in. (30 cm) high, based upon crosses between *B. socotrana, B.* × *cheimantha,* various Andean species, and cultivars of *B.* × *tuberhybrida.* These combine the winter-flowering habit of *B.* × *cheimantha* with the large flowers and many bright colors of *B.* × *tuberhybrida.* The Reiger hybrids belong in this group. Autumn to winter. Greenhouse only.

× *tuberhybrida* p. 213
A group of hybrids and cultivars from a series of species native in the Andes. Stems fleshy, erect or spreading, to 18 in. (45 cm) high. Flowers large, in a wide range of colors from white to red, to 4 in. (10 cm) in diameter. Normally flowering in summer (and used for summer display) and dormant in winter. There are numerous shapes and a range of flower sizes; flowers may be single or double, and many are classified as rose, camellia, carnation, or ruffled forms. Zone 10.

Boophone
Amaryllis family
Amaryllidaceae

Bow-of'on-ee. A few species of tropical and South African bulbous herbs. (*Boophone* is from the Greek *bous,* "ox," and *phonos,* "to slaughter," referring to the poisonous character of this genus.)

Description
Leaves sword-shaped or strap-shaped, in 2 ranks. Flowers small, many, in an umbel with 2 spathes. Flowers with a narrow tube and broadly spreading lobes. Stamens 6.

How to Grow
Culture is as for *Amaryllis.*

disticha *p. 215*
Gifbol. Bulb to 9 in. (22.5 cm) in diameter.
Leaves 8–16, to 18 in. (45 cm) long,
sword-shaped, in 2 vertical rows. Flowering
stalk to 12 in. (30 cm) high. Flowers red,
the tube to ½ in. (13 mm) long, the
spreading, linear lobes to 1½ in. (4 cm)
across, on stalks to 4 in. (10 cm) long; in an
umbel to 12 in. (30 cm) in diameter.
Tropical Africa. Foliage is poisonous if eaten.
Summer to autumn. Zone 10.

Brimeura
Lily family
Liliaceae

Bry-me-oo′ra. Two species of hyacinthlike
bulbous herbs, native in s. Europe. The
genus differs from *Hyacinthus* in details of
the fruit. (Named for Marie de Brimeur, a
French gardener of the 16th century.)

Description
Leaves 4–8, linear, all from the bulb. Flowers
borne on an erect flowering stalk; cup-
shaped, with 6 perianth lobes.

How to Grow
Culture is as for *Hyacinthus.*

amethystina *p. 262*
A slender, graceful, hardy, bulbous herb,
4–10 in. (10–25 cm) high, well suited to
rock gardens. Leaves to 8 in. (20 cm) long.
Flowers to ⅜ in. (9 mm) long, nodding,
light blue, bell-shaped. There is also a
white-flowered form. Spain and Yugoslavia.
Early spring. Formerly called *Hyacinthus
amethystinus.* Zone 6.

Brodiaea
Amaryllis family
Amaryllidaceae

Bro-di-ee′a. About 40 species of attractive
perennials with crocuslike corms and narrow,
grasslike leaves. Native on western coasts of
North and South America, they are mostly
grown in Calif., but a few species can be
grown in the East. (Named for James
Brodie, a Scottish botanist.)

Description
Leaves few, narrow. Flowers mostly funnel-shaped, solitary or in loose umbels that arise from spathelike membranous bracts. Petals and colored sepals 6. Stamens 6, sometimes 3 of them sterile. Fruit a capsule, splitting by valves.

How to Grow
The triplet lilies, as they are often called, are easily grown in Calif., and do well in most soils except wet or shaded ones, but prefer gritty or sandy sites. In the East they must have protection north of Zone 8, and they are unlikely to survive outdoors north of Zone 6. Plant in pots in autumn and store over winter in a cold frame or cold cellar, as with other bulbs potted for forcing; plant in the garden in early spring. They also can be forced for indoor bloom. After flowering, when leaves die down, dig corms from garden and store dry over summer, as they are intolerant of excessive summertime moisture.

coronaria p. 261
12–18 in. (30–45 cm) high. Flowers funnel-shaped, violet-purple, 1½ in. (4 cm) long. This is often offered as *Hookera* (or *Hookeria*) *coronaria,* and as *Brodiaea grandiflora.* British Columbia to Calif. Summer. Zones 7–8.

Calochortus
Lily family
Liliaceae

Kal-o-kor′tus. Mariposa Lily; Star Tulip; Butterfly-Tulip. A charming group of 60 species of chiefly Californian bulbous herbs, grown there for ornament, and hardy with protection, as indicated below, in other parts of the country. (*Calochortus* is from the Greek for "beautiful grass.")

Description
They bear bulbs, erect stems, and narrow, grasslike, but somewhat fleshy, leaves. Flowers terminal, solitary or in small clusters, usually very showy and almost tuliplike. The flower has 3 showy inner segments and 3 sepal-like outer segments. Stamens 6. Fruit a 3-angled capsule.

How to Grow

Mariposa lilies are simple to grow in their native region of w. U.S., and in Calif. they do well in a light, sandy, porous soil, preferably slightly acid, but not too rich. Manure is not advised. In the East, although they can stand considerable cold, they do not tolerate alternate freezing and thawing and especially dislike mucky conditions. They are thus best grown in pots in a light, sandy potting mixture. Plant bulbs in late fall and plunge pots in a cold frame for winter. After spring growth and blooming, and after leaves have died down naturally, lift bulbs and keep in a dry place until fall planting time, when they can be repotted. In Calif. they can stay in the ground continuously if kept dry during summer, and in the East as far north as Washington, D.C., *C. albus* will often overwinter without lifting. Two of the most satisfactory in the East are *C. Gunnisonii* and *C. macrocarpus.*

albus p. 160

White Globe Lily; Fairy Lantern. About 2 ft. (60 cm) high. Flowers nodding, more or less globe-shaped, white, the petals purplish at the base, 1½ in. (4 cm) long. Cen. Calif. Early spring. Zone 5.

Gunnisonii p. 175

Mariposa Lily; Sego Lily. About 18 in. (45 cm) high, the flowers nearly 1¾ in. (4.5 cm) long, white but purple-streaked. Cen. U.S. Late spring. Zones 4–5.

luteus p. 196

Yellow Mariposa. From 1–2½ ft. (30–75 cm) high, the stem sometimes branching. Flowers 1½–2 in. (4–5 cm) long, the petals yellow or orange but brown-spotted at the base, and brown-striped. Cen. Calif. Late spring. *C. concolor,* with lemon-yellow flowers, and *C. vestae,* with white to purple flowers, have been treated in the past as varieties of *C. luteus.* Both are brown-spotted. Zones 5–6.

macrocarpus p. 222

Green-banded Mariposa. Nearly 2 ft. (60 cm) high, the flowers 2 in. (5 cm) long, pinkish purple, with a green stripe down the center of each segment. British Columbia and Mont. south to extreme n. Calif. Summer. Zones 4–5.

splendens p. 223

From 1¼–2 ft. (38–60 cm) high. Flowers numerous (sometimes 30), lilac or purple and unspotted, 2 in. (5 cm) long. Cen. and sw. Calif. Late spring. There is also a reddish-lilac variety. Zones 5–6.

Camassia
Lily family
Liliaceae

Ka-mas′si-a. A small genus of North American bulbous herbs, those described below grown for their showy flowers. (Latinized form of the Indian *camas* or *quamash*.) The plants are occasionally called *Quamasia*.

Description
They have narrow or grasslike leaves, mostly basal, and a bracted stalk to the raceme, which usually overtops the leaves. Flower not tubular, of 6 separate segments, each with a stamen inserted at the base. Fruit a 3-valved capsule, the seeds black.

How to Grow
Plant the bulbs in fall and do not disturb. Place them 3–5 in. (7.5–12.5 cm) apart in a loamy soil containing some sand. The plants prefer heavy, moist but well-drained soil, and should not be allowed to dry out during growing season. *C. Leichtlinii* is especially desirable in open borders.

Cusickii p. 271

A perennial with large, rather foul-smelling bulbs. Leaves 1½ in. (4 cm) wide and nearly 20 in. (50 cm) long, bluish green. Flower-stalk 3½ ft. (105 cm) high, crowned with a terminal raceme of 50–300 pale blue flowers that are 1 in. (2.5 cm) long. Ne. Oreg. Late spring. Zones 4–5.

Leichtlinii p. 270

Flowering stem to 4 ft. (120 cm) high. Leaves narrow, tough, 2 ft. (60 cm) long and 1 in. (2.5 cm) wide. Flowers 1 in. (2.5 cm) long, blue or creamy white, the withered remains tightly clasping the pods. British Columbia to n. Calif. Late spring. Zones 4–5.

Quamash p. 269
Camas; Bear Grass. Usually 1–2 ft. (60–90 cm) high, the leaves basal, long and strap-shaped. Flowers blue or white in a long terminal raceme, the whole cluster often 1 ft. (30 cm) long, the individual flowers 1 in. (2.5 cm) long. British Columbia and Alberta south to n. Calif. and Idaho. Late spring. Zones 4–5.

scilloides p. 270
Wild Hyacinth. Not over 2½ ft. (75 cm) high, the leaves keeled, 2 ft. (60 cm) long and scarcely ½ in. (13 mm) wide. Flowers pale blue or whitish, ½ in. (13 mm) long, persistent even after withering. Pa. to Minn., south to Ga. and Tex. Late spring. Often offered as *C. esculenta.* Zones 4–5.

Canna
Canna family
Cannaceae

Kan'na. A very useful and handsome genus of tropical herbs. These popular bedding plants have been hybridized so much that it is doubtful if any modern canna can now be definitely assigned to any of its wild ancestors, and even the parentage of many of them is wholly unknown. (*Canna* is an old name for some reedlike plant.)

Description
They have mostly tuberous rootstocks and stately, broad, often colored leaves, without marginal teeth, but prominently veined, the leafstalk sheathing. In the Garden Canna (there are 40 other, mostly nonhorticultural species), the flowers are very showy, in a terminal cluster, and very irregular. Sepals 3 and greenish. Petals 3, resembling the sepals. Nearly all the color comes from the much-enlarged, colored, and petal-like sterile stamens. Fruit a 3-angled, roughish capsule, surrounded by the withered calyx.

How to Grow
Over most sections of the country, cannas must be grown as summer bedding plants, for they are tropical and will not tolerate freezing. In parts of Calif. and the far South, however, they may be left in the ground and treated like any other perennial herb.

Preparing a Bed

If soil is poor or stony, prepare a bed 1½–2 ft. (45–60 cm) deep; dig it out and fill in with any good garden loam to which about one-quarter its bulk in compost has been added. Leave center of bed 4–6 in. (10–15 cm) higher than edges. Space rootstocks or potted plants 18 in. (45 cm) apart each way, and plant tall varieties at center of bed. Cannas are so strikingly different from most other garden plants that they need careful placing with relation to the rest of the garden. Cannas look best when planted in a bed by themselves or in the center of a formal courtyard, or when planted in large patches in a border.

Care and Propagation

Cannas do well during summer over most of the U.S. provided there is plenty of heat. Keep beds thoroughly watered over drought periods and free of weeds. When autumn frosts threaten, dig up plants and store like dahlias. In early spring, if you intend to raise your own plants, divide rootstock so that there will be at least 1, but not more than 2, buds per piece. Pot the pieces in early spring and put in a warm greenhouse or by a sunny window in the house. To start outdoors, plant rootstocks directly in the bed, but not before soil temperature at 6 in. (15 cm) deep is at least 65°F (18.5°C); in other words, tomato-planting time or later. Many home gardeners prefer to buy pot plants ready for outdoor planting.

Pests and Diseases

Leaf-feeding insects and leaf-rolling caterpillars can be stopped by regular applications of carbaryl. Bacterial bud rot, the most serious disease of canna, starts as a water-soaked leafspot and stem rot, after which buds and flowers rot. Overwatering, overcrowding, and poor aeration worsen the problem. Select healthy planting stock. Dip rootstocks in a streptomycin solution before planting.

X *generalis* pp. 214, 215

Common Garden Canna. Plant 3–6 ft. (0.9–1.8 m) high. Flowers not tubular at the base; to 4 in. (10 cm) across, petals less than ½ in. (13 mm) long, not reflexed. Colors various, from whitish to red. Summer. Zone 8.

Cardiocrinum
Lily family
Liliaceae

Kard-ee-o-kry'num. Three species of bulbous
herbs, ranging from the Himalayas through
China to Japan. (*Cardiocrinum* is from the
Greek *kardia,* meaning "heart," and *krinon,*
"lily," referring to the shape of the leaves.)

Description
Cardiocrinum species have frequently been
included in *Lilium,* but differ most markedly
from that genus by the conspicuously heart-
shaped bases of the leaves. Flowers funnel-
shaped.

How to Grow
They like a cool, moist, humus-rich soil and
should be planted shallow, because the stems
do not form roots above the bulbs.

giganteum p. 185
An immense lilylike plant, to 12 ft. (3.5 m.)
high. Leaves in a basal rosette and scattered
along the stem, the lower ones 12–18 in.
(30–45 cm) long. Flowers funnel-shaped,
drooping, fragrant, nearly 6 in. (15 cm)
long, white, but green-tinged outside and
with reddish-purple stripes inside. Himalayas.
Summer. Zone 7.

Chionodoxa
Lily family
Liliaceae

Ki-on-o-dock'sa. Five or 6 species of bulbous
herbs, mostly from Crete and Asia Minor, 1
or 2 widely planted in the blue garden or
rock garden for their attractive bloom. They
are commonly called glory-of-the-snow
because of their early flowering. (*Chionodoxa*
is Greek for "glory of the snow.")

Description
Very short stalk from bulb; leaves narrow
and toothless, flowers small, blue, in tiny
racemes at end of stalk. Corolla bell-shaped,
the tube very short, its 6 stamens attached to
the throat. Fruit a 3-angled capsule.

How to Grow
Chionodoxas are among the earliest and
most beautiful of spring-flowering bulbs.
They are very hardy and increase freely in

good, well-drained soil where there is plenty of light and some moisture during growing season. Planted in low, sunny sections of the rock garden, or massed closely about such shrubs as *Magnolia stellata,* forsythias, and Flowering Almond (*Prunus glandulosa*), their blue color shows to perfection. Their best display comes in the years following their first blossoming, so they should not be disturbed; allow them to seed and increase from year to year to attain a carpet of color. A regular mulch of compost or old manure in autumn keeps the soil in good condition. Plant bulbs 3 in. (7.5 cm) deep and 3 in. (7.5 cm) apart as soon as available in autumn. *C. Luciliae* and *C. sardensis* are the best for general use.

Luciliae p. 260
About 3 in. (7.5 cm) high while in flower, to 6 in. (15 cm) high in fruit. Leaves nearly grasslike, shorter than stalk of flower cluster, longer when in fruit. Flowers about 5 in a cluster, the lower nodding, blue with a white center, to 1 in. (2.5 cm) in diameter. Asia Minor. Early spring. There are also pink- and white-flowered varieties. Zone 4.

sardensis p. 260
Plant 3–6 in. (7.5–15.0 cm) high. Similar to *C. Luciliae,* but the blue flowers slightly smaller and lacking the white eye. Asia Minor. Early spring. Zone 4.

Clivia
Amaryllis family
Amaryllidaceae

Kly′vi-a. Three South African species of perennial herbs, one a widely popular greenhouse plant and well suited for house decoration when in bloom. (Named for a Duchess of Northumberland, one of the Clive family.)

Description
They have fleshy roots, and a bulblike swelling of the lower part of the stem, formed by the expanded leaf bases. Leaves strap-shaped, evergreen. Flowers in a terminal umbel, the corolla funnel-shaped, the 3 inner segments wider than the outer ones. Fruit a red berry.

How to Grow
Clivias are robust evergreen herbs with fleshy roots and without a true bulb. They resent disturbance at the roots and flower best when root-bound. They need fairly moist, very well drained soil, and grow in sun or partial shade. Immediately after flowering in spring, and through summer, give plenty of water, light, and liquid fertilizer. In fall, reduce water and lower temperature to 50° F (10° C). In late winter, when flower-spikes begin to elongate, provide more light, water, and heat.

miniata pp. 212, 213
Flowering stalk 1½–2 ft. (45–60 cm) high. Leaves thick, to 18 in. (45 cm) long, two-ranked, more or less strap-shaped, and 1–2 in. (2.5–5.0 cm) wide. Flowers 10–18 in the cluster, lilylike, scarlet with yellowish throat, the corolla 2–3 in. (5.0–7.5 cm) long. Berry 1 in. (2.5 cm) long. Early spring. The species is far surpassed by some of the hybrid or improved horticultural varieties, which have about 20–40 red to yellow, sometimes green-tipped, flowers per cluster and bloom in spring. Among the best known is *C.* × *cyrtanthiflora,* a cross between *C. miniata* and *C. nobilis.* Zone 9.

Colchicum
Lily family
Liliaceae

Kol'chi-cum. A genus of 60–70 species of mostly autumn-blooming, crocuslike, cormous herbs, very popular in the autumn garden and in the rock garden. They are commonly called autumn crocus or meadow saffron, although there are several autumn-blooming plants of the genus *Crocus.* (*Colchicum* is derived from Colchis, an ancient country bordering on the Black Sea, now part of Georgian Republic, U.S.S.R.)

Description
Leaves sometimes appear with the flowers, sometimes later; both arising from the ground, the plant apparently stemless. Flowers tubular, the segments 6, and the 6 stamens inserted within the tube. Color generally light pink to mauve, with varieties in deeper shades. Petals sometimes tessellated in white and pink, or light and dark pink. Fruit a 3-valved capsule.

How to Grow

Purchase corms in summer, when they are dormant. Several extremely good, widely grown hybrid forms are available. Set corms so that their tops are 3–4 in. (7.5–10.0 cm) below surface of soil. They produce leaves in spring, so do not plant them where their lush but coarse foliage will mar the appearance of the garden. They look best in a corner by themselves with a ground cover of Creeping Myrtle (*Vinca minor*). Flowers shoot up without any leaves in autumn, and in the North bloom in succession from Sept. to Nov. To divide them or move them in the garden, clumps may be lifted when in bloom, but should be replanted immediately because root growth is active then.

Growing from Seed

Seeds of the previous year's flowers mature in midsummer, when leaves turn brown. Sow the seeds at once. Although they often lie dormant until the second or third spring, in time they do germinate, and after 3 or 4 years' growth, the corms reach the blooming stage.

autumnale p. 220

Leaves produced in spring, 8–10 in. (20–25 cm) long and 1½ in. (4 cm) wide, the plant leafless in summer. Flowers 2 in. (5 cm) long and 3–4 in. (7.5–10.0 cm) wide, pink to purple-lilac. Fruit usually maturing with the leaves in spring. Europe and n. Africa. Autumn. This species is the most common in cultivation. There is a wild pink form, a white single variety, and a double pink and a double white. Zone 5.

speciosum p. 221

Leaves produced in spring, nearly 12 in. (30 cm) long and 3–4 in. (7.5–10.0 cm) wide. Flowers to 4 in. (10 cm) wide and 12 in. (30 cm) long, cup-shaped, crimson-purple with a white tube. Caucasus, Asia Minor. Autumn. There is also a variety with pure white flowers, var. *album*. Zone 5.

Crinum
Amaryllis family
Amaryllidaceae

Kry'num. A genus of perhaps 130 species of thick- or bulbous-rooted, lilylike herbs, mostly tropical, a few cultivated for their very showy flowers. (*Crinum* is the Greek name for a lily.)

Description
Leaves persistent or evergreen, thick or almost fleshy, strap- or sword-shaped, stalkless. Flowers in an umbel at the end of a tall, solid stalk, beneath the umbel 2 spathelike bracts. Corolla funnel-shaped, or with a long, slender tube, the summit ending in narrow or broad segments. Fruit an irregularly bursting capsule.

How to Grow
These handsome plants, sometimes called crinum lilies, are grown outdoors chiefly in the South, although some can be wintered over up to Zone 7 with a good mulch of straw and manure. They are naturally rich feeders and do best in good soil with plenty of water. In the South they should be left where planted, because they dislike moving and may not flower for 2 or 3 seasons after being lifted. If left alone, however, they are apt to make striking large clumps. If grown in the greenhouse, the roots of most kinds should be stored over winter in a cool but frost-free place; pot up in early spring and put in a warm, moist spot. Evergreen kinds grown in the greenhouse must be potted up continuously and rested during winter by reducing heat and partially drying them out. Most species produce small offsets from base of the bulblike root. These can be detached, and provide the simplest method of propagation because they root easily.

americanum *p. 168*
Swamp Lily. Leaves few, long and narrow. Flowers white, 3 in. (7.5 cm) wide, the tube 3–4 in. (7.5–10 cm) long, segments long and narrow. Stalk of flower cluster 1½–2 ft. (45–60 cm) long, usually arising before leaves appear. Fla. to Tex. Late spring to summer. Zone 9.

bulbispermum *p. 243*
The commonest crinum in cultivation and hardy, with protection, up to Zone 7. A vigorous plant, to 3 ft. (90 cm) high. Leaves long and narrow, the margins roughish. Flowers pink or white, about 12 in the cluster, to 4 in. (10 cm) wide, the tube to 4 in. (10 cm) long and curved. Segments 1 in. (2.5 cm) wide. South Africa. Late spring. Also known as *C. capensis* and *C. longifolium*. Zones 8–9.

latifolium p. 180
Milk-and-Wine Lily. To 2 ft. (60 cm) high.
Bulb globose, to 8 in. (20 cm) in diameter.
Leaves about 4 in. (10 cm) wide and 3 ft.
(90 cm) long. Flowers in a cluster of 10–20,
greenish white with pink stripes, the curved
tube to 4 in. (10 cm) long, the spreading
lobes to 8 in. (20 cm) across. Tropical Asia.
Late spring. Zone 9.

Moorei p. 176
Flower-stalk to 5 ft. (1.5 m) high, the leaves
at least 3 in. (7.5 cm) wide and smooth on
the edges. Flowers nearly 4 in. (10 cm)
wide, white, with a pink stripe. South Africa.
Summer. Zone 9.

× *Powellii* p. 242
A hybrid *Crinum* (*bulbispermum* × *Moorei*),
with a globular, long-necked bulb, and about
20 narrow leaves, to 4 ft. (1.2 m) long.
Flowers curved, 3 in. (7.5 cm) long, reddish,
green at base, with 6–8 flowers in a terminal
umbel that stands 2 ft. (60 cm) high.
Summer. Zone 8.

Crocosmia
Iris family
Iridaceae

Kro-kos′mee-a. Five species of gladiolus-like
herbs from South Africa. (*Crocosmia* is from
the Greek *krokos*, "saffron," and *osme*, "a
smell," because of the saffron smell that is
evident when the dried flowers are soaked in
warm water.)

Description
Leaves sword-shaped, flowers yellow to
orange-red.

How to Grow
Should be treated like *Gladiolus*.

× *crocosmiiflora* p. 208
Common Montbretia. A cormous plant, like
Gladiolus. Leaves few, scattered, sword-
shaped, the lower shorter than the upper.
The erect flower stem to 4 ft. (1.2 m) high
terminating in a panicle of bright orange-
yellow flowers. Flowers regular, star-shaped,
with a tube about 1 in. (2.5 cm) long,
spreading to about 2 in. (5 cm) wide. There
are many color forms of this popular garden
plant. The original cross (*C. aurea* × *C. Pottsii*)

that produced this favorite was made about 1800. Summer to autumn. Zone 7.

Masoniorum *p. 209*
Flowering stem 2–4 ft. (60–120 cm) high. Flowers 12–30, orange-red, about 1 in. (2.5 cm) long. South Africa. Summer. Zone 7

Crocus
Iris family
Iridaceae

Kro'kus. A genus of about 80 species of very popular garden plants, ranging from the Mediterranean region to sw. Asia. They are usually stemless plants arising from a corm. (*Crocus* is the Greek name for the saffron crocus, *Crocus sativus.*)

Description
Leaves narrow or grasslike, appearing before, with, or after the flowers. Flowers bloom very early in spring or in autumn, but the plants commonly called autumn crocus belong to the genus *Colchicum. Crocus* flowers are produced at ground level, are stemless or very short-stalked, and have 6 segments and 3 stamens. Stamens and pistils showy yellow to orange. Fruit a capsule ripening at, or below, ground level.

How to Grow
The small corms resemble those of *Gladiolus.* Plant 3–4 in. (7.5–10.0 cm) deep in a sunny spot with warm, well-drained soil where they may self-sow. If planted with other plants, choose ground covers that are not too dense to hold moisture in summer. *Crocus* naturalizes well in lawns, but do not mow lawn until crocus foliage has begun to die down. If autumn-blooming species are naturalized in a lawn, do not mow lawn once buds emerge from soil. Although most *Crocus* species come from areas where there is intense heat in summer, they usually need definite cold in winter.

biflorus *pp. 165, 257*
Scotch Crocus. Flowers to 4 in. (10 cm) long, white or lilac-blue, striped, veined, or strongly tinged with purple-blue or brown-purple, the throat yellow. Se. Europe and Asia. Early spring. Useful for the rock garden. *Adamii,* a violet variety, is one of

several named forms, most of them color variants. Zone 5.

chrysanthus pp. 164, 165, 199

Leaves keeled, 12 in. (30 cm) long, and very narrow, appearing after the bloom. Flowers to 4 in. (10 cm) long, pale yellow to orange-yellow. Greece and Asia Minor. Early spring. There are many good horticultural forms. Among them are 'Snow Bunting', white with a yellow throat; 'Blue Pearl', pale lavender outside and white inside, with a yellow throat; and 'E. P. Bowles', a yellow form. Zone 4.

etruscus p. 255

Leaves very narrow, with a white band, appearing with the flowers. Flowers 4 in. (10 cm) long, purple or lilac, often with purple veins. Italy. Early spring. Zone 3.

flavus p. 199

Leaves appear with the flowers. Flowers pale yellow to deep orange-yellow, 2½–7 in. (6.0–17.5 cm) long. Balkan Peninsula. 'Dutch Crocus', 'Dutch Yellow', 'Golden Yellow', and 'Yellow Giant' are cultivar names for a sterile hybrid (*C. flavus* × *C. angustifolius*) that has been in cultivation for at least 200 years and remains extremely popular. Early spring. Zone 4.

Goulimyi p. 221

Leaves present at flowering time. Flowers fragrant, pale to deep pinkish purple, 4–10 in. (10–25 cm) long. S. Greece. Autumn. Does well in s. Calif. Zone 8.

Imperati p. 255

Leaves appear with the flowers. Flowers 2½–5½ in. (6–14 cm) long, buff or yellowish outside, purple inside, with yellow throat. W. Italy. Early spring. One of the first to bloom. Zone 6.

longiflorus p. 254

Leaves present at flowering time. Flowers 2¾–5½ in. (7–14 cm) long, lilac to purple, the throat yellow. S. Europe. Autumn. Zone 5.

medius p. 256

Leaves appear after flowering time. Flowers 4–10 in. (10–25 cm) long, lilac to deep purple, throat with purple veins. Nw. Italy and se. France. Autumn. Zones 6–7.

niveus p. 166
Leaves appear with the flowers. Flowers
4½–9½ in. (11.5–24 cm) long, usually
white but sometimes pale lilac. S. Greece.
Autumn. Zone 7.

Tomasinianus p. 256
Leaves appear with the flowers. Flowers lilac
to purple with white throat, 2½–5½ in.
(6–14 cm) long. S. Hungary to nw.
Bulgaria. Early spring. Zones 4–5.

vernus pp. 254, 257
Common Crocus; Dutch Crocus. Leaves
present at flowering time. Flowers white,
purple, or striped, 1½–8 in. (4–20 cm) long.
Cen. and s. Europe. The large-flowered
Dutch Crocus are selections or hybrids of
this species and come in a variety of colors.
Spring. Zone 4.

versicolor p. 164
The parent of many horticultural varieties.
Leaves appear at flowering time. Flowers
3½–5½ in. (9–14 cm) long, white, lilac, or
purple, conspicuously striped with purple on
the outside; throat pale yellow or nearly
white. 'Picturatus' is a white form with
stripes. Se. France. Early spring. Zone 5.

Curtonus
Iris family
Iridaceae

Ker-ton'us. A single species from South
Africa, allied to *Gladiolus.* (*Curtonus* is from
the Greek *kyrtos,* "bent" or "hunch-backed,"
perhaps alluding to the bent corolla tube.)

Description
Flowers in dense spikes at tips of branches,
red and yellow, the perianth tube curved.
Differs from *Gladiolus* by the branched,
zigzag axis of the flower spikes.

How to Grow
Should be treated like *Gladiolus.*

paniculatus p. 209
Corm large, globular. Stem to 4 ft. (120 cm)
high, branched. Leaves 1½–2 ft. (45–60 cm)
long, to 3 in. (7.5 cm) wide. Flowers 2 in.
(5 cm) long. Natal Prov. (South Africa).
Summer. Zone 7.

Cyclamen
Primrose family
Primulaceae

Sy'kla-men, also sick'la-men. About 15
species of perennial herbs with tuber-corms,
native in Europe and Asia Minor. Hybrids
are very popular florists' pot plants, grown
for their handsome flowers. (*Cyclamen*,
regarded in s. Europe as a favorite food of
swine, is from the Greek meaning
"sowbread.")

Description
Leaves all at base of stem, long-stalked, the
blade roundish or kidney-shaped. Flowers
solitary on each stalk, which is less than
12 in. (30 cm) high. Calyx with 5 divisions.
Corolla with a very short tube, the 5 lobes
much longer, contorted, and with strongly
recurved tips. Fruit a 5-valved capsule
splitting from the top downward.

How to Grow
Most species can be grown as hardy
perennials from Zone 7 southward, and are
especially suited to rock gardens or shaded
borders. They need good garden loam
enriched with organic matter, and moisture.
North of Zone 7 they may overwinter in
pots in a cold frame or a cold greenhouse.
Cyclamen coum and *C. hederifolium* are
relatively hardy but usually cannot be grown
outdoors in the East without protection.
Cultivation in places with soil that is not
too cold and wet is relatively easy if the
situation is free of alternate freezing and
thawing.

Florists' Cyclamen
Cyclamen persicum, the common florists'
cyclamen, needs special attention and fares
best in a cool greenhouse. For good bloom
plants should be started from seed; however,
it takes 18 months before they are ready to
flower. Sow seeds in mid- to late summer in
pots or flats containing one-third each
garden soil, compost or potting soil, and
perlite. Before sowing, soak seeds for 12
hours in water at 70° F (21° C) to leach
germination-inhibiting chemicals from seed
coat. Sow 2 in. (5 cm) apart, and cover to a
depth of about ¼ in. (6 mm). Cover surface
of medium with black plastic until seedlings
begin to appear. Maintain a temperature
of 65–68° F (18.5–20.0° C); higher
temperatures will inhibit germination. It

may take 2–2½ months for first leaf to
appear. Then grow young seedlings with
highest light intensity possible at a
temperature of 60–65° F (15.5–18.5° C);
higher temperatures may cause leaf burn.
Maintain this temperature constantly until
plants flower. After flowering, reduce water
until leaves die down; then withhold water
entirely. Leave tuber-corms in their pots and
place pots in a cool, moderately dry spot for
3 months. Then repot tuber-corms and place
in a bright but lightly shaded spot at a
temperature of 60–65° F (15.5–18.5° C).

Pests and Diseases
Microscopic mites twist plants and stunt
growth; use uninfested stock. Fumigate
greenhouse before planting, and immerse
tuber-corms in water for 15 minutes at
110° F (43° C). New miticides have been
developed. Leafspot, caused by a fungus, may
mar appearance of leaves but usually does
not become serious enough to prevent
growing the plant. During very humid
weather gray mold may become serious,
rotting crown or center of leaf cluster. Apply
ferbam or zineb, and repeat once or twice at
10- to 14-day intervals.

× *Atkinsii* p. 156
Reputedly *C. coum* × *C. persicum,* but
cultivated material is probably selected forms
of *C. coum.* Relatively hardy, 3–6 in.
(7.5–15.0 cm) high. Leaves similar to
C. coum, but with white markings. Flowers
¾–1 in. (2.0–2.5 cm) long, whitish or pale
pink, spotted or streaked with red. Early
spring. Zone 7.

coum p. 226
Plant 3–6 in. (7.5–15.0 cm) high.
Tuber-corm to 1½ in. (4 cm) in diameter,
globular but flattened on top. Leafstalks to
4 in. (10 cm) long. Leaf blades nearly round
or kidney-shaped, to 3 in. (7.5 cm) long.
Leaves plain green or marbled above, red-
purple beneath. Flowers to ¾ in. (19 mm)
long, white to carmine, with a purple
blotch. Se. Europe. Early spring. Zone 7.

hederifolium p. 225
Sowbread. Plant 3–6 in. (7.5–15.0 cm) high.
Tuber-corm to 6 in. (15 cm) in diameter,
globular but flattened on top. Leaf blades
heart-shaped, to 5½ in. (14 cm) long,
marbled above, plain green or red beneath.
Flowers to 1 in. (2.5 cm) long, pink or

white, with a crimson blotch. S. Europe. Late summer to autumn. Formerly called *C. neapolitanum.* Zone 7.

persicum p. 227

Common Cyclamen. Plant 6–12 in. (15–30 cm) high. Tuber-corm to 6 in. (15 cm) in diameter, globular but flattened on top. Leaf blades roundish heart-shaped, to 5½ in. (14 cm) long and wide, the margins with rounded teeth. Flower-stalk 6–8 in. (15–20 cm) high, the flowers 2 in. (5 cm) long, rose or white, dark purple at the mouth. Much variation exists in the cultivars. Of the many forms in cultivation, one has flowers nearly twice the normal size, others have double flowers, and some have crested or shredded petals. Greece to Syria. Blooms in early spring where grown outdoors, but winter-flowering as grown under glass by florists. Zone 9.

purpurascens p. 226

Plant 3–6 in. (7.5–15.0 cm) high. Tuber-corm to 1½ in. (4 cm) in diameter, globular. Leaf blades kidney- to heart-shaped, to 3½ in. (9 cm) long, plain green or marbled above, green to red beneath. Flowers ¾ in. (19 mm) long, pink to magenta, with a darker blotch. Fragrant. Cen. and s. Europe. Late summer to autumn. Zone 7.

repandum p. 227

Plant 3–6 in. (7.5–15.0 cm) high. Tuber-corm to 2½ in. (6 cm) in diameter, globular. Leaf blades heart-shaped, to 5 in. (12.5 cm) long and wide, plain green or marbled above, reddish purple beneath. Flowers 1¼ in. (3 cm) long, white to red, darker at the base. Cen. and e. Mediterranean region. Early spring. Zone 7.

Cypella
Iris family
Iridaceae

Kyp-el´la. About 20 species of cormous or bulbous herbs native to tropical and extra-tropical South America. (*Cypella* is from the Greek *kypellon,* meaning "goblet" or "cup," referring to the shape of the flowers.)

Description
Leaves elongate, folded lengthwise. Flowers

in a cluster at top of stalk, the outer 3 floral segments spreading, the inner 3 erect.

How to Grow
Should be treated like *Gladiolus*.

Herbertii p. 189
To 18 in. (45 cm) high. Leaves about ¼ in. (6 mm) wide, tapering at both ends. Flowers orange-yellow, about 3 in. (7.5 cm) across. The individual flowers last for only a day, but are produced in succession for a week or more. S. Brazil, Paraguay, Uruguay, and n. Argentina. Late spring to summer. Zone 9.

Dahlia
Daisy family
Compositae

Dahl′ya, also day′li-ya. A small but very important genus of approximately 27 species of tuberous-rooted herbs, mainly from the uplands of Mexico and Guatemala. (Named for Andreas Dahl, a pupil of Linnaeus.)

Description
Leaves opposite, often compound or twice-compound, the leaflets or segments toothed or cut. Flowers vary greatly due to breeding. Wild types always have both ray and disk flowers and are generally open-centered with a single row of petals, while most garden varieties are double-flowered. These range from small, ball-shaped pompons to large, multipetaled blossoms with curled, quill-like petals.

How to Grow
Dahlias thrive best on a well-drained loam enriched with phosphorus, potash, and organic matter. They tolerate mildly acid soil; add lime to improve results. Improve heavy clay soil by mixing in sand to a depth of 4 or 5 in. (10.0–12.5 cm). Dahlias prefer full sun, but will do well with only 5 or 6 hours of direct sunlight a day. They like plenty of water after they begin to bloom.

Planting
Plant dahlias outdoors as soon as danger of frost is past. If necessary they can be started first in the house or in cold frames. Set plants 1–3 ft. (30–90 cm) apart in rows 3–4 ft. (90–120 cm) apart (bedding plants should be closer). If growing large

exhibition flowers, place plants at least 4 ft. (120 cm) apart in all directions. All but dwarf varieties should be staked; drive stakes before planting.

Ensure that each root has a section of stem with a bud. To plant, lay root down horizontally, eye upward and toward stake, in a hole 6 in. (15 cm) deep. Cover with 2–3 in. (5.0–7.5 cm) of soil, adding more soil as shoot grows until hole is filled or a little concave to facilitate watering. Let only 1 or 2 shoots develop. After plants have made a good start, feed from surface with top-dressing of raw bone meal and muriate of potash, keeping it about 6 in. (15 cm) away from base of plant and raking into surface. To produce large exhibition flowers, repeat this treatment after 2 weeks, or use diluted liquid manure in a shallow trench 1 ft. (30 cm) from plant. A mulch of stable manure, compost, or granulated peat will help hold moisture and supply food. During blooming period, water plants copiously at least once a week.

Dahlias can also be grown from stem cuttings or from seed; plants started in a greenhouse in very early spring will flower the same season and develop tuberous roots at base of stem.

Pruning and Disbudding
Plants will bloom more freely if you remove dense, shrubby growth to allow better lighting and air circulation. To develop exhibition-quality flowers, pinch out lateral buds and branches for 2, 3, or 4 pairs of leaves directly underneath bud terminating main stem. If you prefer bushy plants with more blooms, pinch out center repeatedly when 4–6 leaves have developed so that side shoots will form.

Storage
Soon after first killing frost, carefully dig up roots, shake off soil, and dry 3 or 4 hours in the sun. Divide clumps to propagate new plants, being certain that each tuberous root has part of the stem with a bud. Cover roots with sand, granulated peat, ashes, or vermiculite to prevent excessive shrinkage and possible death during winter storage. Keep in cellar or other cool, barely moist place at 35–50° F (1.5–10.0° C).

Pests and Diseases
Control leaf feeders, aphids, and Tarnished Plant Bugs with malathion. Control

European Corn Borer with a mixture of carbaryl and dicofol as eggs hatch, and repeat weekly for 3 to 4 weeks. Virus infections such as mosaic, ringspot, oak leaf, or stunt, transmitted by insects, can be serious and usually appear as blotches or patterns in the leaves. Destroy infected plants. The virus does not persist from year to year in soil, but a fungus that causes wilt may build up if dahlias are grown continuously in same area. Use only healthy stock for propagation. Wet, humid weather at flowering time may cause rot in blooms. Remove old blooms and apply gentle mist of zineb over flowers at 3- or 4-day intervals.

***pinnata* hybrids** *pp. 194, 201, 202, 203, 232*
Species to 6 ft. (1.8 m) high, with flowerheads 2–4 in. (5–10 cm) wide, purple or lavender-purple. *D. pinnata* is an important parent species of the modern garden dahlia. Thousands of named varieties have been introduced to the trade, with perhaps 2000 on the market at any given time. For exhibition and commercial purposes they are classified into 14 different groups based on size, shape, and petal formation. For gardening purposes they can be divided into 2 groups: medium-size to tall plants with long-stemmed blossoms sometimes more than 8 in. (20 cm) wide, used for cutting; and dwarf or low-growing types only 1 ft. (30 cm) high, used for bedding. Cultivars yellow, red, orange, pink, purple, white, or bi-colored. Mexico. Summer to autumn. Zone 9.

Dichelostemma
Amaryllis family
Amaryllidaceae

Dy-kel-os′tem-ma. Six species of cormous perennials native in w. North America, allied to *Brodiaea.* (*Dichelostemma,* from the Greek, means "bifid corona," referring to appendages on stamens.)

Description
Leaves linear, flattened, keeled beneath and grooved above. Flower cluster subtended by usually colored spathe bracts. Flowers inflated or cup-shaped. The fruit a capsule.

How to Grow
Should be treated like *Brodiaea.*

pulchellum *p. 238*
Blue Dicks. Stems to 2 ft. (60 cm) high.
Leaves nearly round, to 16 in. (40 cm) long.
Spathe bracts purplish. Flowers violet or
white, to ¾ in. (2 cm) long. Oreg. to
Lower Calif. Early spring. Zones 5–7.

Dierama
Iris family
Iridaceae

Dy-ray'ma. A small genus of South African
herbs. (*Dierama,* from the Greek for
"funnel," is an allusion to the shape of the
flowers.)

Description
Leaves chiefly basal, long, and rigid. Flowers
on a long, showy, bending raceme; corolla
funnel-shaped but expanded at throat.
Stamens 3. Corms like those of *Gladiolus.*
Fruit a 3-valved capsule.

How to Grow
Should be treated like *Ixia.*

pendulum *p. 240*
Nearly 5 ft. (1.5 m) high. Leaves chiefly at
base of stem, 12–20 in. (30–50 cm) long,
¼ in. (6 mm) wide. Flowers 1 in. (2.5 cm)
long, white to lavender, grouped in slender,
drooping spikes. Summer. Zone 9.

Eranthis
Buttercup family
Ranunculaceae

E-ran'thiss. Seven species of tuberous-rooted
Eurasian herbs, the roots perennial, a new
one produced each year and flowering the
following spring. (*Eranthis* is Greek for
"flower of spring.")

Description
Leaves rounded, lobed, and segmented.
Flowers single and terminal on short, erect
aerial stems from a tuberous base.

How to Grow
The species below thrives in well-drained soil
that does not dry out in summer. Plant in
full sun or beneath deciduous shrubs. It
self-seeds freely and should be left

undisturbed for as long as possible. After
seed matures, plant dies down and roots rest
during summer. Growth begins in early
autumn, so get roots into the ground as
soon as possible, preferably in late summer
or early fall. Plant 3 in. (7.5 cm) deep and
no more than 3 in. (7.5 cm) apart. For best
results, soak dried root clusters overnight in
warm water before planting. Mice and
chipmunks may be a problem.

hyemalis p. 197

Winter Aconite. An erect, usually
unbranched, perennial, 3–8 in. (7.5–20.0 cm)
high. Leaves at base of stem, roundish,
long-stalked. Flowers solitary, 1 in. (2.5 cm)
wide, petals none and much reduced. Sepals
5–8, yellow and petal-like, ½ in. (13 mm)
long. Fruit a collection of small follicles,
resembling miniature bean pods. S. Europe.
Early spring. Zones 4–5.

Erythronium
Lily family
Liliaceae

E-ri-throw′ni-um. About 25 species of
generally woodland, bulbous spring-
blooming perennial herbs, all but one North
American. Some are among the most
attractive of American wildflowers and are
generally called Dogtooth Violet,
Adder's-Tongue, Trout Flower, or Trout
Lily. (*Erythronium* is from the Greek for
"red," apparently referring to the color of
the flower of the European species or the
marbling on the leaves.)

Description
Leaves 2, often mottled, and at base of
stems. Flowers rather handsome, nodding,
borne in small clusters or solitary atop
flower-stalk. Petals and sepals not easily
distinguishable as such, but the segments
separate. Stamens 6. Fruit an oblongish,
3-angled pod.

How to Grow
Dogtooth violets are best suited to the wild
garden, where they do well in partial or light
deciduous shade, and in moist, humus-rich
soil that is not especially acid. Plant corms
6 in. (15 cm) deep. Propagate by offsets, or
raise from seeds if you are willing to wait
3–4 years for the first flowers. Or force them

under glass, treating them like *Crocus* and never letting temperature exceed 50° F (10° C).

americanum p. 190

Yellow Adder's-Tongue; Dogtooth Violet. To 12 in. (30 cm) high. Leaves 4–6 in. (10–15 cm) long, blades mottled with brown. Flowers yellow, 1½ in. (4 cm) long, segments curved backward, fragrant. Nova Scotia to Minn., south to Fla., especially in rich, moist woods. Early spring. Often grown in the rock garden, but also suited to the wild garden. Zone 4.

californicum p. 162

Fawn Lily. About 12 in. (30 cm) high. Leaves strongly mottled with brownish or whitish spots. Flowers 1½ in. (4 cm) long, cream-white, fragrant. Native in n. Calif. but will grow well in the East. Early spring. Zone 6.

citrinum p. 162

Similar to E. californicum, but 10–12 in. (25–30 cm) high and the flowering stem bears 1–9 pale lemon-yellow flowers to 1½ in. (4 cm) long. N. Calif. and s. Oreg. Early spring. Zone 6.

Dens-canis p. 224

Dogtooth Violet of Europe. A blotched-leaved perennial, 6–12 in. (15–30 cm) high. Leaves ovalish, stalked, with a slender point. Flowers nodding, about 1 in. (2.5 cm) long, 2 in. (5 cm) wide, purplish pink. S. and s.-cen. Europe. Early spring. Zone 4.

grandiflorum p. 190

Avalanche Lily; Adam-and-Eve; Chamise Lily. 1–2 ft. (30–60 cm) high. Unmottled leaves. Flowers 1–6, bright yellow, 1–2 in. (2.5–5.0 cm) long, segments strongly bent backward. British Columbia to Oreg., e. to Mont. and Utah. Said to grow well in the East, but not at low elevations. Early spring. Zone 6.

Hendersonii p. 224

To 12 in. (30 cm) high. Leaves mottled. Flowers about 1½ in. (4 cm) long, pinkish purple, segments bent strongly backward. S. Oreg., but grows well in the East. Early spring. Zone 6.

montanum p. 163
Alpine Fawn Lily. To 12 in. (30 cm) high.
Leaves not mottled. Flowers 1½ in. (4 cm)
long, white with orange inside base,
segments somewhat curved. Wash. and
Oreg. Early spring. Zone 6.

revolutum p. 225
Coast Fawn Lily. To 16 in. (40.5 cm) high.
Leaves mottled. Flowers lavender-white,
ultimately turning purple, 1¾ in. (4.5 cm)
long. British Columbia to Calif. A fine rock
garden herb. Early spring. Zone 4.

tuolumnense p. 191
To 12 in. (30 cm) high. Foliage bright
green and not mottled. Leaves to 12 in.
(30 cm) long, broadly lance-shaped, stalk
clasping. Flowers 1¼ in. (3 cm) long,
yellow, but greenish yellow or paler at base.
Calif., but grows well in the East. Early
spring. Zone 4.

Eucharis
Amaryllis family
Amaryllidaceae

You'kar-is. South American bulbous herbs.
(*Eucharis* is from the Greek, meaning "very
graceful.")

Description
Leaves broad, contracted to a leafstalk at
base. Flowers large, white, tubular, with
lobes spreading.

How to Grow
Pot in rich, open soil mixture and water
copiously. Grow in minimum night
temperature of 65–70° F (18.5–21.0° C).
Induce flowering by lowering night
temperature to 55–60° F (13.0–15.5° C)
and withholding water until leaves droop;
continue for 2–3 weeks, then return to
normal night temperature and copious
watering. Flowering will occur in a few
months.

grandiflora p. 177
Amazon Lily. Popular greenhouse and pot
plant, grown outdoors in s. Fla. and Calif.
Stout bulb, to 3 in. (7.5 cm) in diameter.
Leaves several, with leafstalks to 1 ft.
(30 cm) long and egg-shaped blades, about
1 ft. (30 cm) long and 6 in. (15 cm) wide,

with wavy margins. Stalk 1–2 ft. (30–60 cm) high, topped with an umbel of 5–6 intensely fragrant flowers. Corolla cylindrical and tubular below, lobes spreading, in all about 4 in. (10 cm) wide and very showy. Stamens 6, their bases expanded and united to form a cup at mouth of corolla tube. Fruit a 3-lobed capsule. Colombia. Chiefly an indoor pot plant; blooms can be forced at any time of year. Also called *E. amazonica.* Zone 10.

Eucomis
Lily family
Liliaceae

You-kow'mis. A small genus of South African perennial bulbous herbs related to *Scilla,* from which it differs by the crown of leafy bracts at top of flower-stalk. (*Eucomis,* from the Greek for "beautiful topknot," alludes to the form of the flower cluster.)

Description
Leaves in rosette atop bulb. Flowers starlike, in a raceme topped with a cluster of leaflike bracts.

How to Grow
Grow in full sun. Allow bulbs to overwinter in the ground south of Zone 7, but handle as pot plants in a cool greenhouse in the North.

comosa p. 186
Pineapple Flower. Grows 1–2 ft. (30–60 cm) high. Leaves brown-spotted beneath, nearly 2 ft. (60 cm) long and 3 in. (7.5 cm) wide, in a rosette at base of stem. Flowers greenish white, ½ in. (13 mm) long, the segments separate, borne in a leafy-topped, terminal raceme. Stamens 6. Fruit a 3-valved capsule. Summer. Sometimes offered as *E. punctata.* Zone 7.

Ferraria
Iris family
Iridaceae

Fer-ra'ree-a. A genus of about 17 species of cormous herbs native in South Africa, one of which is sometimes cultivated. (The name commemorates Giovanni Battista Ferrari

(1584–1655), an Italian botanist and writer on cultivated plants.)

Description
Leaves swordlike. Flowers lasting only a day or less, 3 outer segments spreading and much longer than the 3 erect inner segments.

How to Grow
Should be treated like *Gladiolus*.

crispa p. 252
Branching stem to 18 in. (45 cm) high. Leaves sword-shaped, to 18 in. (45 cm) long. Flowers purplish brown to greenish brown, 3–4 in. (7.5–10.0 cm) wide, with a sickly-sweet odor. Although individual flowers bloom only a day, each plant remains in flower for a month or more. South Africa. Late spring to summer. Zone 9.

Freesia
Iris family
Iridaceae

Free′zi-a. Very fragrant and beautiful South African branched herbs, deservedly popular, especially among florists, for their winter-blooming flowers. Freesias have been heavily hybridized and there are many named forms. (Named for F. H. T. Freese, a pupil of the christener of the genus.)

Description
Bulblike corms and mostly narrow, basal, sword-shaped leaves. Flowers typically white or yellow, in terminal, not dense, spike-like racemes, which are mostly at right angles to stem. Corolla funnel-shaped or tubular, the limb slightly irregular. Stamens 3. Fruit a small capsule.

How to Grow
In colder climates, plant corms in late summer and keep in a cool greenhouse, ensuring that night temperature does not exceed 45–50° F (7–10° C). Keep them reasonably moist. The first flowers of the earliest varieties should appear in about 3½ months. When this occurs, water plants freely. For a succession of bloom, stagger planting time over 2–3 weeks. Plants are weak-stemmed, so provide stakes or other support as the flowering spike elongates.

Whenever they finish blooming, reduce
water, and when leaves begin to die, shake
out corms and store in a cool, slightly moist,
dark place until the next planting season.
Corms can be started in mid- to late winter
for window-box blooming in spring.

× *hybrida* pp. *178, 188*

Group of horticultural hybrids, probably all
derived from *F. refracta*. Cormous perennials
with slender, usually branched stems,
1½–2 ft. (45–60 cm) high. Leaves
sword-shaped, 2-ranked, to 6 in. (15 cm)
long. Flowers funnel-shaped, with flaring
mouth, to 2 in. (5 cm) long, in many colors
including white, yellow, and others notably
tinted or veined with pink, purple, blue,
orange, or even brown. South Africa. Chiefly
grown in the greenhouse; blossom time
varies. Zone 9.

Fritillaria
Lily family
Liliaceae

Fri-til-lay′ri-a. Fine, old-fashioned garden
flowers, all 100 known species from the
north temperate zone and usually called
fritillary, although *F. imperialis* is the
well-known Crown Imperial. (*Fritillaria,*
from the Latin for "dicebox," refers to the
flower markings of some species.)

Description
Bulbous, mostly unbranched herbs with
alternate or whorled leaves, sometimes with
a terminal cluster above the flowers, which
bloom in early spring. Flowers lilylike,
pendant, the 6 segments alike, and no
apparent calyx. Stamens 6. Fruit a
many-seeded, 3-valved capsule.

How to Grow
The Old World fritillaries, especially the
Crown Imperial, are old garden favorites that
persist for years and are easy to grow. Plant
4–6 in. (10–15 cm) deep in humus-rich, well-
drained soil in full sun or light deciduous
shade. They produce abundant offsets. Lift,
divide, and reset every second or third
season. Purchase bulbs as soon as available in
autumn and plant immediately, since they
dry out quickly. Most species from the w.
U.S. do not do well in the cold, wet winters
of the East.

imperialis p. 211

Crown Imperial. Stout, unpleasant-smelling herb, 2–4 ft. (60–120 cm) high. Stem purple-spotted. Leaves many along lower two-thirds of stem, sometimes with a terminal whorl above the flowers, usually lance-shaped, to 6 in. (15 cm) long. Flowers nearly 2 in. (5 cm) long, reddish, yellowish, or purplish, the segments veined. Iran to n. India. Early spring. Zone 5.

lanceolata p. 191

Checker Lily; Mission Bells. To 2 ft. (60 cm) high. Leaves oval or lance-shaped, to 6 in. (15 cm) long, sometimes in 2 or 3 whorls. Flowers 1–4, about 1½ in. (4 cm) long, the segments purple mottled with greenish yellow. British Columbia east to Idaho, south to n. Calif. Not happy in eastern gardens. Keep crown of plant dry; good drainage is very important. Early spring. Zone 6.

Meleagris pp. 161, 241

Guinea-Hen Flower; Checkered Lily; Snake's-Head. Erect herb, 12–18 in. (30–45 cm) high. Leaves few, oblongish or narrower, 3–6 in. (7.5–15.0 cm) long. Flowers usually solitary, bell-shaped, about 1½ in. (4 cm) long, the segments checkered and veined purplish or maroon. There is also a white- and a yellow-flowered form. Best grown in rock garden. Europe. Early spring. Zone 4.

pallidiflora p. 192

Handsome bulbous perennial. 6–14 in. (15–35 cm) high. Lower leaves opposite, oblong, to 3 in. (7.5 cm) long, the rest narrower and scattered, all bluish green. Flowers mostly at upper leaf joints, 1½ in. (4 cm) long, bell-shaped, yellowish white but green-tinged outside and with reddish-purple dots inside. S. Siberia. Early spring. Zone 5.

pudica p. 193

Yellow Fritillary; Yellow Bell. To 9 in. (22.5 cm) high. Leaves narrow, broader toward the tip, to 8 in. (20 cm) long. Flowers about ¾ in. (2 cm) long, only 1–3 in a cluster, the segments yellow or orange tinged with purple. W. North America. Early spring. Will grow in the East, but requires full sun, perfect drainage, and very little humus. Zone 4.

verticillata p. 240

Stem to 2 ft. (60 cm) high. Leaves narrowly
lance-shaped, opposite or whorled, upper
leaves with tips drawn out into short
tendrils. Flowers to 1¼ in. (3 cm) long,
cup-shaped, purplish inside and white or
yellow flecked with green outside. Cen. Asia,
China, and Japan. Early spring. Zone 6.

Galanthus
Amaryllis family
Amaryllidaceae

Ga-lan'thus. Snowdrops; Candlemas Bells.
Pretty little spring-blooming, bulbous herbs,
all Eurasian, and a handful of the 12 known
species cultivated for their handsome, very
early bloom. (*Galanthus,* from the Greek for
"milk" and "flower," alludes to the white
blooms.)

Description
They have small bulbs, a solid flowering
stalk, and only 2–3 narrow leaves at the base
of stem. Flowers solitary at end of stalk,
usually nodding, outer segments white, inner
green or greenish, without a tube. Stamens
6. Fruit a 3-valved capsule.

How to Grow
Plant in large numbers in light, rich soil in
full sun or beneath deciduous trees and
shrubs. Plant bulbs in late summer to early
fall. Set them 3 in. (7.5 cm) deep and 3 in.
(7.5 cm) apart. They increase freely and may
be left undisturbed for years to form large,
densely packed colonies.

byzantinus p. 160

3–9 in. high. Leaves broad, bluish green,
margins recurved. Flowers ½–1 in. (1.3–
2.5 cm) long, oblongish, inner flower white,
with green patch at base. Nw. Anatolia
(Turkey). Early spring. Zone 5.

Elwesii p. 159

Giant Snowdrop. Flowering stalk 4–11 in.
(10.0–27.5 cm) high. Leaves 8 in. (20 cm)
long, ¾ in. (2 cm) wide, very bluish green.
Flowers 1–1½ in. (2.5–4.0 cm) long, inner
segments with green patches at base and tip,
outer segments white. Se. Europe. Prefers
full sun and sandy soil, and a mulch of
well-decayed manure or compost in autumn.
Early spring. Zones 4–5.

Galtonia
Lily family
Liliaceae

Gall-tow′ni-a. A small genus of South
African bulbous herbs. (Named for Sir
Francis Galton, British anthropologist.)

Description
Flowers large, drooping, whitish, on a tall
raceme. Leaves fleshy, strap-shaped. Related
to *Veltheimia* and *Lachenalia*.

How to Grow
Plant bulbs 6 in. (15 cm) deep in
well-drained soil liberally enriched with
compost. Top dress every autumn with at
least 2 in. (5 cm) of compost. Prefers full
sun. Not really hardy north of Zone 6 unless
well mulched. Propagated by offsets from the
bulbs, or by seed.

candicans p. 181
Summer Hyacinth; Giant Summer Hyacinth.
Garden plant with showy, fragrant flowers.
Erect, flowering stalk 2–4 ft. (60–120 cm)
high, terminated by a long, rather sparsely
flowered raceme. Leaves basal, strap-shaped,
2–3 ft. (60–90 cm) long, 1–2 in. (2.5–
5.0 cm) wide. Flowers white, short-tubed,
1½ in. (4 cm) long, narrowly bell-shaped,
segments longer than tube. Stamens 6. South
Africa. Summer. Often sold as *Hyacinthus
candicans*. Zone 6.

Gladiolus
Iris family
Iridaceae

Gla-dy′o-lus; also glad-i-o′lus. Very popular
summer-blooming plants, many from South
Africa, but a few from tropical Africa and
elsewhere. More than 250 species are known,
and from a few of them several thousand
named forms have been developed, some
very striking. Modern garden varieties are
bred for increased disease resistance, greater
substance, better-germinating cormels, wider
color range, and better keeping qualities.
They are classified by size from miniatures,
with flowers less than 2½ in. (6 cm) wide,
to giants, with flowers 5½ in. (14 cm) wide.
The almost endless range of forms includes
ruffled, waved, crimped, horned, frilled,
needle-pointed, and plain-petaled flowers.

(*Gladiolus,* Latin for "small sword," alludes
to the shape of the leaves.) Old names for
them are Sword Lily and Corn Lily.

Description
Gladiolus bear corms from which grows a
usually erect, unbranched, leafy stem. Leaves
commonly sword-shaped, long, narrow, and
handsome. Flowers very showy, in a long,
terminal, spike-like cluster composed of leafy
bracts, between every 2 of which there is a
single stalkless flower. They bloom from the
bottom upward. Flowers funnel-shaped, but
with the tube dilated, and usually curved
upward. Flower segments 6, upper 3 larger
than the lower, hence flower is slightly
irregular. Stamens 3. Fruit a large capsule, its
seeds usually flattened or winged.

How to Grow
Plant corms from early spring to
midsummer, up to a time that will allow a
90-day growth before the first killing frost.
Size of corm will determine planting depth:
small corms, ½ in. (13 mm) or less, 3 in.
(7.5 cm) deep; medium corms, ½–1 in.
(1.3–2.5 cm) in diameter, 4–5 in. (10.0–
12.5 cm) deep; and large corms, 1¼ in.
(3 cm) and up, 6–8 in. (15–20 cm) deep.
Deep planting holds large plants erect when
they bloom, eliminating staking, and
prevents corms from splitting or producing
many small cormels.
Plant in full sunlight in well-drained, deeply
prepared soil, away from other deep-rooted
plants. Dig trench 2 in. (5 cm) deeper than
prescribed planting depth and add fertilizer
such as 5-10-10 or 4-12-12 plus bone meal,
using 1 cup per 10 ft. (3 m) of row. Cover
fertilizer with 2 in. (5 cm) of soil. Plant
corms from 3–6 in. (7.5–15.0 cm) apart;
wider spacing produces taller plants and
larger flowers. Rows in a cutting garden
should be from 2–2½ ft. (60–75 cm) apart;
in a border planting, allow 6 in. (15 cm)
between plants. Cover corms with several
inches of soil and work in soil as plants
grow. Keep plants free of weeds. Water well
during growth once bloom spikes emerge
above ground level. If season is dry, soak soil
every third day until first flower opens.

Other Planting Methods
In the South, where *Gladiolus* is grown for
cut flowers during winter, dormant corms
can be planted at any time. For continuous
bloom, make successive plantings 10–14 days

apart; try varieties that have different maturity periods and blooming spans.

Gladiolus is rarely forced in greenhouses, but for mid-spring blooms corms can be planted in a heated cold frame outside in mid-winter, with plastic covering during cold weather or late-spring frosts to keep plants from freezing. Plant corms 3 in. (7.5 cm) deep and 4 in. (10 cm) apart in the hotbed and do not allow night temperature to drop below 50° F (10° C).

Cutting Flowers

For cutting purposes, cut spike when first flower opens and place in water in a cool room for 24 hours to allow it to develop. When cutting, allow at least 5 leaves to remain on plant to provide growth and food for developing corm. Low cutting will produce immature, undersized corms.

Harvesting and Storage

Corms can be harvested 4–6 weeks after blooming; it is not necessary to allow the plants to die. Remove leaves flush with top of corm as soon as dug. Destroy or compost the foliage, which could harbor insects and fungus diseases.

As soon as easily separated, remove and discard the old corms and place new corms and cormels in open container to dry. Dust with fungicide, then store in cool, dry, well-ventilated cellar. Remove husks from corms before planting in spring. In temperate zones, cool weather causes corms to become dormant. In warm regions, however, you should place corms in cold storage for 3 months to induce dormancy and a sufficient rest period for good growth.

Propagation

Gladiolus is propagated from cormels clustered around the corm, but their thick protective husk usually prevents speedy growth. Seed culture requires several seasons to produce blooming-size corms.

Pests and Diseases

To control thrips, dust corms with Diazinon or a systemic, or soak for 3 hours in 1¼ tablespoons (18.5 ml) Lysol in 1 gal. (3.8 l) of water just before planting. Spray or dust Diazinon on plants in field to prevent damage there, particularly during early part of growing season. Flowers may be damaged by insecticides.

Small sunken spots with a varnishlike coating on corms are symptoms of bacterial scab. If only a few spots are present, corms can be planted with good results, but large decayed areas indicate fungus disease, so discard these corms. When plants turn yellow and die before flowering, it is usually due to fungus yellows. Do not plant gladiolus in that area for at least 3 years. Light gray streaks in leaves and abnormal white streaks in flower petals indicate mosaic virus; discard the corms. During humid weather, leaves and flowers may develop gray mold spots. Spray with zineb at weekly intervals to prevent further spotting.

byzantinus p. 244
To 3 ft. (90 cm) high. Leaves 3–5, to 1 ft. (30 cm) long. Spikes loosely many-flowered. Flowers pinkish purple, segments to 1½ in. (4 cm) long, some with a white stripe. There is a form with white flowers and one with cerise-scarlet flowers. Mediterranean region. Summer. Material sold as this species is often actually *G. illyricus*. Zone 5.

carneus p. 173
About 2 ft. (60 cm) high, stems sometimes branched. Leaves usually 4, nearly 1 ft. (30 cm) long. Flowers 4–8 in spike, 2–3 in. (5.0–7.5 cm) wide, white, red-tinged, or pink, segments pointed. South Africa. Summer. Zone 9.

× *Colvillei* p. 172
G. cardinalis × *G. tristis*. To 2 ft. (60 cm) high. Leaves sword-shaped, about 18 in. (45 cm) long. Flower spikes short, early-blooming. Flowers scarlet with yellow oblong blotches, 2 in. (5 cm) long. 'The Bride', shown, is a pure white cultivar. Late spring to summer. Zone 7.

× *gandavensis* p. 217
A very popular and long-cultivated, late-blooming garden gladiolus. About 3 ft. (90 cm) high. Leaves broad. Flowering spike long and dense. Flowers mostly red or reddish yellow, often streaked or penciled, 2–3 in. (5.0–7.5 cm) long. Summer. It is the origin of many named forms. Zone 9.

× *hortulanus* pp. 187, 218, 219
Name for vast number of fancy-named cultivated forms for which no definite parentage can be assigned. Sturdy plants, to 3 ft. (90 cm) high or more. Leaves sword-

shaped, 12 in. (30 cm) long or more. Spikes of large, funnel-shaped flowers in many colors, 3–4 in. (7.5–10.0 cm) long or more. Garden origin. Summer. Zone 9.

illyricus *p. 245*
Cormous herb, 1–3 ft. (30–90 cm) high. Leaves only 2 or 3, narrow, 6–12 in. (15–30 cm) long. Flowers in loose, 1-sided spikes, tube slightly curved, crimson-purple, 1½ in. (4 cm) wide. Europe. Late spring to summer. Plants offered as *G. anatolicus* and *G. byzantinus* are apt to be *G. illyricus*. Zone 9.

segetum *p. 245*
Cornflag. A cormous herb, 1½–2 ft. (45–60 cm) high. Leaves ½ in. (13 mm) wide. Flowers in loose 1-sided spike, corolla 1½ in. (4 cm) long, pinkish purple, segments flaring. Mediterranean region. Summer. Zone 7.

tristis *p. 182*
To 2 ft. (60 cm) high, unbranched. Leaves 3, round in section, 18 in. (45 cm) long, and ribbed. Flowers night-blooming, white or yellowish white, purple streaked, very fragrant in the evening, tube 2 in. (5 cm) long. Var. *concolor* has pure white flowers. South Africa. Summer. Zone 7.

Gloriosa
Lily family
Liliaceae

Glow-ri-o´sa. Glory-lily. Weak-stemmed, tuberous-rooted, showy vines, natives of tropical Africa and Asia, mostly grown in the greenhouse, but suited to outdoor culture in the far South. (*Gloriosa,* from the Latin for "glorious," alludes to the showy flowers.)

Description
They have narrow leaves, tips prolonged into tendril-like organs by which the plants climb. Flowers lilylike, solitary in upper leaf axils, mostly red or yellow, segments separate, rather narrow, sometimes crisped. Stamens 6. Fruit a capsule.

How to Grow
Greenhouse culture demands a day temperature of 55–65° F (13.0–18.5° C).

Tubers potted in midwinter will bloom in late summer and autumn, after which they need a rest; reduce their water. In the North, often grown as a summer annual, thus tubers are stored over winter. For outdoor culture, plants need a long growing season, full sun, and must be staked. Propagate by division of tubers during dormancy.

Rothschildiana p. 210
A climbing vine, to 8 ft. (2.4 m) high. Leaves broadly lance-shaped, 5–7 in. (12.5–18.0 cm) long. Flowers bent downward, red, edged in yellow, segments to 3 in. (7.5 cm) long, not crisped, but sometimes wavy. Tropical Africa. Blooms outdoors late spring to summer. Zone 10.

superba p. 189
Vine to 12 ft. (3.5 m) long. Leaves narrowly lance-shaped, 4–6 in. (10–15 cm) long. Flowers at first yellow or yellowish green at base of segments and red at tips, changing totally to dark red with age. Segments narrow, 2–3 in. (5.0–7.5 cm) long, much-crisped and appearing twisted. A very handsome plant and the most widely grown of the genus. The cultivar 'Lutea' has yellow flowers. Tropical Africa. Summer. Zone 10.

Habranthus
Amaryllis family
Amaryllidaceae

Ha-bran'thuss. A small genus of bulbous herbs from North and South America, the 3 species described below cultivated in the greenhouse or in frostless regions outdoors. Closely related to *Zephyranthes,* from which they are separated only by technical characteristics. May be offered in the trade as *Hippeastrum* or *Zephyranthes.* (*Habranthus* means "delicate flower.")

Description
They have coated bulbs, narrow leaves, and showy, but rather fleeting, flowers. Petals recurved at the tip (erect in *Zephyranthes*). Fruit a 3-lobed pod.

How to Grow
Habranthus may be grown outdoors in Zones 9 and 10, and elsewhere as pot plants. Plant bulbs singly in pot 6 in. (15 cm) deep containing a mixture of one-third each

garden soil, compost, and perlite. Neck of bulb should be at or above level of soil. Keep soil moist, but not wet, until growth begins; then add more water. Regular fertilizing during growing period is beneficial. After plant has flowered and leaves begin to die, reduce water and cease fertilizing. When leaves have completely died down, keep pot almost dry until growth commences the following spring. Plants can stay in same pots for several years. Propagation is by offsets or by seed.

Andersonii p. 223

To 6 in. (15 cm) high, the grassy leaves to 6 in. (15 cm) long. Flowers 1½ in. (4 cm) long, yellow, with red veins outside; may appear pinkish. South America. Late spring. Zone 9.

brachyandrus p. 222

Bulb football-shaped, 1 in. (2.5 cm) thick. Leaves 12 in. (30 cm) long, sparse. Flowering stalk 12 in. (30 cm) high, topped by a solitary, funnel-shaped flower that may be up to 3 in. (7.5 cm) wide; pink above, but shading to a much darker (almost blackish) base. S. Brazil. Summer. Zone 10.

tubispathus p. 220

Similar to *H. brachyandrus,* but to only 9 in. (22.5 cm) high. Flowers to 3 in. (7.5 cm) long, rose-pink. Argentina. Along the Gulf Coast it self-sows and repeats its bloom. Summer to autumn. Zone 9.

Haemanthus
Amaryllis family
Amaryllidaceae

Hy-man′thus. Blood Lily. Showy, bulbous African herbs comprising 60 species, those described below grown in greenhouses for their handsome flowers. (*Haemanthus,* Greek for "blood flower," alludes to the red flowers of many species.)

Description
They have chiefly basal, broad, blunt leaves and a somewhat flattened, solid flower-stalk, crowned by a dense head of usually red flowers, beneath which is a whorl of spathelike bracts. Flowers more or less tubular, segments erect or spreading.

Stamens sometimes showy and protruding.
Fruit berrylike, not splitting.

How to Grow
Grow in a cool greenhouse with a night
temperature not over 55° F (13° C). Under
these conditions, they flower in late summer
and early autumn; then bulbs should be
rested through winter and started into
growth in spring. Dig up bulbs and store in
a cool, dark, frost-free cellar, or gradually dry
off pots and store similarly.

albiflos p. 193
To 12 in. (30 cm) high. Leaves thick, fleshy,
6–8 in. (15–20 cm) long, nearly 4 in.
(10 cm) wide, hairy on margins. Flowers
¾ in. (2 cm) long, white with numerous
yellow stamens, crowded at end of solid stalk
in dense umbels that may be 2 in. (5 cm)
wide. South Africa. Summer. Zone 9.

coccineus p. 217
Blood Lily. Flowering stalk 12 in. (30 cm)
high. Leaves thick, fleshy, to 2 ft. (60 cm)
long and 8 in. (20 cm) wide. Flowers red,
1 in. (2.5 cm) long, cluster 3 in. (7.5 cm)
wide. South Africa. Summer. Zone 9.

Katherinae p. 216
Catherine-Wheel. 12–18 in. (30–45 cm)
high. Leaves thin, 10–14 in. (25–35 cm)
long, 6 in. (15 cm) wide. Flowers bright red,
nearly 2½ in. (6 cm) long, the cluster nearly
9 in. (22.5 cm) wide and very showy. South
Africa. Summer. Zone 9.

Hemerocallis
Lily family
Liliaceae

Hem-mer-o-kal′lis. Daylily. About 15 wild
species of perennial herbs, found from
Central Europe to Japan, and having many
hybrid forms. (*Hemerocallis* is from the Greek
for "beautiful for a day.")

Description
Roots somewhat fleshy. Leaves nearly all
basal, narrow, sword-shaped, and keeled.
Stem or stalk of flower cluster is often
branched and usually exceeds leaves. Flowers
funnel-form or bell-shaped, widely expanding
above. Stamens 6, inserted on throat of
corolla. Fruit a capsule.

How to Grow
Daylilies flower freely, are easy to grow, and resist disease. They thrive in sun or partial shade and adapt well to most any location, whether massed on dry slopes or in moist soil by the waterside, or planted in clumps in the flower garden. Individual flowers last only a day, but others follow on the branched stems to prolong the display, and some may flower a second time in the season. By selecting varieties that bloom at different times, it is possible to have some plants in flower from late spring until fall. The leaves of all species and varieties are attractive throughout the growing season. Evergreen daylilies are better suited for the South, but with protection may survive a northern winter.

Propagation
Daylilies are readily increased by root division. Clumps can remain undisturbed for several years, but whenever growth gets too congested, divide and replant. This is best done in late summer or early spring. Pry off divisions of about 3 growths from outside of clump and replant in well-worked soil enriched with organic material. Trim foliage back about half when done in summer. To protect against frost, mulch heavily. Plantlets that sometimes develop on flower stem can be detached and planted, and will grow and flower like the parent. Plants propagated by seed—the method hybridizers use to create named forms—will first bloom when 2–3 years old.

aurantiaca p. 148
To 3 ft. (1 m) high, with spreading rhizomes. Leaves to 3 ft. (90 cm) long, 1 in. (2.5 cm) wide. Flowers burnt-orange or salmon-orange, to 4 in. (10 cm) across. China. Summer. Zone 7.

citrina p. 141
To 4 ft. (1.2 m) high. Leaves 3 ft. (1 m) long, 1 in. (2.5 cm) wide. Flowers light lemon-yellow, nearly 6 in. (15 cm) long, fragrant. China. Summer. Zones 3–4.

Dumortieri p. 143
To 18 in. (45 cm) high. Leaves 18 in. (45 cm) long, ½ in. (13 mm) wide. Flowers pale orange, fragrant, 2½ in. (6 cm) long, tube short. Japan. Late spring. Zones 3–4.

fulva p. 149
To 5 ft. (1.5 m) high. Leaves 2 ft. (60 cm) long, to 1½ in. (4 cm) wide. Flowers to 5 in. (12.5 cm) long, orange-red, often with dark lines. Eurasia. Summer. Quite common as a roadside escape in e. U.S. Zones 3–4.

hybrids *pp. 130, 141, 142, 143, 153*
Popular interest in daylilies has steadily increased with the development of countless new garden varieties. These named forms, numbering in the thousands, grow 1–5 ft. (30–150 cm) high, some with flowers to 6 in. (15 cm) wide, with petals single, double, or ruffled. Colors alone or in combination include cream through many shades of yellow, orange, red, pink, lavender, and purple. Late spring to summer. Zones 3–4.

Lilioasphodelus p.139
Lemon Daylily. Flowering stalk 3 ft. (1 m) high. Leaves ¾ in. (2 cm) wide. Flowers yellow, 3–4 in. (7.5–10.0 cm) long, fragrant, stalks weak and arching. E. Asia. Rarely an escape in e. U.S. Late spring. Also known as *H. flava.* Zone 4.

Middendorfii p. 144
To 18 in. (45 cm) high. Leaves 1 in. (2.5 cm) wide. Flowers pale orange, 2¾ in. (7 cm) long, fragrant, segments curving backward with age. Siberia (U.S.S.R.). Late spring. Zones 3–4.

Hermodactylus
Iris family
Iridaceae

Her-mo-dak'ti-lus. A single irislike bulbous herb from s. Europe. (*Hermodactylus,* Greek for Hermes and "finger," aludes to the shape of the root.)

Description
Differs from *Iris* chiefly in its 1-celled pod. Flowers cup-shaped, 3 outer segments spreading, inner segments erect.

How to Grow
Grow in full sun in well-drained, compost-enriched soil. European sources recommend a neutral or alkaline pH. Plant 3 in. (7.5 cm) deep. Mulch area well in autumn and winter. Propagate by seed or, preferably, divide the clumps.

tuberosus p. 186
Snake's Head Iris. About 18 in. (45 cm) high. Leaves somewhat 4-angled, 2 ft. (60 cm) long, bluish green. Flower solitary, outer segments very dark purple, inner greenish, to 2 in. (5 cm) long. S. Europe. Early spring. Zone 6.

Hesperocallis
Lily family
Liliaceae

Hes-per-o-call'is. A single species of bulbous, perennial herbs, native in the deserts of s. Calif. and w. Ariz. (From the Greek for "western beauty.")

Description
The bulb produces a single stem with leaves borne at the base and a raceme of funnel-shaped flowers at the top.

How to Grow
Suitable for gardens in desert areas of Zones 8–10; plant in deep, sandy soil. Propagated by seed.

undulata p. 184
Desert Lily. Stems to 2½ ft. (75 cm) high. Leaves linear, to 18 in. (45 cm) long and 3/5 in. (15 mm) wide, crisped along whitish margins. Flowers funnel-shaped, to 2½ in. (6 cm) long, white. Spring. Zone 9.

Hippeastrum
Amaryllis family
Amaryllidaceae

Hipp-e-as'trum. Amaryllis-like, mostly tropical, American bulbous herbs comprising 70 or more species and many garden hybrids, the horticultural sorts commonly called Dutch Amaryllis and grown like them. They differ from true *Amaryllis* in their hollow flower-stalk. (*Hippeastrum* is from the Greek words for "horse" and "star," but has no known application here.)

Description
Leaves basal and strap-shaped in the horticultural kinds. Flowers large, showy, lilylike, prevailingly red or sometimes white-lined, generally funnel-shaped, borne in

a large terminal umbel. Fruit a globe-shaped capsule. Some species occasionally known as *Habranthus.*

How to Grow
Plant bulbs mid- to late autumn in equal parts garden soil, compost, and perlite in pot about 2 in. (5 cm) wider than bulb. Keep soil moist but not wet, and night temperature above 65° F (19° C). After root growth and flowering, transfer to pot 4 in. (10 cm) wider than bulb and fertilize. When roots fill pot, repot in container at least 12 in. (30 cm) in diameter. Set outdoors in full sun for summer, never letting soil dry out. Fertilize regularly through late summer. Before first frost, place indoors in sunny window. As leaves fall off, reduce watering, but do not let pot become dry. New flower spikes appear mid-winter. Increase watering and resume fertilizing when leaves appear. Periodically remove offsets and pot separately. Seedlings are unlikely to equal parent hybrid plant.

hybrids *pp. 218, 219*
Dutch Amaryllis. Developed from complex crosses of *H.* × *Johnsonii, H. reginae, H. vittatum,* or other species. To 2 ft. (60 cm) high. Leaves 2 in. (5 cm) wide or more. Flowers brilliant red, pink, orange, white, or striped, 6 in. (15 cm) long or more. Most often forced indoors for winter bloom. Early spring. Zone 9.

Homeria
Iris family
Iridaceae

Ho-meer′i-a. A small genus of South African bulbous plants. (*Homeria* is from the Greek *homereo,* "to meet," referring to the united stamens.)

Description
Usually a basal solitary leaf, with others on the stem. Flowers in a leafy cluster, funnel- or cup-shaped but segments free and spreading, stamens forming a united tube.

How to Grow
Should be grown like *Ixia.*

Breyniana *p. 207*
About 18 in. (45 cm) high. Stem leaves
concave, 2 ft. (60 cm) long. Flowers
salmon-pink or orange-red and yellow,
1½ in. (4 cm) long. Flowers of the cultivar
'Aurantiaca' are yellow at base of petals. In
Calif. it seeds freely and is apt to spread. Late
spring. Zone 9.

Hyacinthoides
Lily family
Liliaceae

Hy-a-sin-thoi'deez. Three species of bulbous
herbs native in w. and s. Europe; also known
as *Endymion*. (*Hyacinthoides* means
hyacinthlike.)

Description
Hyacinthoides species are similar to *Scilla* but
differ in that they renew their bulbs each
year and have 2 bracts for each flower.

How to Grow
Plant *Hyacinthoides* in damp, humus-rich soil
in open borders or under light, deciduous
shade. Set them 3 in. (7.5 cm) deep and
6 in. (15 cm) apart in an area where they
will not be disturbed from year to year.
Hyacinthoides will self-sow readily, as well as
make abundant offsets.

hispanicus *pp. 158, 262*
Spanish Bluebells; Spanish Jacinth. Flowering
stems to 20 in. (50 cm) high. Leaves strap-
shaped, nearly 1 in. (2.5 cm) wide. Flowers
¾ in. (19 mm) wide, bell-shaped, blue in
the typical form. Clusters 12- to 15-flowered.
There are several cultivars, including a
white-flowered form. Spain and Portugal.
Late spring. Sometimes called *Endymion
hispanicus* or *Scilla campanulata*. Zone 5.

italicus *p. 268*
Italian Squill. Flowering stems to 12 in.
(30 cm) high. Leaves linear to linear-
lance-shaped, to 10 in. (25 cm) long and ½
in. (13 mm) wide. Flowers fragrant, bluish
violet, the segments to ¼ in. (6 mm) long,
spreading. Portugal, se. France, and nw.
Italy. Late spring. Zone 5.

non-scriptus *p. 263*
Bluebells of England; Wood Hyacinth.
Flowering stems to 18 in. (45 cm) high, the

leaves ½ in. (13 mm) wide. Flowers
fragrant, bell-shaped, blue, to ¾ in.
(19 mm) long, in 6- to 12-flowered clusters.
There are pink- and white-flowered cultivars.
W. Europe. Late spring. Zone 6.

Hyacinthus
Lily family
Liliaceae

Hy-a-sin'thus. A genus of a single species
of bulbous herbs from the Mediterranean
region. (Named for the mythological
character.)

Description
It has narrow, basal, sometimes almost
grasslike leaves without marginal teeth.
Flowers fragrant in a showy, stiff, regular
terminal raceme, each individual flowering
stalk with a narrow bract at the base. Corolla
more or less bell-shaped, its 6 lobes or
segments spreading or turned backward.
Stamens 6. Fruit a 3-angled capsule.

How to Grow
All garden hyacinths are forms derived
under cultivation from *Hyacinthus orientalis*.
Plant bulbs in full sun 5–6 in. (12.5–
15.0 cm) deep in good soil rich in nutrients.
Although *Hyacinthus* is reasonably cold-
hardy, in the North, a winter mulch applied
late in autumn helps protect young shoots
as they push through the soil. Bulbs sold
commercially have been cultivated to
produce a large bloom-stalk the first time
they flower, but will not give equal
performance each year. They resume the
growth cycle during their second year in the
garden, and if well fertilized, will again come
to the same size and stage as when first
purchased. Some natural multiplication also
occurs at this time, resulting in several
smaller flower-stalks.

Indoor Forcing
Hyacinths force well in pots; follow dates
that appear in catalogues. Do not hurry the
plants. First let roots fill bottom of pot, then
bring pots into the light to allow flower-
stalk to develop. They can also be grown in
water in hyacinth glasses; keep them in the
dark until base of glass is well filled with
roots.

Diseases
Plants that wilt suddenly and die may be victims of a fungus rot. In wet soil especially, bulbs may become soft and rotten as a result of bacterial soft rot; in wet or dry soil, small, hard, black objects on the neck of a solid bulb indicate another fungus. In either case, dig out bulbs and destroy. If bulb rots become serious after continuous yearly planting in the same area, do not replant with hyacinths for at least 3 years.

orientalis p. 261
Common Garden Hyacinth. Flowering stalk to 18 in. (45 cm). Leaves nearly 1 ft. (30 cm) long and ¾ in. (19 mm) wide. Flowers many colors, very fragrant, about 1 in. (2.5 cm) long, sometimes double-blooming. Range of varieties changes from season to season. Those with deep rose or yellow flowers produce smaller spikes than others. Var. *albulus* (Roman Hyacinth) is usually white or blue, smaller, less hardy, blooms earlier, and has several flower-stalks per bulb but with fewer, less stiff blooms than the common hyacinth. Greece to Asia Minor. Early spring. Zone 5.

Hymenocallis
Amaryllis family
Amaryllidaceae

Hy-men-o-kall′is. Showy, chiefly tropical American bulbous herbs, commonly known as spider-lilies. Of the 25 known species, only a few are of much interest, although wild species from S.C. to Fla. are sometimes transferred to gardens in their own region. (*Hymenocallis,* from the Greek for "beautiful membrane," alludes to the cuplike base of the stamens.)

Description
They have narrow, strap-shaped basal leaves and few-flowered umbels of white flowers at the end of a stout, solid stalk. Corolla white, cylindric, and united below, broadening at top and with narrow segments. Stamens 6, their filaments much broadened and united at base into a conspicuous, white, cuplike structure. Fruit a 3-valved capsule.

How to Grow
Spider-lilies are popular for outdoor tropical

gardens. In the North they need greenhouse care and should be planted in large pots or small tubs, because their bulbs become large. Grow in a warm-temperate greenhouse.

caribaea p. 174
Bulb with little or no neck. To 3 ft. (90 cm) high; leaves 12–20, usually 1–2 ft. (30–60 cm) long, nearly 3 in. (7.5 cm) wide. Flowers fragrant, 6 in. (15 cm) long, half tubular. Perianth lobes narrow, longer than tube. Cuplike base of stamens 1 in. (2.5 cm) high and wide, stamens protruding beyond it nearly 2 in. (5 cm). West Indies. After blooming, bulbs must be rested for a season. Blooms indoors in winter, outdoors in late spring to summer. Zone 10.

narcissiflora p. 175
Basket-Flower; Peruvian Daffodil. Bulb with a long, stout neck from which arise 6–8 leaves, which are nearly 2 ft. (60 cm) long and 2 in. (5 cm) wide, 2-ranked. Flowers fragrant, nearly 8 in. (20 cm) long, half tubular, segments narrow. Cuplike base of stamens nearly 2 in. (5 cm) wide, fringed, stamens protruding beyond it about ½ in. (13 mm). Peruvian and Bolivian Andes. Lift bulbs from ground to rest during winter. Summer. Often offered as *Pancratium calathinum* and *Ismene calathina*. Zone 8.

Ipheion
Amaryllis family
Amaryllidaceae

If-ee'on. A small genus of South American bulbous herbs. (*Ipheion* is a name of unknown derivation.)

Description
Leaves linear; flowers borne singly on the stems. Flowers funnel-shaped with spreading lobes. Related to *Brodiaea*.

How to Grow
Plant bulbs mid- to late summer, 3 in. (7.5 cm) deep and up to 6 in. (15 cm) apart, in full sun. Propagation by offsets is very rapid. Leaves appear in autumn and persist through winter. After flowering, plants go dormant. To grow bulbs indoors, provide plants with at least 4 hours of full sun each day, and maintain night temperature of 50–65 ° F (10.0–18.5 ° C).

uniflorum p. 259
Spring Starflower. The best-known and most
widely cultivated species. Usually not over
8 in. (20 cm) high. Flowers solitary, white
tinged with blue or bluish, about 1 in.
(2.5 cm) long and 1½ in. (4 cm) across.
Bruised leaves give off strong onionlike odor.
Argentina and Uruguay. Early spring. Also
known as *Milla uniflora* and *Leucocoryne
uniflora*. Zone 6.

Iris
Iris family
Iridaceae

Eye′ris. A large genus of perennial herbs
comprising over 150 species, mostly from the
north temperate zone, and thousands of
horticultural varieties. There are 2 basic
types: those that grow from stout rhizomes,
and those that grow from bulbs. Only the
bulbous kinds will be covered here. (*Iris* was
named for the goddess of the rainbow.)

Description
Leaves narrow, sometimes grasslike. Flowers,
in 6 segments, arise from spathelike bracts.
The 3 outer segments are reflexed and
generally called falls; the inner 3 are usually
smaller, erect, and known as standards. Falls
and standards have a narrow claw, or haft, at
base. Flowers followed by a large, 3-celled
seed pod.

How to Grow
Plant bulbous iris in autumn in a sunny
location sheltered from the north and west,
in well-drained soil enriched with compost.
Iris reticulata grows at least as far north as
Zone 5 in the rock garden and persists year
after year, as long as the tiny foliage is left in
the ground. Varieties of *I. Xiphium* and
I. xiphioides will flower in the North the
first season but tend to die out after that.
Lift bulbs in early summer and store in a
warm, dry place, and replant in autumn.
From Zones 7–9 *I. Xiphium* and
I. xiphioides are perennial.

Danfordiae p. 197
A short-stemmed iris, to 4 in. (10 cm)
high. Stem brown-spotted. Leaves appearing
after the bloom, 8–12 in. (20–30 cm)
long, 4-sided, and hollow. Flowers 2–3 in.
(5.0–7.5 cm) long, yellow, standards

reduced to bristlelike structures. Falls to
1¼ in. (3 cm) long. Asia Minor. Plant 4 in.
(10 cm) deep to discourage bulbs from
breaking up into many small nonflowering
bulblets. Early spring. Zone 5.

Histrio p. 253
Bulbous herb to 6 in. (15 cm) high at
flowering time. Leaves 4-sided, 8 in. (20 cm)
long at flowering time, elongating to 12 in.
(30 cm) later. Flowers borne singly, about
3 in. (7.5 cm) wide, blue with yellow line
bordered with white in center. Var.
aintabensis is a small-flowered form. S. Turkey
to Lebanon. A good pot plant northward in
a cold greenhouse or cold frame. Early
spring. Zone 5.

histrioides p. 251
Bulbous herb 4–9 in. (10.0–22.5 cm) high.
Leaves 4-sided, to 20 in. (50 cm) long after
flowering. Flowers to nearly 3 in. (7.5 cm)
wide, blue. 'Major' has bright blue flowers.
N. cen. Turkey. A better garden plant than
I. Histrio, since the bulbs have less tendency
to break up into nonflowering-size bulblets.
Early spring. Zone 5.

reticulata pp. 250, 251
A stemless iris (until the fruit matures),
6–18 in. (15–45 cm) high. Leaves 2–4,
narrow, grasslike, 4-sided, in a tuft,
ultimately to 18 in. (45 cm) long. Flower
solitary, violet-purple, fragrant; falls with an
orange ridge, bordered with white, tube of
flower 3–6 in. (7.5–15.0 cm) long.
'Harmony' and 'Violet Beauty' are 2
horticultural forms. Caucasus. Best grown in
a cool greenhouse. Early spring. Zone 5.

xiphioides p. 250
English Iris. A bulbous iris imported to
Bristol, England, and thought by the Dutch
to be native there; hence called English Iris.
Leaves narrow, channeled, equal in length to
the stem, which may be 8–15 in. (20–
38 cm) long. Flowers 2–3, deep purple-blue,
usually golden-patched, to 3 in. (7.5 cm)
long; falls wedge-shaped. Pyrenees. Can be
grown outdoors in mild climates. Late spring
to summer. Also known as *I. latifolia.*
Zone 5.

Xiphium p. 252
Spanish Iris. Similar to *I. xiphioides.* To 2 ft.
(60 cm) high. Leaves almost cylindrical, to
2 ft. (60 cm) long. Flowers to 4 in. (10 cm)

long, falls fiddle-shaped, flower blue-purple (in the wild form) with a yellow or orange patch. There are many horticultural forms, including the Dutch Iris, which is one of the best for forcing winter bloom and is often used by florists. Mediterranean region. Late spring. Zones 6–7.

Ixia
Iris family
Iridaceae

Ick′si-a. South African bulbous herbs of about 30 species. Many named horticultural forms. (*Ixia,* from the Greek for "bird lime," possibly refers to the juice of some species.)

Description
Leaves grasslike, generally 2-ranked. Flowering stalk generally much longer than leaves. Flowers bell-shaped. Fruit a small capsule.

How to Grow
Hardy generally only from Zone 7 southward; occasionally safe northward with protection, but autumn leaf growth tends not to be frostproof. Elsewhere treat as greenhouse bloomers: Plant corms of blooming size in 4–5-in. (10.0–12.5-cm) pots or pans in autumn, 4–7 to a pot, and treat them like crocus or grape-hyacinths forced for early spring bloom. They grow readily outdoors in s. Calif., where they multiply quickly.

maculata pp. 183, 188
6–12 in. (15–30 cm) high. Leaves as long, linear and ribbed. Flowers bright yellow, 1 in. (2.5 cm) long, in dense and erect spikes, with black mark in throat. There is also a cream-white form with a purplish blotch in throat. Late spring to summer. Zone 7.

viridiflora p. 182
To 20 in. (50 cm) high, usually less as cultivated. Leaves narrowly sword-shaped. Flowers 1 in. (2.5 cm) long, numerous in a loose spike, the corolla pale green with black spot at base, filaments of anthers also black. Difficult to grow; needs extremely well drained soil. Late spring to summer. Zone 7.

Lachenalia
Lily family
Liliaceae

Lack-en-a'li-a. South African greenhouse and
bulbous herbs, a few of the 50 known
species grown in pots for their showy
flowers, and usually called Cape Cowslip.
(Named for Werner de Lachenal, a Swiss
professor.)

Description
Leaves 1 or 2 (or a few), basal, and without
marginal teeth. Flowers red and yellow,
drooping (in cultivated species), borne in
terminal spike or raceme at end of stalk that
rises from leaves. Corolla cylindric, tubular,
the outer 3 segments shorter than the
inner 3. Stamens 6. Fruit a 3-angled
capsule.

How to Grow
Hardy outdoors only in Zone 9 or 10. Grow
as pot plants elsewhere: In late summer,
using light, well-drained, humus-rich soil,
plant 5–6 bulbs 1 in. (2.5 cm) deep in a
5–6-in. (12.5–15.0-cm) pot. Place pots in a
cool, shady place with a minimum
temperature of 45–50° F (7–10° C). Do not
allow pots to dry out or stay wet. In early
winter, place pots in a sunny location.
Increase water and feed regularly with a
liquid fertilizer at half the recommended
strength. After flowering, water and fertilize
until leaves begin to die down, then cease
feeding and reduce watering (but never let
the pots become totally dry) until growth
begins again. *Lachenalia* can be propagated
by offsets or, more rarely, by seeds or by leaf
cuttings.

aloides p. 192
Cape Cowslip. To 12 in. (30 cm) high.
Leaves 2 to each plant, as long as the
flowering stalk, to 1 in. (2.5 cm) wide, often
purple-spotted. Flowers many in cluster,
corolla 1 in. (2.5 cm) long, shorter outer
segments yellow but green-tipped, inner ones
yellow but red-tipped. The cultivar 'Luteola'
has lemon-yellow flowers tipped with green;
white and lavender cultivars are also
available. Early spring. Zone 9.

Lapeirousia
Iris family
Iridaceae

La-pay-roo′si-a. South African bulbous herbs comprising 50 species, related to *Freesia,* but more hardy. (Named for Philippe Picot de la Peirouse, French savant.) Sometimes called *Anomatheca.*

Description
Corms small, leaves mostly basal, narrow, 2-ranked. Flowers small, not fragrant, red or blue, between spathe-like bracts. Corolla tubular, slender, slightly swollen where the spreading, nearly equal segments diverge. Fruit a small, 3-valved capsule.

How to Grow
Plant corms 3–4 in. (7.5–10.0 cm) deep in spring, in ordinary garden soil. The plants are hardy from Zone 7 southward, but north of this they should have a winter mulch of straw or litter. Wherever hardy they self-sow freely. Divide every few years to prevent overcrowding.

laxa p. 206
Leaves 6–10 in. (15–25 cm) long, thin and flat. Flowering stalk about as long, the few flowers in a 1-sided spike or raceme. Corolla red, nearly 1½ in. (4 cm) long, the tube very slender. Summer. Zone 7.

Ledebouria
Lily family
Liliaceae

Led-ee-bore′ee-a. About 15 species of bulbous plants closely related to *Scilla,* most native in South Africa, one in India. One species, *L. socialis,* cultivated in greenhouses.

Description
Leaves at tops of bulbs frequently spotted with brown or red. Flowers in a raceme, more or less cup-shaped.

How to Grow
Bulbs grow on surface of soil, forming large masses by producing offsets at bases. Pot in well-drained, humus-rich soil. Grow in full sun at minimum temperature of 50° F (10° C).

socialis p. 157

To 6 in. (15 cm) high. Bulbs reddish, narrowly pear-shaped or cylindrical. Leaves 2–5, lance-shaped, fleshy, 2–6 in. (5–15 cm) long, mottled green and silver above, unmottled red below. Flowering stalk 2–4 in. (5–10 cm) long. Flowers cup-shaped, segments reflexed at tips, green with white edges, to ¼ in. (6 mm) across. South Africa. Late spring. Zone 10.

Leucojum
Amaryllis family
Amaryllidaceae

Lew-ko'jum. Spring- or autumn-flowering bulbous herbs, 3 of the 9 known species often cultivated in the flower garden. All are native in Europe. (*Leucojum,* from the Greek for "white violet," probably alludes to the violetlike odor of its flowers.)

Description
They have small bulbs and a hollow flower-stalk usually taller than the narrow basal leaves. Leaves appear with the flowers in spring-flowering species, but after the bloom in fall-flowering sorts. Flowers bell-shaped, mostly nodding, inner and outer segments alike, but often differently colored, generally white and tinged with green or red. Stamens 6. Fruit a 3-valved capsule, its seeds nearly globe-shaped.

How to Grow
Plant in humus-rich, sandy, well-drained soil, 4–5 in. (10.0–12.5 cm) deep, 4 in. (10 cm) apart. Once planted, they need not be disturbed for years. Effective in clumps between shrubs, in borders of ferns, or in rock gardens. Propagate by separating offsets that develop around bulbs once leaves wither and plants are dormant.

aestivum p. 158

Giant Snowflake; Summer Snowflake. Flowering stalk 9–12 in. (22.5–30.0 cm) high, hollow, compressed, 2-winged. Leaves as long or a little longer, and ⅕–¾ in. (5–19 mm) wide. Flowers to ¾ in. (19 mm) long, generally in clusters of 2–5. Segments white with green spot just below apex. Europe. Spring. Zone 4.

autumnale p. 161
Flowering stalk 3–6 in. (7.5–15.0 cm) high.
Leaves very narrow, 5–6½ in. (12.5–
16.0 cm) long. Flowers white tinged with
red, to ½ in. (13 mm) long, borne in loose
clusters of 1–3. S. to sw. Europe. Summer to
autumn. Zone 6.

vernum p. 159

Spring Snowflake. Flowering stalk 5–14 in.
(12.5–35.0 cm) high, hollow, 2-winged.
Leaves strap-shaped, to 10 in. (25 cm) long.
Flowers fragrant, white with green or yellow
spot below apex of each segment, to 1 in.
(2.5 cm) long. Cen. Europe. Early spring.
Zone 4.

Lilium
Lily family
Liliaceae

Lil'i-um. A large genus of showy bulbous
herbs of outstanding garden importance.
There are more than 80 known species, and
about 50 have been cultivated in the U.S. at
one time or another. Hybrids are numerous
and have been classified into groups based on
origin and flower shape. (*Lilium* is the old
Latin name for the lilies, derived from the
Greek name for the Madonna Lily.)

Description
Erect, perennial, leafy-stemmed herbs with
scaly bulbs. Leaves scattered or in whorls,
without marginal teeth, usually narrow.
Flowers extremely showy, erect, horizontal,
or nodding, either solitary or in racemes,
sometimes densely flowered. Petals and
sepals often colored alike and scarcely
distinguishable as such (tepals), sometimes
narrowed at base into a claw. The whole
flower is more or less funnel-shaped. Stamens
6. Fruit a many-seeded capsule.

How to Grow
Handle lily bulbs carefully, leaving any stem
roots intact. Plant in fall or early spring, 3
times as deep below surface of ground as the
bulb is high. Thus if bulb is 2 in. (5 cm)
high, its bottom should be 6 in. (15 cm)
below ground level. *L. candidum* and its
hybrids are an exception and should have
only 1 in. (2.5 cm) of soil above top of
bulb. All lilies prefer light, loamy soil with a
deep organic mulch, and require perfect

drainage. Fertilize at beginning of growing season to encourage larger plants. If the season is dry, keep ground moist but not wet by watering thoroughly once a week until plants flower. After flowering, reduce water and allow them time to dry.

Light and Placement
Some lilies do better in partial shade, others in sun. Flowers may bleach in bright sunlight but will keep color if grown in slight shade. Most lilies benefit from a ground cover 12–18 in. (30–45 cm) high to shade their roots and leave upper portions of stem and flowers in the sun, and to protect young shoots emerging in early spring. However, avoid planting with strong perennials that might smother them, or among strong-growing shrubs that might crowd them out. Small, low-growing lilies can be grown in rock gardens if roots are shaded. Once lilies are established in the garden, do not move them until clumps become too thick. To divide, dig up clumps very gently, separate, and plant excess bulbs elsewhere immediately so that they do not dry out.

Propagation
Lilies can be propagated from small bulbs that form at base of parent bulb, and also from bulb scales. Pull scales away from parent bulb in early summer. Dust with captan or ferbam and store in light shade in sealed plastic bags of moist vermiculite. In late summer place bags in vegetable compartment of refrigerator for 6–8 weeks to allow bulblets to form; then transplant to pots of well-drained compost, grow for 3 months, and refrigerate again for 6–8 weeks. Do not allow them to dry out. In early spring repot the new bulbs or set in cold frame, and grow as usual. In some species, bulbils grow in the leaf axils; remove and plant the same as bulblets. Raising lilies from seed is another propagation method, but it takes 2–4 years to obtain a flowering plant.

Pests and Diseases
To discourage moles and mice during the first year, roll bulbs in sulfur or copper oxide before planting. Use pyrethrum or malathion for chewing pests and aphids. Leafspot often becomes severe on some lily varieties; apply zineb when spots first appear, and repeat 3 or 4 times at 10-day intervals. Yellow streaks in

foliage indicate mosaic disease, and stunted or "flat" plants indicate another virus. Dig up and discard bulbs of infected plants. Dip Easter Lily bulbs (varieties of *L. longiflorum*) for 30 minutes in ferbam and terraclor before planting to prevent basal root rot.

amabile p. 146
To 3 ft. (90 cm) high. Stem hairy. Leaves lance-shaped, spreading, 1½–3½ in. (4–9 cm) long. Flowers drooping, about 2 in. (5 cm) long, red-orange and dark-spotted, segments recurved. Korea. Late spring. Zone 4.

auratum p. 137
One of the favorites, 3–9 ft. (0.9–2.7 m) high. Leaves narrowly lance-shaped, spreading, scattered, to 8½ in. (22 cm) long. Flowers bowl-shaped, fragrant, somewhat drooping, 6–10 in. (15–25 cm) wide, white with crimson spots and a central gold stripe on each petal. Japan. Susceptible to virus. Summer. Zone 5.

canadense pp. 138, 151
Meadow Lily. Stem to 5 ft. (1.5 m) high. Leaves lance-shaped, usually whorled, to 6 in. (15 cm) long. Flowers bell-shaped, drooping, segments recurved or spreading, to 3 in. (7.5 cm) across, yellow, orange-yellow, or red, usually dark-spotted. Var. *editorum* has red flowers and elliptic to oblong leaves. Nova Scotia to Va., west to Ohio. Best grown in the bog garden. New bulbs produced annually at ends of stolons. Summer. Zone 4.

columbianum p. 144
Stem 3–5 ft. (0.9–1.5 m) high. Leaves scattered above, in whorls below, to 5½ in. (14 cm) long. Flowers nodding, 2 in. (5 cm) long, 3 in. (7.5 cm) wide, yellow to red and conspicuously dark-spotted, segments recurved. British Columbia to Calif. Summer. Zone 7.

concolor p. 152
Star Lily. Stem 3–4 ft. (90–120 cm) high, purplish, with whitish hairs. Leaves linear or narrowly lance-shaped, scattered, to 2½ in. (6 cm) long. Flowers erect, cup-shaped, somewhat fragrant, to 2 in. (5 cm) long and 3½ in. (9 cm) wide, bright red and unspotted. China. Summer. Zone 5.

formosanum p. 135
5–7 ft. (1.5–2.1 m) high. Leaves numerous, linear to narrowly lance-shaped, scattered, crowded near base of stem, 3–8 in. (7.5–20.0 cm) long. Flowers horizontal, funnel-shaped, fragrant, 5–8 in. (12.5–20.0 cm) long, white inside, stained purplish red outside. Taiwan. Susceptible to virus. Summer to autumn. Zone 6.

Hansonii p. 145
Japanese Turk's-Cap Lily. 4–5 ft. (1.2–1.5 m) high. Leaves long, elliptical, in whorls, to 7 in. (17.5 cm) long. Flowers drooping, segments reflexed, fragrant, 1½ in. (4 cm) long and 3 in. (7.5 cm) wide, orange-yellow with purple spots. Ne. Asia. Late spring. Zone 4.

Henryi p. 147
7–9 ft. (2.1–2.7 m) high. Stems branch several times at right angles to main stem. Leaves lance-shaped, scattered, 3–6 in. (7.5–15.0 cm) long. Flowers drooping, the segments reflexed, not fragrant, 3 in. (7.5 cm) long and wide, orange with brown spots. Cen. China. Needs staking. Tolerates virus and is resistant to wilt disease. Summer. Zone 5.

× *hollandicum* p. 152
Candlestick Lily. *L. bulbiferum* × *L.* × *maculatum.* Stems to 2½ ft. (75 cm) high. Leaves narrowly lance-shaped, scattered, 3–6 in. (7.5–15.0 cm) long. Flowers erect, cup-shaped, 4 in. (10 cm) wide, yellow to red. Summer. Zone 5.

japonicum p. 132
To 3 ft. (90 cm) high. Leaves narrowly lance-shaped, scattered, 2–6 in. (5–15 cm) long. Flowers more or less horizontal, funnel-shaped, fragrant, 6 in. (15 cm) long and wide, light pink or rose-colored. Japan. Susceptible to virus. Summer. Zone 6.

lancifolium p. 151
Tiger Lily. 4–6 ft. (1.2–1.8 m) high. Leaves narrowly lance-shaped, numerous, scattered, to 7 in. (17.5 cm) long, often with small, shiny black bulbils in leaf axils. Flowers drooping, segments reflexed, to 5 in. (12.5 cm) across, orange spotted with purple. E. Asia. One of the most vigorous garden lilies. Easily infected by lily mosaic virus, but apparently unharmed by it and serving as source of infection for other lilies, so

isolate them. Summer. Also called
L. tigrinum. Zone 4.

longiflorum *p. 135*

White-Trumpet Lily. To 3 ft. (90 cm) high.
Leaves numerous, scattered, narrowly
lance-shaped, to 7 in. (17.5 cm) long.
Flowers more or less horizontal, fragrant,
pure white, trumpet-shaped, nearly 7 in.
(17.5 cm) long. Much better known is the
var. *eximium,* the Easter Lily, which is taller
and has longer flowers. This and other
varieties are especially popular for forcing.
Japan. Blooms in spring in the greenhouse,
in midsummer where grown outdoors.
Zone 8.

× maculatum *p. 148*

L. concolor × *L. pensylvanicum.* To 2 ft.
(60 cm) high. Smooth or hairy. Leaves
narrowly lance-shaped, scattered, 3–6 in.
(7.5–15.0 cm) long. Flowers erect, cup-shaped,
4 in. (10 cm) wide, yellow to deep red, with
or without spots. Long cultivated in Japan
and Europe. Summer. Frequently called
L. × *elegans.* Zone 5.

Martagon *pp. 127, 137*

Turk's-Cap Lily; Martagon Lily. 4–6 ft.
(1.2–1.8 m) high. Leaves whorled, to 6 in.
(15 cm) long. Flowers drooping, segments
reflexed, ill-scented, to 2 in. (5 cm) wide,
typically purplish pink and dark-spotted, but
varying from white (var. *album*) to almost
black. Many horticultural forms. Eurasia.
Late spring. Zone 4.

michiganense *p. 150*

Stem to 5 ft. (1.5 m) high. Leaves narrowly
lance-shaped, whorled, 3½–4½ in. (9.0–
11.5 cm) long. Flowers drooping, to 3 in.
(7.5 cm) wide, segments reflexed, orange-red
with darker spots. Ontario and Manitoba to
Tenn. and Ark. For garden purposes, similar
to *L. canadense.* Summer. Zone 5.

monadelphum *p. 138*

Caucasian Lily. Stems to 5 ft. (1.5 m) high.
Leaves narrowly lance-shaped, numerous,
scattered, to 5 in. (12.5 cm) long. Flowers
drooping, cup-shaped, segments reflexed,
fragrant, to 5 in. (12.5 cm) wide, golden
yellow, (rarely) tinged or spotted with
purple. Caucasus. Late spring. Zone 4.

Parryi p. 139
Lemon Lily. 4–6 ft. (1.2–1.8 m) high. Leaves lance-shaped, scattered or whorled, to 6 in. (15 cm) long. Flowers more or less horizontal, funnel-shaped, fragrant, to 4 in. (10 cm) long, lemon-yellow, with or without maroon spots. Calif. Summer. Zone 7.

philadelphicum p. 153
Wood Lily. 2–3 ft. (60–90 cm) high. Leaves lance-shaped, whorled, 2–4 in. (5–10 cm) long. Flowers erect, cup-shaped, to 4 in. (10 cm) long, orange-red with darker spots. E. North America. Late spring to summer. Zone 5.

pyrenaicum p. 147
Yellow Turk's-Cap Lily. 3–4 ft. (90–120 cm) high. Leaves linear to lance-shaped, numerous, scattered, to 5 in. (12.5 cm) long, sometimes with silver edge. Flowers nodding, segments reflexed, ill-scented, to 2 in. (5 cm) long and wide, yellow with purple spots. There is a deeper yellow and an orange-scarlet form. Pyrenees. Late spring. Zone 5.

regale p. 133
Regal Lily. 4–6 ft. (1.2–1.8 m) high. Leaves narrowly lance-shaped, numerous, scattered, 2–5 in. (5.0–12.5 cm) long. Flowers horizontal, funnel-shaped, fragrant, to 6 in. (15 cm) long, white inside, purplish outside, yellow throat. W. China. Summer. Zone 4.

speciosum pp. 128, 131
Japanese Lily. An old garden favorite. 4–5 ft. (1.2–1.5 m) high. Leaves lance-shaped, scattered, to 7 in. (17.5 cm) long. Flowers fragrant, drooping, segments much reflexed so that flower appears flat, 4–6 in. (10–15 cm) across, white variously suffused with pink or red, the conspicuous raised spots darker. Many garden forms. The cultivar 'Rubrum' has carmine-red flowers. Japan. Susceptible to virus. Summer to autumn. Zone 5.

superbum p. 150
Turk's-Cap Lily. 5–8 ft. (1.5–2.4 m) high. Leaves lance-shaped, whorled, to 3 in. (7.5 cm) long. Flowers drooping, segments reflexed, to 3 in. (7.5 cm) across, orange-red and dark-spotted. E. U.S. Summer. Zone 5.

Washingtonianum p. 133
Washington Lily. 4–6 ft. (1.2–1.8 m) high.
Leaves whorled, to 6 in. (15 cm) long.
Flowers horizontal, funnel-shaped, fragrant,
to 4 in. (10 cm) wide, white, often
purple-spotted. Calif. Summer. Zone 7.

Hybrid Classes
In addition to the true species there are
numerous hybrid lilies. New varieties
are under constant development, resulting in
an increasing number of named forms on the
market each year. They are often easier to
grow than the species. Hybrids are divided
into several classes based primarily on
geographical or horticultural origin and on
shape. Examples of flowers from 5 of these
categories are represented here.

American hybrids *p. 127*
Hybrids of lilies native to North America,
cultivated mainly from *L. Parryi* and
L. pardalinum. 'Bellingham' grows 4–8 ft.
(1.2–2.4 m) high. Leaves whorled. Flowers
4–6 in. (10–15 cm) wide, nodding, spotted,
many colors including red, pink, orange, and
yellow. Summer. Zones 4–8.

Asiatic hybrids *pp. 131, 140, 145, 146, 149*
Based distantly on Asiatic species and
includes the well-known Mid-Century
hybrids. 2–5 ft. (60–150 cm) high. Flowers
4–6 in. (10–15 cm) wide, subdivided by
shape: upright ('Enchantment', 'Impact');
outward-facing ('Connecticut Lemonglow');
and pendant ('Connecticut Yankee', 'Tiger
Babies'). Colors in a range of shades from
white through yellow, orange, pink,
lavender, and red, alone or in combination,
with or without spotting. Summer. Zones
4–7.

Aurelian hybrids *pp. 126, 132, 134, 140, 142*
Based on crosses of several Asiatic species;
formerly known as Trumpet and Olympic
hybrids. 3–8 ft. (0.9–2.4 m) high. Flowers
usually fragrant, 6–8 in. (15–20 cm) long,
some to 8 in. (20 cm) wide, subdivided by
shape: Chinese trumpet ('Black Dragon',
'Golden Splendor', 'Green Magic', 'Pink
Perfection'); bowl-shaped ('Heart's Desire');
pendant ('Golden Showers'); and sunburst.
Colors in a range of shades from white
through greenish white, yellow, orange,
pink, and gold, alone or in

combination, some with yellow throats or
maroon stripes. Summer. Zones 4–7.

Candidum hybrids *p. 136*
Madonna Lily; Annunciation Lily. Hybrids
of *L. candidum*. 3–4 ft. (90–120 cm) high.
Leaves lance-shaped. Flowers pure white,
fragrant, 4–5 in. (10.0–12.5 cm) wide.
'Cascade' is a popular named variety. Plant
only 1 in. (2.5 cm) below ground level.
Summer. Zone 5.

Oriental hybrids *pp. 126, 128, 129, 130, 136*
Primarily hybrids of *L. auratum* and
L. speciosum, and others based on *L. japonicum*,
L. rubellum, and crosses with *L. Henryi*.
2½–7 ft. (75–210 cm) high. Flowers
fragrant, 3–10 in. (7.5–25.0 cm) wide,
subdivided by shape: bowl-shaped ('Little
Rascal' strain); flat-faced ('Imperial Crimson',
'Imperial Pink', 'Imperial Silver',
'Maharajah'); backswept petals ('Jamboree').
White; white with yellow, pink, or crimson
stripes; or pink to crimson, edged with
white; generally spotted. Summer.
Zone 5.

Lloydia
Lily family
Liliaceae

Loyd′ee-a. Genus of 10–20 species of
perennial, mostly alpine, herbs with bulbs
formed at ends of elongated rhizomes.
(Name commemorates Welsh botanist
Edward Lhuyd [Lloyd], 1660–1709.)

Description
Leafy stems. Flowers 1–3, terminal, cup-
shaped. Related to *Erythronium*.

How to Grow
Plant 2 in. (5 cm) deep in early autumn, in
well-drained, compost-rich soil in sun to
partial shade. Propagate by offsets from
bulbs.

serotina *p. 167*
Stem 2–6 in. (5–15 cm) high. Leaves 2,
basal, linear, 2¾–8 in. (7–20 cm) long, stem
leaves shorter. Flowers usually solitary, white,
to ½ in. (13 mm) long, segments with
reddish or purplish veins. Mts. of Wales,
Europe, and n. Asia, and the Rocky Mts.
Spring. Zone 5.

Lycoris
Amaryllis family
Amaryllidaceae

Ly-kow′ris. Asiatic, bulbous, amaryllis-like
herbs, including perhaps a dozen species.
(Named for the mistress of Mark Antony.)

Description
Strap-shaped leaves develop after flowers
appear. Flowers fragrant, petals united below
into a short tube, segments usually crisped,
white, yellow, pink, or lilac-pink. Style
protruding but stamens about as long as
petals. Flower cluster a loose umbel at end of
a solid stalk.

How to Grow
Plant dormant bulbs in pots indoors in late
summer in equal parts garden soil, compost,
and perlite. Flowers grow quickly, then leaves
appear. Continue growing in winter. When
leaves die down in spring, let pots dry out,
water about once a month, and maintain
soil temperature at 75–85° F (24–30° C).
Resume regular watering in late summer;
flower spikes will appear. For garden cultivation,
plant in humus-rich soil and full sun.

radiata p. 204
Red Spider-Lily. To 16 in. (40 cm) high.
Foliage green, leaves strap-shaped, ½ in.
(13 mm) wide, 12–14 in. (30–35 cm) long.
Flowers pink to deep red (white in cultivar
'Alba'), to 1½ in. (4 cm) long. China and
Japan. Propagate by offsets. Autumn. Not
reliably hardy north of Zone 7.

squamigera p. 247
Magic Lily; Hardy Amaryllis. Very showy,
more hardy than other species. To 2 ft.
(60 cm) high. Leaves about 1 in. (2.5 cm)
wide and 12 in. (30 cm) long. Flowers nearly
3 in. (7.5 cm) long, rose-lilac (purplish
in a horticultural variety), segments not
wavy-margined or reflexed. Japan. Summer.
Sometimes offered as *Amaryllis Hallii*.
Zone 5.

Milla
Amaryllis family
Amaryllidaceae

Mil′la. A small genus of cormous herbs,
native from sw. U.S. to Guatemala. Related

to *Allium* and *Brodiaea.* (Named for J. Milla, Spanish gardener at the Madrid court.)

Description
Leaves linear or tubular. Flowers with a short tube and widely spreading lobes.

How to Grow
Grow in pots for winter or early spring bloom. Put several bulbs in a pot and grow in a cool greenhouse, allowing about 3 months for bloom. To grow outdoors, treat exactly like gladiolus; the bulbs will not stand severe climates.

biflora p. 169
Mexican Star. Leaves basal, cylindrical. Flowers white, nearly 2½ in. (6 cm) wide, and to 8 in. (20 cm) long, in a loose cluster of 3–5 blooms at end of a naked stalk 6–12 in. (15–30 cm) high. Corolla salver-shaped, segments 3-veined. Stamens 6. Fruit a stalkless capsule. Ariz. and N. Mex. to Guatemala. Blooms outdoors in summer. Zone 9.

Moraea
Iris family
Iridaceae

More-ee'a. Also spelled *Morea.* South African herbs comprising 100 species. (Named for Robert Moore, English botanist.) Some species are offered as *Dietes.*

Description
They bear corms. Leaves basal, sword-shaped or narrower. Flowers similar to *Iris,* which this genus replaces in the Southern Hemisphere.

How to Grow
Moraea is not hardy outdoors in the North. Grow in cool greenhouse with much the same conditions as for *Freesia.* Their flowers last only a day.

ramosissima p. 187
A leafy-stemmed herb, 2–3 ft. (60–90 cm) high. Leaves very narrow, 18 in. (45 cm) long. Flowers numerous, fragrant, in an open corymb, yellow, 1¼ in. (3 cm) long. South Africa. Spring. Zone 9.

Muscari
Lily family
Liliaceae

Mus-cay'ree. Grape-Hyacinth. Small, bulbous, herbaceous perennials, comprising about 40 species, some sweet-scented. They are natives of the Mediterranean region. (*Muscari,* from the Latin for "musky," alludes to the musky odor of some species.)

Description
Leaves 4–6, long, narrow, green. Flowers on a leafless stalk, in a terminal raceme, blue or white. Individual flowers urn-shaped and drooping, segments of corolla usually ending in 6 teethlike points, or much cut. Stamens 6. Fruit a 3-celled capsule.

How to Grow
Grape-hyacinths are easy to grow and make fine spreads of color. They thrive and increase rapidly in sunny areas with deep, rich, somewhat sandy soil. Plant bulbs in fall in generous quantities, 3 in. (7.5 cm) deep and 3–4 in. (7.5–10.0 cm) apart. They require little attention. Propagated by seeds and offset

armeniacum *p. 265*
To 12 in. (30 cm) high. Leaves ¼ in. (6 mm) wide, channeled at base, dark green on lower surface, appearing in autumn. Flowers 30–40 in tight terminal clusters, blue, tipped with white, fragrant, 5/16 in. (8 mm) long. Asia Minor. Early spring. Zone 5.

azureum *p. 264*
To 8 in. (20 cm) high. Leaves bluish green, channeled. Flowers blue, 3/16 in. (5 mm) long, fragrant, in dense, short clusters; lobes of corolla not incurved. Mediterranean region. Early spring. Zone 4.

botryoides *p. 264*
Bluebells; Starch Hyacinth. To 12 in. (30 cm) high. Leaves ¼ in. (6 mm) wide. Flowers ⅛ in. (3 mm) long, fragrant, blue, lower ones fertile, having both stamens and pistil, upper ones sterile. A garden favorite. S. Europe. Early spring. Zone 4.

comosum *p. 271*
Tassel-Hyacinth. To 18 in. (45 cm) high. Leaves 1 in. (2.5 cm) wide. Flowers 5/16 in. (8 mm) long, fragrant, blue or violet. Eurasia. Late spring. Zone 5.

latifolium p. 265
To 12 in. (30 cm) high. Only a single leaf
to each bulb; leaf flat, nearly 1 in. (2.5 cm)
wide. Flowers ¼ in. (6 mm) long, blue, in
loose terminal clusters of 10–20 blooms. Asia
Minor. Early spring. Zone 5.

Narcissus
Amaryllis family
Amaryllidaceae

Nar-sis'sus. Important, chiefly hardy, bulbous
plants comprising about 26 species, most of
them European, very widely grown for
ornament or fragrance. The genus includes
such well-known plants as the daffodil,
jonquil, 'Paper-white' Narcissus, Chinese
Sacred Lily, and Poet's Narcissus.
Horticultural forms are numerous and have
been classified into groups based on flower
shape and species derivation. (*Narcissus* is
named for the mythological youth so fond
of his own reflection in a pool that he was
changed into a flower.) Sometimes called
Lent lilies.

Description
All bear bulbs. Leaves basal, generally
rushlike in the jonquil and its relatives, but
flat or nearly so in the common daffodil;
usually about as long as the flowering stalk.
Flowers prevailingly white or yellow, often
nodding. Calyx and corolla not separable as
such, but modified in 2 ways: the flower
having a long, tubular central crown, or
corona, as in the Trumpet Narcissus, or
daffodil; or the corona reduced to a shallow,
ringlike cup, as in the jonquil and Poet's
Narcissus. Outside this central corolla-like
organ are 6 segments that constitute petals
and sepals. Stamens 6, usually hidden in
crown. Fruit a 3-lobed, many-seeded capsule.
The species have been much hybridized, so
the exact botanical identity of the cultivar
classes described below is somewhat
uncertain.

How to Grow
Plant bulbs outdoors in fall, timing this to
allow at least one month for good root
development before soil is cold. In warm
regions, to avoid basal bulb rot, wait to
plant until soil has cooled to less than 70°F.
Plant 1½ times as deep as the depth of the
bulb itself, always planting deeper in case of

doubt. Shallow planting causes bulb to split up quickly into many small nonflowering offsets. Grow in well-drained soil enriched with compost. Bulbs will not survive in heavy, waterlogged soil; some writers thus recommend setting each bulb on a handful of sand. Mulch annually with compost or partially composted manure. For larger blooms commercial fertilizer, though rarely necessary, can be applied lightly as shoots first emerge.

Dividing Bulbs
In most gardens *Narcissus* bulbs must be divided every fourth year. After the leaves have died off in early summer, lift bulbs, dry in shade, and do not break apart until they separate easily, since damage to base is serious. Replant at once, or store bulbs in a cool, airy place until autumn. Examine periodically for signs of rot.

Forcing Bulbs
All *Narcissus* can be forced; many, such as the popular 'Paper-white' and other forms of *N. Tazetta,* are grown in bowls of pebbles and water. In all cases, allow roots to develop well before bringing pots to light, and keep room or greenhouse temperature low for best flower results.

Diseases
Rots are a common problem on roots and base of bulbs, or on neck of plant between top of bulb and soil line. If leaves suddenly wilt and die, examine neck of bulb for small black or brown seedlike objects. Remove affected bulbs and surrounding soil. Do not buy bulbs with seedlike objects on or under the husks. Yellow streaks in leaves characterize mosaic disease. Dig and discard infected plants to prevent spread of virus.

asturiensis *p. 85*
Tiny plant only 4–5 in. (10.0–12.5 cm) high. Leaves linear, to 4 in. (10 cm) long, ⅛–¼ in. (3–6 mm) wide. Flowers borne singly on stalk, shaped like miniature daffodil, ½–1 in. (12–25 mm) long, corona ⅓–⅖ in. (8–16 mm) long, slightly longer than spreading perianth segments. Spain and cen. Portugal. Very early spring. Zone 5.

Bulbocodium *p. 77*
Hoop-Petticoat Daffodil. 4–18 in. (10–45 cm) high. Leaves channeled or nearly

round in cross section, usually longer than flowering stalk. Flowers solitary, yellow or white, 1–2 in. (2.5–5.0 cm) long, crown longer than narrow corolla segments. S. France, Spain, Portugal. Early spring. Zones 6–7.

cyclamineus p. 76
Leaves linear, to 12 in. (30 cm) long. Flowers solitary, drooping, deep yellow, 1–2 in. (2.5–5.0 cm) long, corolla segments recurved and shorter than orange-yellow crown. Spain and Portugal. Early spring. Zones 6–7.

× *incomparabilis* p. 65
N. poeticus × *N. Pseudonarcissus.* Leaves flat, 12 in. (30 cm) long, ¼–½ in. (6–13 mm) wide. Flower solitary, yellow, 3–4 in. (7.5–10 cm) wide, perianth tube below segments to ¾ in. (2 cm) long, segments equally long, crown half as long. Double-flowered forms exist. Spain to Austria. Early spring. Zone 5.

× *Johnstonii* p. 83
N. Pseudonarcissus × *N. triandrus* var. *cernuus.* Leaves flat, to 10 in. (25 cm) long, ½ in. (13 mm) wide. Flowers solitary or occasionally 2, pale yellow, horizontal or nodding, to 2 in. (5 cm) long, crown as long as corolla segments. Portugal. Early spring. Zone 5.

Jonquilla p. 75
Common Jonquil. Leaves to 18 in. (45 cm) long, rushlike. Flowers in clusters of 2–6, fragrant, yellow, tube 1 in. (2.5 cm) long, corona less than half as long as segments. Double-flowered forms exist. S. Europe and n. Africa. Spring. Zone 4.

juncifolius p. 75
A jonquil, its rushlike leaves to 6 in. (15 cm) long. Flowers in clusters of 1–4, about 1 in. (2.5 cm) long, yellow, fragrant, tube ½ in. (13 mm) long; corona half as long as segments, darker yellow, wavy-edged. Double-flowered forms exist. S. France and Spain. Early spring. Zones 6–7.

minor p. 78
A yellow trumpet narcissus, perhaps merely a form of *N. Pseudonarcissus.* To 6 in. (15 cm) high. Leaves 5 in. (12.5 cm) long, ¼ in. (6 mm) wide. Flowers yellow, 1¼ in. (3 cm) long, corona sulfur-yellow. S. France and

n. Spain. A rock garden species. Early spring. Zone 5.

moschatus *p. 86*
White Trumpet Narcissus. Perhaps merely a form of *N. Pseudonarcissus.* To 18 in. (45 cm) high. Leaves to 16 in. (40 cm) long and ½ in. (13 mm) wide. Flowers white, 2–3 in. (5.0–7.5 cm) long, fragrant, segments slightly twisted, sulfur-yellow-tinged, turning white, corona as long as segments and pure white. S. France and n. Spain. Early spring. Zone 7.

obvallaris *p. 82*
Tenby Daffodil. To 12 in. (30 cm) high. Leaves linear, 8–12 in. (20–30 cm) long, ⅓–⅖ in. (8–10 mm) wide. Flowers yellow, 1–2½ in. (2.5–6.0 cm) long, borne singly on stalk 8–12 in. (20–30 cm) high. Possibly a cultivated form of *N. Pseudonarcissus,* which has become naturalized in Britain. Early spring. Zones 6–7.

✕ odorus *p. 78*
N. Jonquilla ✕ *N. Pseudonarcissus.*
Campernelle Jonquil. Leaves 12 in. (30 cm) long, very narrow or rushlike. Flowers in clusters of 2–4, to 2 in. (5 cm) long, fragrant, yellow, tube ¾ in. (2 cm) long, wavy or lobed corona half as long as segments. Double-flowered forms exist. Spain and France. Early spring. Zone 6.

poeticus *p. 65*
Poet's Narcissus; Pheasant's-Eye Narcissus. Leaves 18 in. (45 cm) long, wide, flat, grasslike. Flowers very fragrant, white, 1 in. (2.5 cm) long, 2–3 in. (5.0–7.5 cm) wide; corona very shallow, much shorter than segments, edges wavy and conspicuously red-margined. Double-flowered forms exist. S. Europe. Late spring. Zone 5.

Pseudonarcissus *p. 79*
Common Daffodil; Trumpet Narcissus. Stout, long-cultivated plant now having many forms and available in innumerable named garden types. Leaves flat, 12–18 in. (30–45 cm) long, usually just reaching flowers. Corolla 2 in. (5 cm) long, typically pale yellow, segments and corona mostly a different shade; corona very long, deeply wavy or even slightly fringed. Europe. Early spring. Zone 5.

rupicola p. 74
To 6 in. (15 cm) high. Leaves 3-sided, 3–6 in. (8–15 cm) long, 1/16–⅛ in. (1.5–3.0 mm) wide. Flowers borne singly on stalk to 4 in. (10 cm) high. Flower yellow, fragrant, ¾–1¼ in. (2–3 cm) wide, corona only 1/10–1/5 in. (2.5–5.0 mm) long. Cen. Spain and n. Portugal. Early spring. Zones 6–7.

triandrus p. 77
Leaves 12 in. (30 cm) long, rushlike or nearly round in cross section. Flowers pure white, 1–1½ in. (2.5–3.5 cm) long, tube ¾ in. (2 cm) long. Corona cuplike, with margins not crisped or wavy, half as long as segments. The var. *concolor* has pale yellow flowers. Sw. Europe. Early spring. Zone 5.

Hybrid Classes
The numerous *Narcissus* hybrids and varieties are classified into several groups either by size of floral parts and their coloration, or by species derivation. Here, categories based on shape precede those based on species, and are arranged alphabetically within each section.

Double Narcissus *pp.* 68, 69, 70, 71
Double-flowered varieties, i.e., having more than 1 layer of petals; all colors and dimensions. 'Angkor', 'Ascot', 'Cheerfulness', 'Golden Ducat', 'Irene Copeland', and 'White Lion' are popular cultivars that range 14–18 in. (35–45 cm) high, with flowers 2–3 in. (5.0–7.5 cm) wide. Mid-spring to late spring. Zones 4–7.

Large-cupped Narcissus *pp.* 66, 67, 70, 73, 82, 84, 86
Cup is more than one-third but less than total length of perianth segments. One flower per stem. Color subdivisions: yellow perianth and colored cup, which may be yellow or yellow stained with another color; white perianth, colored cup; white perianth, white cup; and any not in the above, including all varieties of the proper proportions but with other colors, such as pink or salmon, in the cup. Popular cultivars are 'Aranjuez', 'Binkie', 'Carlton', 'Flower Record', 'Ice Follies', 'Roulette', and 'Rushlight', ranging 14–20 in. (35–50 cm) high, with flowers to 4½ in. (11.5 cm) wide. Early spring to mid-spring. Zones 4–7.

Small-cupped Narcissus *p.* 73
Cup is no more than one-third the length of the perianth segments. One flower per stem.

Color subdivisions same as for Large-cupped forms. Cultivar 'Birma' to 15 in. (38 cm) high, with flowers 2–3 in. (5.0–7.5 cm) wide. Early spring. Zones 4–7.

Split-corona Narcissus *p. 67*
Corona, or cup, is split for at least one-third its length. Cultivar 'Egard' is 16–20 in. (40.5–50.0 cm) high, with flowers to 3 in. (7.5 cm) wide. Mid-spring to late spring. Zones 4–7.

Trumpet Narcissus *pp. 66, 80, 81*
Trumpet, or corona, is as long or longer than the perianth segments. One flower per stem. Color subdivisions: pure yellow flowers; bicolors, in which trumpet is yellow and perianth white; and pure white flowers. Popular cultivars 'Foresight', 'King Alfred', and 'Unsurpassable' range 16–20 in. (40.5–50.0 cm) high, with flowers 3–4 in. (7.5–10.0 cm) wide. Early spring to mid-spring. Zones 4–7.

Cyclamineus Narcissus *pp. 64, 80, 81, 84, 87*
Hybrids of *N. cyclamineus.* All characterized, in varying degrees, by perianth segments that curve distinctly backward. 'Beryl', 'February Gold', 'February Silver', 'Peeping Tom', and 'Tête-à-Tête' are popular cultivars that range 6–10 in. (15–25 cm) high, with flowers ½–2 in. (1.3–5.0 cm) wide. Early spring. Zones 4–7.

Jonquilla Narcissus *pp. 74, 83, 85*
Hybrids of *N. Jonquilla.* Characterized by small cups, reedlike leaves, and fragrance. 'Lemon Tarts', 'Suzy', and 'Sweetness' are popular cultivars; most to 12 in. (30 cm) high, with flowers ½–1 in. (1.3–2.5 cm) wide. Spring. Zones 4–7.

Poeticus Narcissus *pp. 63, 64*
Wild and garden forms of *N. poeticus.* Characterized by glistening white perianth and very flat center, or "eye," which may vary from yellow with a red margin to almost pure red, to others with green emerging from the throat. All scented. Cultivar 'Actaea' to 18 in. (45 cm) high, with flowers to 3 in. (7.5 cm) wide. Mid-spring to late spring. Zone 5.

Tazetta Narcissus *pp. 62, 63, 69, 72*
Forms of *N. Tazetta,* including various garden hybrids once known as "Poetaz." In

the species (sometimes called Polyanthus
Narcissus) leaves are flat, 18 in. (45 cm)
long, nearly ¾ in. (2 cm) wide. Flowers
often white, to 1 in. (2.5 cm) wide, fragrant,
usually in clusters of 4–8; corona much
shorter than segments and usually pale
yellow. Popular horticultural forms, ranging
12–18 in. (30–45 cm) high with flowers
½–1¼ in. (1.3–3.0 cm) wide, are 'Canary
Bird', 'Cragford', 'Geranium', 'Paper-white',
and 'Soleil d'Or'; these last 2 are tender and
are often forced indoors in pebbles and
water. Spring. Zone 7.

Triandrus Narcissus *pp. 76, 87*
Hybrids and varieties of *N. triandrus.* Among
popular cultivars are 'Hawera', a miniature
form to 8 in. (20 cm) high, with yellow
flowers 1 in. (2.5 cm) long, and 'Thalia', to
16 in. (40.5 cm) high, with white flowers to
2 in. (5 cm) wide. Mid-spring to late spring.
Zones 4–7.

Nectaroscordum
Amaryllis family
Amaryllidaceae

Nek-tar-os-kor'dum. One or two species of
woodland plants, native in s. Europe. (The
name is from the Greek for "nectar" and
"garlic.")

Description
Closely related to *Allium,* from which it
differs in having a half-inferior (not a
superior) ovary and 3–7 veins (not one) in
perianth segments.

How to Grow
Should be treated like *Allium.*

bulgaricum p. 243
To 4 ft. (120 cm) high. Like *N. siculum,* and
sometimes regarded as a variety or
subspecies, but flowers greenish white tinged
with pink, about ½ in. (13 mm) long. Se.
Europe. Early spring. Zone 6.

siculum p. 242
Bulbous perennial herb with strong,
garliclike odor. Flowering stalk to 4 ft.
(120 cm) high, lower third enclosed in an
erect, sheathing leaf. Leaves narrowly lance-
shaped, to 2 ft. (60 cm) long, 2 in. (5 cm)
wide. Flowers many, pendulous (erect in

fruit), dull greenish red, cup-shaped, about
½ in. (13 mm) long. France and Italy. Early
spring. Zone 6.

Nerine
Amaryllis family
Amaryllidaceae

Ne-ry′ne. A genus of South African bulbous
herbs. Several of the 20 known species are
cultivated for their handsome autumn and
early-winter bloom. (Named after the
Nereids, the daughters of Nerius, or perhaps
for one of them.)

Description
Leaves all basal, strap-shaped. Flowers
funnel-shaped, in a close terminal umbel on
a solid stalk. Corolla with almost no tube, its
segments scarcely separable as petals or
sepals, red, often crisped on margins.
Stamens 6, sometimes protruding, but 3
shorter than others. Fruit a 3-valved capsule.

How to Grow
Grow in the North in pots in a cool
greenhouse, where they flower in late
autumn, or force almost anytime if the bulbs
have been rested for 4–5 months before
planting. Bulbs started in Oct. will bloom at
Christmas if given plenty of water. When
blooming stops, the leaves will develop; then
water generously until the leaves die back.
While dormant, the pots can be plunged in
a sunny place in the garden. In Calif. and
similar climates, they can be grown outdoors
and left in the ground for several years
before dividing.

Bowdenii p. 246
Stalk 1–2 ft. (30–60 cm) high. Leaves 6–12
in. (15–30 cm) long and 1 in. (2.5 m) wide.
Flowers pink, to 3 in. (7.5 cm) long, in
clusters of 8–12. South Africa. Autumn.
Zone 9.

sarniensis p. 236
Guernsey Lily (not native there, but grown
there after its importation from South
Africa). To 18 in. (45 cm) high. Leaves

appearing after the bloom, 12 in. (30 cm) long, ¾ in. (19 mm) wide, not curved. Flowers crimson-pink, about 10 in cluster. Corolla 1½ in. (4 cm) long, segments somewhat crisped, stamens protruding. Several varieties in a range of flower colors from rose-pink to deeper scarlet. Autumn. The common name of this species alludes to a story that the bulbs were originally cast up on the English Channel island of Guernsey after a shipwreck. Zone 9.

Notholirion
Lily family
Liliaceae

Noth-ol-i´ree-on. A genus of 4–6 species, related to *Lilium* and *Fritillaria* and native in the Himalayas from Afghanistan to w. China. (From the Greek for "false lily," because of its resemblance to the true lilies.)

Description
Bulbs producing many bulbils in the scale axils. Basal leaves very long, stem leaves shorter. Flowers in racemes, funnel-shaped, red, pink, or lavender.

How to Grow
Hardy only in Zones 7–9 on the West Coast where summers are not hot. Elsewhere grow in pots in a cool greenhouse. Pot up in early fall in well-drained, compost-rich soil, one bulb to a 5 in. (12.5 cm) pot. Cover 2 in. (5 cm) deep. Keep moist but not wet. When flowering stem appears in early spring, increase water. After flowering, decrease water as leaves die, and turn out pot. The old bulb generally dies, but leaves many small bulblets, which should be potted up individually and reach flowering size in 3–4 years.

Thomsonianum p. 244
Stems 3–4 ft. (90–120 cm) high. Basal leaves to 12 in. (30 cm) long, ¾ in. (19 mm) wide. Flowers in a raceme of 10–20, fragrant, pink to rose, funnel-shaped, to 2 in. (5 cm) long. Afghanistan and nw. Himalayas. Early spring. Zone 7.

Nothoscordum
Amaryllis family
Amaryllidaceae

Noth-os-kor′dum. 20–30 species of American bulbous perennials related to *Allium.* (From the Greek for "false" and "garlic.")

Description
Leaves linear. Perianth segments united at bases (not free from each other as in *Allium*). Flowers yellow or white, bell-shaped.

How to Grow
Set bulbs 3 in. (7.5 cm) deep in well-drained, compost-rich soil in full sun.

bivalve p. 168
Stems to 16 in. (40.5 cm) high. Leaves linear, to 16 in. (40.5 cm) long. Flowers to ½ in. (13 mm) long, few in a cluster, whitish or yellowish. S.-cen. U.S. to Mexico. Early spring. Zone 8.

Ornithogalum
Lily family
Liliaceae

Or-ni-thog′a-lum. Hardy or tender bulbous herbs comprising about 100 species, the hardy ones natives of Europe and w. Asia, the tender species natives of Africa. (*Ornithogalum,* from the Greek words for "bird" and "milk," alludes to the egglike color of some species.)

Description
Leaves narrow or broad, tapering to a point at tip. Flowers in racemes on leafless stems, sometimes as high as 3 ft. (90 cm). Individual flowers stalked and have a small, leafy bract. Petals 6, separate, spreading, white, yellow, or orange-red. Stamens 6. Fruit a dry 3-valved capsule.

How to Grow
Outdoor species require no attention and are generally used for wild gardens, since the bulbs increase so quickly that they become a nuisance in beds or borders. Grow tender species as border plants in the South, or in cool greenhouses or sunny windows in temperate regions. Using a compost of sandy loam, leaf mold, and sand, plant bulbs in

autumn to midwinter, 1 in. (2.5 cm) deep,
in pots, bowls, or boxes with good drainage.
Water moderately when growth begins,
freely in full growth. Apply liquid manure
when flower buds appear. Gradually
withhold water when foliage begins to turn
yellow. Bulbs can be dried and stored for use
the following year. Propagate by offsets
removed from old bulbs when dormant.

arabicum p. 181
Star-of-Bethlehem. Bulb oval. Leaves 5–8,
pale green, 1–1½ ft. (30–45 cm) long, ¾ in.
(19 mm) wide. Flower stem 1–2 ft. (30–
60 cm) high. Flowers 6–12, white, 1 in.
(2.5 cm) long, with prominent black pistils.
Makes good pot plant. Mediterranean region.
Summer. Zone 8.

nutans p. 179
Star-of-Bethlehem. Bulb oval, 1 in. (2.5 cm)
thick, producing offsets freely. Leaves pale
green, 1–1½ ft. (30–45 cm) long, ¼–½ in.
(6–13 mm) wide. Flower-stalks 8–12 in.
(20–30 cm) long. Flowers 3–12, to 2 in.
(5 cm) wide, white inside, green outside
with a white margin, fragrant, nodding.
Asia Minor. Can be used for naturalizing.
Early spring. Zone 6.

Saundersiae p. 180
Giant Chincherinchee. Flowering stem to
4 ft. (120 cm) high. Leaves strap-shaped, to
1 ft. (30 cm) long, 2 in. (5 cm) wide, limp,
gray-green, in rosette atop bulb. Flowers
white with blackish ovary, to 1 in. (2.5 cm)
wide, many in cluster. South Africa.
Summer. Zones 7–8.

thyrsoides p. 173
Wonder Flower; Chincherinchee. Bulb
globe-shaped, 1½ in. (4 cm) thick. Leaves
5–6, 1–2 in. (2.5–5.0 cm) wide, 6–12 in.
(15–30 cm) long, margins slightly hairy.
Flower stems 6–18 in. (15–45 cm) long.
Flowers ¾ in. (19 mm) long, 12–30 in
dense raceme, white or cream-colored. A
good cut flower. South Africa. Late spring to
summer. Zone 8.

umbellatum p. 167
Star-of-Bethlehem; Summer Snowflake. Bulbs
round, 1 in. (2.5 cm) thick. Leaves 6–12 in.
(15–30 cm) long, ¼–½ in. (6–13 mm)
wide, veined or spotted with white.
Flowering stem 6–8 in. (15–20 cm) long.
Flowers 12–20 in cluster, 1 in. (2.5 cm)

wide, starlike, white, 3 outer segments
having green margins. Mediterranean region.
Widely naturalized in e. North America,
where it is often an invasive pest in gardens.
Early spring. Zone 5.

Oxalis
Oxalis family
Oxalidaceae

Ox'a-lis; also ok-sal'is. Wood Sorrel. Over
800 species of sour-juiced herbs, most
abundant in South America and South
Africa, but only a few of horticultural
interest. Some forms grow wild in U.S.
woods, and several others as yellow-flowered
roadside weeds. (*Oxalis,* from the Greek for
"sour," alludes to the sour juice of most
species.)

Description
All have compound, cloverlike leaves, the
leaflets always arranged finger-fashion, often
folding up at night or in dark. Flowers
solitary, or more often in few-flowered
clusters, white, pink, red, or yellow. Sepals
and petals 5 each. Stamens 10, with 5 longer
than the others. Fruit a capsule.

How to Grow
Oxalis species come from such widely
different regions that no general cultural
directions apply. See individual species for
growing information.

adenophylla *p. 229*
A perennial herb with tuberous roots, to 6
in. (15 cm) high. Leaflets 12–22, notched, ½
in. (13 mm) long, bluish green. Flowers
pink, veined with deeper pink, about 1 in.
(2.5 cm) wide. Chile. Grow in a cool
greenhouse in neutral or slightly alkaline
soil; when done flowering, lift and store
tubers in a cool, dark place, and plant again
in autumn. Blooms indoors in winter;
outdoors in summer. Zone 8.

Bowiei *p. 228*
A perennial herb with a thickened rootstock.
To 12 in. (30 cm) high. Leaflets 3, notched.
Flowers 1–1½ in. (2.5–4.0 cm) wide, rose to
purple. South Africa. Not hardy over winter.
Grow exactly like *Gladiolus*. Summer.
Zone 8.

braziliensis p. 232

A perennial with a small bulb. 5–10 in. (12.5–25.0 cm) high. Leaflets 3, almost round, notched at tip, green. Flower solitary, 1 in. (2.5 cm) wide, magenta with yellow in throat, petals slightly notched. Brazil. Grow like *O. adenophylla*. Thrives outdoors along Gulf Coast. Summer. Zone 8.

corymbosa p. 230

Taproot strongly swollen and producing a mass of bulbils at its top. To 12 in. (30 cm) high. Leaves all basal, forming a sort of rosette, leaflets 3. Flowers in clusters, on stalks longer than leaves, purplish pink, to ¾ in. (19 mm) wide. Tropical America. Widely distributed as a weed. Summer. Zone 10.

Deppei p. 207

Good-Luck Plant. A perennial, 4–12 in. (10–30 cm) high. Leaflets 4, minutely toothed on the margin, nearly round, 1 in. (2.5 cm) long, blunt at tip. Flowers in long-stalked umbel exceeding the leaves, red or purplish violet, ½–1 in. (1.3–2.5 cm) long, petals slightly notched. There is also a white-flowered variety. Mexico. Grow like *O. adenophylla*. Summer. Zone 8.

lasiandra p. 231

A perennial from many small scaly bulbs. To 12 in. (30 cm) high. Leaflets 5–10, usually 8, tongue-shaped, slightly notched at tip, red-blotched beneath. Flowers in tight umbel, petals ½ in. (13 mm) wide, rounded, not notched, pinkish red. Mexico. Summer. Zone 9.

Pes-caprae p. 196

Bermuda Buttercup (neither native in Bermuda nor a buttercup, but naturalized there). A bulbous herb to 12 in. (30 cm) high. 3 notched leaflets. Flowers yellow, 1½ in. (4 cm) wide, nodding. South Africa. Hardy in the far South; in the North treat like *O. adenophylla*. Early spring. Zone 9.

purpurea p. 231

Bulbous perennial to 6 in. (15 cm) high. Leaves to 3 in. (7.5 cm) long, 3 leaflets to ¾ in. (19 mm) long. Flowers solitary, on stalks shorter or longer than leaves, pink, violet, or white, to 2 in. (5 cm) wide. South Africa. Autumn. Zone 9.

rubra p. 230

A perennial herb, 6–12 in. (15–30 cm) high. Leaflets 3, notched. Flowers in umbels higher than leaves. Petals rose-pink but darker-veined, sometimes lilac or even white, to ¾ in. (19 mm) long. Brazil. Sometimes grown in window gardens or greenhouses, or outdoors far southward. Treat like *O. adenophylla.* Winter. Zone 8.

violacea p. 229

Purple, Violet, or Wood Sorrel. A perennial woodland herb, to 10 in. (25 cm) high. Leaflets 3, notched at tip. Flowers ¾ in. (19 mm) long, several in a cluster; stalk rises from ground. Petals rose-purple (rarely pinkish white). Quebec to Fla. and west to Rocky Mts. Needs rich woods soil and partial shade. Suitable for the wild garden. Late spring. Zone 5.

Pamianthe
Amaryllis family
Amaryllidaceae

Pam-ee-an'thee. A small genus of 1 or 2 species of South American bulbous perennials. (Named for Major Albert Pam, 1875–1955, a British financier and horticulturist, who introduced this plant into cultivation.)

Description
Bulb with long neck, formed by sheathing leaf bases. Leaves evergreen and linear. Flowering stalk longer than the leaves. Flowers tubular, with a very conspicuous corona.

How to Grow
Should be grown like *Hippeastrum.*

peruviana p. 176

Flowering stalk to 2 ft. (60 cm) high. Leaves to 20 in. (50 cm) long, about 1 in. (2.5 cm) wide. Flowers 1–4, fragrant, with a green tube to 5 in. (12.5 cm) long, white perianth lobes to 5 in. (12.5 cm) long, and a corona to 3 in. (7.5 cm) long. Peru. Early spring. Zone 10.

Paramongaia
Amaryllis family
Amaryllidaceae

Par-a-mon-ga'ee-a. A single Peruvian bulbous
perennial, related to *Pamianthe*. (From the
Greek for "near," and Paramonga, a coastal
city north of Lima, Peru.)

Description
Bulb without a neck. Leaves strap-shaped,
2-ranked. Flowers yellow, daffodil-like but
much larger, tubular with spreading perianth
lobes and prominent corona.

How to Grow
Should be grown like *Hippeastrum*.

Weberbaueri p. 79
To 2 ft. (60 cm) high. Leaves to 2½ ft.
(75 cm) long, 2 in. (5 cm) wide. Flowers 1
or 2, fragrant, tube to 4 in. (10 cm) long,
segments to 4 in. (10 cm) long, spreading,
corona to 3 in. (7.5 cm) long. Peru. Spring.
Zone 10.

Polianthes
Agave family
Agavaceae

Po-li-anth'eez. Tender, tuberous perennial
herbs, comprising about 12 species, all
natives of Mexico. (*Polianthes,* probably from
the Greek for "white, shining flowers,"
alludes to the waxy-white corolla.)

Description
Leaves grasslike. Flowers tubular and bent at
the middle.

How to Grow
The tuberose is easy to grow where summers
are long and warm. They are propagated by
offsets of the tubers. Plant offsets as soon as
danger of frost is over, or start in cool
greenhouse. Set them 2 in. (5 cm) deep and
4 in. (10 cm) apart in rich garden soil.
These will not flower the first year. Dig
tubers before frost and store in dry, warm
place during winter. The following year,
plant the tubers in full sun, 3 in. (7.5 cm) deep
and 6 in. (15 cm) apart; they will bloom
late summer to autumn. Tubers must show
signs of life to be worth planting. Can also
be forced indoors in winter for spring bloom.

tuberosa p. 178

Tuberose. The only commonly cultivated species; not found wild. To 3 ft. (90 cm) high. Basal leaves 12–18 in. (30–45 cm) long and ½ in. (13 mm) wide, bright green, reddish at base. Stem leaves clasping, smaller. Flowers waxy-white, 2½ in. (6 cm) long, extremely fragrant, in short terminal racemes. Calyx of 3 white sepals; corolla of 3 white petals. Stamens 6. Fruit a 3-celled capsule. Mexico. Usually double-flowered forms are grown. Widely cultivated in France for the perfume trade. Summer to autumn. Zone 9.

Puschkinia
Lily family
Liliaceae

Push-kin′i-a. A small genus of bulbous herbs, comprising 2 species, related to *Chionodoxa*. (Named for Count A. A. Mussin-Puschkin.)

Description
Strap-shaped leaves with tubular base and spreading lobes longer than the tube. Flowers pale, striped bells gathered in dense clusters on slender stems.

How to Grow
Plant 3 in. (7.5 cm) deep and 3 in. (7.5 cm) apart in early autumn in sandy, nourishing soil in full sun or partial shade. Bulbs need not be disturbed for several years. If flowering diminishes, dig up bulbs after foliage has fully ripened and replant in fresh soil. Detach bulblets for propagation.

scilloides p. 157

Striped Squill. Stems to 6 in. (15 cm) high. Leaves basal, 6 in. (15 cm) long, ½ in. (13 mm) wide. Flowers small, striped, bluish, bell-shaped, ½ in. (13 mm) long, in terminal raceme at end of flowering stalk. Not very showy. Asia Minor. Early spring. Zone 4.

Ranunculus
Buttercup family
Ranunculaceae

Ra-nun′kew-lus. The crowfoots, or buttercups, comprise a large group of mostly north temperate-zone herbs. Besides field buttercups, they include Persian Buttercup, or common Florists' Ranunculus, which is often grown for winter bloom. (*Ranunculus,* Latin for "little frog," alludes to the meadow habit of many wild species.)

Description

Roots tuberous or fibrous, or sometimes a swollen stem base. Leaves simple or compound, often much cut, lobed, or divided. Flowers prevailingly yellow, but red in florists' plants. Petals 5 or more, sepals 5. Stamens numerous. Fruit a tiny cluster of dry achenes.

How to Grow

Persian Buttercup is hardy from Zones 8 to 10; elsewhere grow it in pots. Plant in damp, light, well-drained, compost-rich soil in autumn or as late as early winter. Bulbs will rot if planted in hot weather. Grow in full sun. Keep cool, 45–50° F (7–10° C) at night, in greenhouse or window, until plant sprouts, keeping soil moist but not wet. Maintain cool temperature, since high temperatures will produce spindly plant and short-lived blossoms. After plant flowers and leaves wither, cease watering, turn tuber out of pot, and store dry over summer. Can also be raised from seed.

asiaticus p. 200

Persian Buttercup; Florists' Ranunculus. Roots swollen, tuberous, attached to stem base. Stem simple, rarely branched, 6–18 in. (15–45 cm) high. Leaves compound, the 3 leaflets toothed and somewhat blunt. Flowers 1–4 on a stem, long-stalked, 1–2 in. (2.5–5.0 cm) wide in older varieties, to 4 in. (10 cm) wide in newer strains. Colors range from white to yellow, orange, pink, and red. Most commercial varieties are double or semidouble. Eurasia. Early spring. Zone 8.

Romulea

Iris family
Iridaceae

Rom-ul-ee′a. A large genus of cormous perennial herbs, related to *Gladiolus* and *Crocus*. Most species native in South Africa, 6 or 7 in s. Europe. (Name commemorates Romulus, the mythical founder of Rome.)

Description
Corms small, crocuslike, but asymmetrical.
Leaves grasslike or narrower. Flowers borne
on short stalks, crocuslike, with short tube at
base and very long lobes.

How to Grow
Hardy outdoors only in Zones 8 to 10.
Elsewhere grow in pots like *Freesia*.

Bulbocodium p. 253
To 2–3 in. (5.0–7.5 cm) high. Leaves
narrowly sword-shaped, 2–12 in. (5–30 cm)
long. Flowers crocuslike, yellow-cream below,
violet above middle, about 1–1½ in.
(2.5–4.0 cm) long. S. Europe from Spain to
Bulgaria. Early spring. Zone 8.

sabulosa p. 204
To 4 in. (10 cm) high. Leaves bristlelike, to
4 in. (10 cm) long. Flowers cup-shaped, to
1–1½ in. (2.5–4.0 cm) long, deep rose-pink
to cherry red. South Africa. Late spring.
Zone 9.

Scilla
Lily family
Liliaceae

Sill'a. Squill. A large genus of bulbous herbs,
most of the 80 known species from the
temperate regions of Eurasia, and several
cultivated for their cheery, mostly early-
spring blooms. (*Scilla* is the old Latin and
Greek name for these plants.)

Description
Leaves narrow, almost grasslike in some
species, basal and usually appearing with the
blooms. Flowers small, blue, white, or
purple, bell-shaped, in terminal racemes at
end of naked stalks that arise from the leaf
clusters. Corolla segments 6, not actually
jointed. Stamens 6. Fruit a 3-lobed or
3-angled capsule.

How to Grow
Scillas are easy to grow and increase rapidly
in rich, sandy soil in sun or partial shade.
The low-growing early kinds, such as
S. siberica, should be planted in hundreds
or thousands beneath spring-flowering,
deciduous shrubs and trees, at the edge of
woodland, or in rock gardens. *S. siberica* will
thrive under evergreen trees where little else

will survive. Scillas also are good as carpet plants for beds of May tulips. Plant them in early autumn, setting bulbs 3 times their own depth in soil, 3–4 in. (7.5–10.0 cm) apart. Easily increased by bulblets from older bulbs taken in autumn. An occasional top-dressing of old manure or good soil is also beneficial in autumn.

bifolia p. 269
Flowering stems to 6 in. (15 cm) high. Leaves 2–3, linear, to 8 in. (20 cm) long. Flowers blue, to ½ in. (13 mm) wide, nodding, in clusters of 3–8. Europe. Early spring. Zone 4.

peruviana p. 267
Cuban Lily. A showy squill, to 18 in. (45 cm) high. Leaves nearly 1 ft. (30 cm) long, 1 in. (2.5 cm) wide. Flowers purple or reddish (white in a horticultural variety), ½ in. (13 mm) long, in handsome clusters of 50 or more. Mediterranean region. Early spring. Zone 9.

siberica p. 263
Siberian Squill. 4–6 in. (10–15 cm) high. Leaves ½ in. (13 mm) wide. Flowers deep blue, ½ in. (13 mm) wide, rarely more than 3–5 to a cluster. Eurasia. Good for rock gardens. Early spring. Zone 4.

Tubergeniana p. 156
Like *S. siberica,* but only to 5 in. (12.5 cm) high and flowers cup-shaped, white or pale blue, to 1½ in. (4 cm) wide. Iran. Early spring. Zone 5.

Sparaxis
Iris family
Iridaceae

Spa-racks′is. Harlequin Flower; Wand-flower. South African perennial cormous herbs, comprising 4 to 6 species. Closely related to *Ixia, Streptanthera,* and *Tritonia.* (*Sparaxis,* from the Greek for "torn," alludes to the torn spathe.)

Description
Leaves basal, narrow, sword-shaped, with parallel veins. Flowers yellow, rose, red, or purple, often tinged brown, in short spikes, each flower enclosed in cut or fringed spathe. Calyx of 3 colored sepals. Corolla of 3 petals

alternating with sepals. Stamens 3. Fruit a 3-celled capsule.

How to Grow
Should be treated like *Ixia*.

tricolor p. 205
To 18 in. (45 cm) high. Leaves lance-shaped, to 12 in. (30 cm) long. Flowers funnel-shaped, 1 in. (2.5 cm) long, dark purplish red, or yellow tinged with brown-purple, with yellow in throat and deep purple blotch at bottom. South Africa. Late spring. Zone 9.

Sprekelia
Amaryllis family
Amaryllidaceae

Spreck-kee′li-a. A single species of tender bulbous herbs, related to *Zephyranthes*. (Name commemorates J. H. van Sprekelsen, a lawyer in Hamburg who was visited by Linnaeus.)

Description
Distinctive because of its strongly 2-lipped flower.

How to Grow
Should be treated like *Hippeastrum*.

formosissima p. 211
Aztec Lily; Jacobean Lily; St. James's Lily. Bulb ovalish. Leafless stalk to 12 in. (30 cm) high, appears before leaves. Leaves few, narrow, thick, to 12 in. (30 cm) long. Flower solitary, 4 in. (10 cm) long, enclosed in membranous spathe. Calyx of 3 sepals, bright red, cylinderlike. Corolla of 3 petals, narrow and erect, bright red, alternating with sepals. Stamens 6. Fruit a 3-celled capsule. Mexico. Summer. Zone 9.

Sternbergia
Amaryllis family
Amaryllidaceae

Stern-ber′ji-a. Winter Daffodil. A genus of late-blooming Eurasian bulbous herbs, related to *Zephyranthes*. (Name commemorates Count Kaspar von Sternberg, an Austrian botanist.)

Description
Leaves narrow, strap-shaped. Flowers solitary, erect, crocuslike, atop leafless stalk that is shorter than the leaves.

How to Grow
Plant in midsummer, 4 in. (10 cm) deep, in gritty nourishing soil. Set in a sheltered position against a south-facing wall, or in a warm nook in the rock garden, where they will receive a good baking. Bulbs increase readily by bulblets. Do not lift and replant frequently. If bulbs are not flowering well, replant in fresh soil after foliage has died away. Foliage persists over winter, withering in early spring. Hardy north to Zone 7; winter in well-drained soil in sheltered places.

lutea p. 198
Winter Daffodil; Lily-of-the-Field. Stout flowering stalk 4–7 in. (10.0–17.5 cm) high. Leaves basal, 8–12 in. (20–30 cm) long, ¾ in. (19 mm) wide, dark green, without teeth, appearing with flowers and usually persisting over winter. Flowers solitary (rarely 2), yellow, with a very short tube, and erect, veined, oblongish segments not over 1½ in. (4 cm) long. Stamens 6. S. Europe and Asia Minor. Attractive for a border or rock garden. Autumn. Zone 7.

Streptanthera
Iris family
Iridaceae

Strep-tan′the-ra. A small genus of bulbous herbs from South Africa, related to *Ixia*. (*Streptanthera,* from the Greek for "twisted anther," alludes to the attachment of the anthers.)

Description
Low herbs with sword-shaped leaves, mostly basal and arranged in fanlike clusters. Flowers solitary or a few, growing in a spathe at the end of a slender stalk. Petals 6, joined at the base into a short tube, to which the stamens are attached.

How to Grow
Should be treated like *Ixia*.

cuprea p. 206

To 9 in. (22.5 cm) high. Leaves weak, slender, pointed, 2–5 in. (5.0–12.5 cm) long, ⅓ in. (8 mm) wide. Flowers 2 or 3, 2 in. (5 cm) wide, tube purple, segments copper-colored, but purplish and yellow-spotted toward base. South Africa. Late spring. Zone 9.

Tigridia
Iris family
Iridaceae

Ty-grid′i-a. Tiger Flower; Flower-of-Tigris. Showy, tender, bulbous herbs. About 25 species scattered from Mexico to Chile. The flowers last only a single day. (*Tigridia,* Latin for "tiger," alludes to markings on the flowers.)

Description
Leaves narrow, sword-shaped. Perianth more or less cup-shaped, with segments spreading or reflexed at tips. Fruit a capsule.

How to Grow
Should be treated like *Gladiolus.*

Pavonia p. 205

Bulb (actually a corm) 1½ in. (4 cm) in diameter, very starchy. 1–2 ft. (30–60 cm) high. Leaves basal, stiffish, sword-shaped, 12–18 in. (30–45 cm) long. Flowers 3–6 in. (7.5–15.0 cm) wide, red with conspicuous spots, generally cup-shaped, growing between leaflike spathes. Petals and sepals scarcely distinguishable, but inner segments shorter than outer; narrow claw purple or yellow. Several color varieties. Mexico and Guatemala. Summer. Zone 7.

Triteleia
Amaryllis family
Amaryllidaceae

Trit-el-eye′a. Fourteen species of cormous perennial herbs, native in w. North America. Related to *Brodiaea* and *Ipheion.* (From the Greek, meaning "completely in threes," because all floral parts are in threes.)

Description

Leaves linear and flattened, keeled below with a channel above. Flowers with short tube and spreading perianth lobes, several in an umbel, subtended by 3 or more papery spathe bracts.

How to Grow

Should be treated like *Brodiaea*.

hyacinthina p. 170

Wild Hyacinth. To 20 in. (50 cm) high. Leaves narrow and nearly grasslike, to 20 in. (50 cm) long, ¼–½ in. (6–13 mm) wide. Flowers about ½ in. (13 mm) long, white or lilac, 20–30 in an umbel. British Columbia and Idaho south to cen. Calif. Summer. Zones 6–7.

Tritonia
Iris family
Iridaceae

Try-to'ni-a. Montbretia; Blazing Star. About 50 species of handsome South African bulbous plants, closely related to *Gladiolus*. (*Tritonia* refers to a weathercock and alludes to the variable direction of the stamens of some species.)

Description

Only *T. crocata* is commonly cultivated. Showy plant growing from fibrous or sheathed corms. Stems short, leaves narrow, sword-shaped. Flowering spike 1–2 ft. (30–60 cm) high. Bracts spathe-like, often 3-toothed. Corolla tubular or bell-shaped, lobes nearly regular. Fruit a membranous capsule.

How to Grow

Should be treated like *Gladiolus*. Plant corms 3–4 in. (7.5–10.0 cm) deep, and 5 in. (12.5 cm) apart each way.

crocata p. 216

Slender, mostly unbranched plant to 18 in. (45 cm) high. Leaves few. Flowers nearly 2 in. (5 cm) wide, orange-red or yellowish brown, in few-flowered, 1-sided racemes. There are also light red, scarlet, and pale pink forms. South Africa. Late spring to summer. Zone 7.

Tulipa
Lily family
Liliaceae

Too′li-pa. Tulip. Bulbous herbs comprising perhaps 100 species and several thousand horticultural forms, the latter including all the common garden tulips. The wild forms all come from the Old World, from the Mediterranean region to Japan. The species, or botanical, tulips are chiefly grown in rock gardens or low borders. The common garden tulips are the result of centuries of breeding and are based mostly on the species *T. suaveolens, T. Gesneriana,* and *T. Fosteriana.* The numerous garden forms have been classified according to bloom time, flower form, and species derivation. (*Tulipa,* a Latinized version of an Arabic word for "turban," alludes to the shape of the flower.)

Description
Bulb generally pointed. Stem single (rarely, branched in some species). Leaves mostly basal, but a few on stem in some tall kinds, generally thick, bluish green, without teeth. Flowers usually solitary, chiefly erect, bell- or saucer-shaped, the petals and sepals indistinguishable as such, totaling 6 (except in double-flowered forms). Stamens 6. Fruit a many-seeded capsule.

How to Grow
Always store tulip bulbs in a cool place prior to planting. Plant in late fall in well-drained, sandy, humus-rich soil. They prefer full sun but will do well on as little as 5–6 hours of sunlight per day. Set bulbs 4–8 in. (10–20 cm) deep and 4–8 in. (10–20 cm) apart, depending on size and variety. Protect from mice and chipmunks. If planted deeper (to 12 in., or 30 cm), bulbs multiply less but produce good-size blooms for several years. In spring apply a light top dressing of balanced commercial fertilizer. After 2–3 years tulips may become crowded and usually produce smaller flowers. Dig up bulbs in midsummer after foliage has withered and replant or discard. Many gardeners treat tulips like annuals and plant new bulbs each fall. They can also be forced in pots. Propagate tulips from offsets that develop around parent bulb; these take 1–3 years to reach blooming size.

Diseases

The most common tulip disease, known as fire, is similar to gray mold. Use ferbam or zineb to prevent spotting of leaves and flowers. Apply when leaves are 4 in. (10 cm) high and repeat weekly until flowers open. When digging or planting bulbs, discard any that have black seedlike objects clustered on surface or just beneath husk. Occasionally mosaic virus disease causes flowers to "break" in color, producing white or green streaks in petals. Discard bulbs of these plants.

***acuminata** p. 110*
Turkish Tulip. Related to *T. Gesneriana,* hence to horticultural varieties. 12–18 in. (30–45 cm) high. Leaves narrow, irregularly curving. Flowers yellow with red lines, segments narrow-pointed, 3–4 in. (7.5–10.0 cm) long. Turkey. Late spring. Zone 4.

***Aucheriana** p. 120*
To 8 in. (20 cm) high. Leaves mostly basal, usually 2–5, strap-shaped, 4–5 in. (10.0–12.5 cm) long. Flowers 1–1½ in. (2.5–4.0 cm) long, starlike, pink with brownish-yellow blotch, inner petals striped green or brown on back. Iran and Syria. Early spring. Zone 4.

***australis** p. 97*
6–10 in. (15–25 cm) high. Leaves usually 2–5, strap-shaped, channeled, 2–4 in. (5–10 cm) long. Flowers fragrant, solitary (rarely, 2); petals yellow inside, reddish outside, pointed at tip, 2 in. (5 cm) long. S. France and Algeria. Late spring. Zone 4.

***Batalinii** p. 97*
A low tulip, 5–6 in. (12.5–15.0 cm) high. Leaves very narrow, grasslike. Flowers to 2 in. (5 cm) long, yellow, blotched gray-yellow, the petals blunt, sometimes notched at tip. Closely related to *T. linifolia.* Bokhara (U.S.S.R.). Early spring. Zone 4.

***Clusiana** pp. 105, 119*

Candy-Stick Tulip. To 15 in. (38 cm) high. Bulb small. Leaves narrow. Flowers fragrant, small, 2 in. (5 cm) long, base reddish purple, pointed tips white or yellowish, the outside striped pinkish red. The var. *chrysantha,* native to India, lacks purple base; inner petals yellow, the outside striped reddish. Iran and Afghanistan; naturalized in s. Europe. Late spring. Zone 4.

Hageri p. 111

A low tulip, to 6 in. (15 cm) high. Leaves 6–8 in. (15–20 cm) long and ½ in. (13 mm) wide. Flowers 1–4 on stalk, bell-shaped, 2 in. (5 cm) long, coppery yellow to scarlet. Asia Minor and Greece. Early spring. Zone 4.

Kolpakowskiana p. 96

To 6 in. (15 cm) high. Leaves 2–4 per bulb, bluish green, 6–8 in. (15–20 cm) long, 1 in. (2.5 cm) wide. Flowers 1 or 2, to 2 in. (5 cm) long, the petals spreading and pointed at both ends, yellow inside, reddish outside, not blotched. Turkestan (U.S.S.R.). Early spring. Zone 4.

linifolia p. 113

A low tulip, 5–10 in. (12.5–25.0 cm) high. Leaves narrow, grasslike. Flowers to 2 in. (5 cm) long, crimson, the base bluish, the petals pointed. Bokhara (U.S.S.R.). Early spring. Zone 4.

montana p. 113

To 8 in. (20 cm) high. Leaves bluish green, long-tapering. Flowers 2 in. (5 cm) long, dark crimson, paler outside, outer petals pointed. Iran and Afghanistan. Late spring. Zone 4.

Orphanidea p. 110

A medium-sized tulip, 8–12 in. (20–30 cm) high. Leaves narrow, folded. Flower solitary, starlike, the petals sharp-pointed, nearly 2 in. (5 cm) long, orange-bronze to yellow, green-stained outside. Turkey and Greece. Early spring. Zone 5.

praestans p. 114

A medium-sized tulip, usually 12 in. (30 cm) high. Leaves narrow, short-tapering. Flowers 1–4, to 2 in. (5 cm) long, light red, petals blunt but with a minute point. Bokhara (U.S.S.R.). Early spring. Zone 4.

pulchella p. 122

4–6 in. (10–15 cm) high. Leaves 2–3, strap-shaped, slightly channeled, smooth. Flowers cup-shaped, but opening flat, 1½ in. (4 cm) long, solitary or few, red to purple, outer petals gray or green. There are violet, violet-pink, and white cultivars. Asia Minor. Early spring. Zone 5.

saxatilis p. 121
New bulbs formed at end of stolons.
Flowering stem to 12 in. (30 cm) high.
Leaves flat, shining green. Flowers 1–3,
cup-shaped, fragrant, pale lilac with yellow
base, to 2 in. (5 cm) long. Crete. Needs less
cold than most species. Mid-spring. Zone 4.

Sprengeri p. 111
Medium-sized, 8–12 in. (20–30 cm) high.
Leaves pointed, long, and narrow. Flowers
2 in. (5 cm) long, the petals almost
prickle-tipped; orange-red, base darker.
Armenia (U.S.S.R.). Late spring. Zone 5.

sylvestris p. 96
Weak-stemmed, 8–12 in. (20–30 cm) high.
Leaves 4–5, strap-shaped, channeled, 8–10 in.
(20–25 cm) long, ⅓ in. (8 mm) wide.
Flowers to 2 in. (5 cm) long, fragrant,
usually only 1 or 2, yellow. Europe, w. Asia,
and n. Africa. Late spring. Zone 4.

tarda p. 92
To 5 in. (12.5 cm) high. Leaves bright
green, forming a flat rosette. Flowers to 2 in.
(5 cm) long, usually several, yellow inside,
the petals edged with white, tinged greenish
and reddish on back. Turkestan (U.S.S.R.).
Early spring. Zone 4.

turkestanica p. 93
To 8 in. (20 cm) high. Leaves lance-shaped.
Flowers 1–6, to 1¼ in. (3 cm) long, white
with an orange-yellow base. Turkestan
(U.S.S.R.). Early spring. Zone 4.

Hybrid Classes
Modern garden tulips are the result of
centuries of horticultural breeding and are
thus of complex botanical ancestry.
Thousands of named forms exist, with
hundreds appearing on the market every
year. They are often easier to grow than the
species tulips. Hybrids are divided into
several classes based on time of bloom,
flower form, and species derivation. The
groups represented here are arranged
alphabetically.

Cottage Tulips pp. 94, 99, 101, 109, 117, 119
Flowers large, egg-shaped, petals pointed or
rounded, on long stems, late-blooming.
Includes some multiflowering or bouquet
forms, such as 'Georgette' and 'Orange
Bouquet', and *viridiflora* types, with green

feathering on the petals. Other popular cultivars are 'Golden Harvest', 'Rosy Wings', and 'Smiling Queen', ranging 1½–3 ft. (45–90 cm) high, with flowers 3–4 in. (7.5–10.0 cm) long. Late spring. Sometimes combined with Darwin Tulips under the heading Single Late Tulips. Zone 4.

Darwin Tulips *pp. 90, 99, 122*
Probably the most popular class. Flowers deep, cup-shaped, on tall stems, late-blooming. Very wide range of colors, from white to purple-black. Cultivars 'Duke of Wellington', 'Golden Age', and 'Queen of the Night' range 1½–2½ ft. (45–75 cm) high, with flowers 3–4 in. (7.5–10.0 cm) long. Late spring. Sometimes combined with Cottage Tulips under the heading Single Late Tulips. Zone 4.

Darwin Hybrid Tulips *pp. 102, 103, 115*
Mainly produced by crossing Darwin Tulips with the species *T. Fosteriana*. Flowers large, on tall stems. Colors range generally from scarlet through deep yellow. Popular cultivars 'Golden Oxford', Gudoshnik', 'Olympic Flame', and 'Oxford' are 1½–2½ ft. (45–75 cm) high, with flowers 3–4 in. (7.5–10.0 cm) long. Late spring. Zone 4.

Double Early Tulips *p. 107*
Flowers many-petaled, peony-like, on sturdy stems. 'Fringed Beauty' is 8–12 in. (20–30 cm) high, with flowers 3–4 in (7.5–10.0 cm) wide. Early spring. Zone 4.

Double Late Tulips *pp. 90, 116, 117*
Flowers many-petaled, peony-like. Popular cultivars 'Eros', 'May Wonder', and 'Mount Tacoma' range 1½–2 ft. (45–60 cm) high, with flowers to 6 in. (15 cm) wide. Late spring. This category often referred to as "peony-flowered tulips." Zone 4.

Fosteriana Tulips *pp. 91, 98, 102, 112*
Hybrids and varieties of *T. Fosteriana*. Species native to Turkestan (U.S.S.R.). White, yellow, gold, orange, and red 'Emperor' forms are especially popular, ranging 12–18 in. (30–45 cm) high; leaves sometimes mottled or striped, as in the species; flowers to 4 in. (10 cm) long. Early spring. Zone 4.

Greigii Tulips *pp. 104, 105, 112, 115, 120*
Hybrids and varieties of *T. Greigii*. Species is 6–9 in. (15.0–22.5 cm) high. Leaves broad, wavy-margined, dark, distinctively mottled

and striped reddish or purplish. Flowers to 3 in. (7.5 cm) long, orange-red with darker base, yellow-margined, the petals minutely pointed. 'Cape Cod', 'China Lady', 'Flaming Star', 'Oriental Splendor', 'Princesse Charmante', and 'Red Riding Hood' are popular cultivars that range 8–12 in. (20–30 cm) high; leaves mottled as in the species; flowers to 6 in. (15 cm) wide. Mid-spring. Zone 4.

Kaufmanniana Tulips *pp. 92, 93, 94, 101, 106, 108*
Hybrids and varieties of *T. Kaufmanniana,* the Water Lily Tulip. Species is 5–10 in. (12.5–25.0 cm) high. Leaves broad, abruptly tapering. Flowers to 3 in. (7.5 cm) long, spreading, white or pale yellow, with red-marked yellow center. Cultivars include 'Giuseppe Verdi', 'Honorose', 'Johann Strauss', 'Scarlet Baby', and 'Shakespeare', most ranging 4–8 in. (10–20 cm) high; leaves sometimes mottled; flowers to 3½ in. (9 cm) wide. Very good in rock gardens. Early spring. Zone 4.

Lily-flowered Tulips *pp. 95, 108, 114, 116, 121, 123*
Flower petals long, pointed, curving outward at tips; many color varieties. 'Ballade', 'Jacqueline', 'Maytime', 'Queen of Sheba', 'Red Shine', and 'West Point' range 1½–2 ft. (45–60 cm) high, with flowers 2–4 in. (5–10 cm) long. Late spring. Zone 4.

Parrot Tulips *pp. 95, 100, 107, 109, 118, 123*
Sports, or chance mutations, from other tulips; flowers large, with petals twisted, cut, and feathered, on fairly long, weak stems. Many color varieties, often with streaking and green flecks. 'Blue Parrot', 'Flaming Parrot,' 'Karel Doorman', 'Texas', and 'Yellow Parrot' range 1½–2 ft. (45–60 cm) high, with flowers 6–7 in. (15.0–17.5 cm) wide. Late spring. Zone 4.

Single Early Tulips *p. 100*
Early-blooming garden forms, some scented; Cottage and Darwin tulips sometimes included in this category. 'Bellona' is a yellow cultivar 14–16 in. (35.0–40.5 cm) high, with flowers 2–4 in. (5–10 cm) long. Early spring. Zone 4.

Triumph Tulips *pp. 106, 118*
Primarily crosses between Single Early Tulips and late-blooming forms; flowers large, on

strong stems, blooming in midseason.
Among popular cultivars are 'Garden Party'
and 'Kees Nelis', 1½–2 ft. (45–60 cm) high,
with flowers 2–4 in. (5–10 cm) long.
Mid-spring. Zone 4.

Urceolina
Amaryllis family
Amaryllidaceae

Ur-see-ol-i'na. 3–6 species of bulbous
perennials, native in Andes of South America
and related to *Eucharis*. (From the Latin,
meaning a small cup or pitcher, referring to
the shape of the flower.)

Description
Leaves with evident stalks, egg-shaped or
oblong. Flowers 2–12 in a cluster at top of
flowering stem, pendulous, urn-shaped, with
very short, spreading lobes.

How to Grow
Grow outdoors only in Zone 10. Elsewhere
pot in autumn in well-drained, compost-
enriched soil. Maintain in cool greenhouse or
room at about 45° F (7° C) until growth
begins in early spring. Keep soil moist, but
not wet. When growth commences, increase
water. After summer flowering, when leaves
have died down, keep soil just barely moist
until autumn, when bulbs may be repotted.

peruviana p. 210
To 18 in. (45 cm) high. Leaves lance-shaped,
to 12 in. (30 cm) long, 1½ in. (4 cm) wide.
Flowers 2–6, bright red, to 1½ in. (4 cm)
long. Bolivia and Peru. Summer. Zone 10.

Urginea
Lily family
Liliaceae

Ur-gin'e-a. Half-hardy bulbous perennials
comprising about 40 species; natives of
Mediterranean region, India, and South
Africa. (*Urginea* was named from an Arabian
tribe in Algeria known as Ben Urgin.)

Description
Bulbs large and scaly. Leaves basal, long,
narrow. Leafless flowering stalk appears
before leaves. Flowers whitish, yellowish, or

pink, small, growing in axils of bracts or in terminal racemes. Calyx of 3 colored sepals. Corolla of 3 petals, alternating with the sepals. Stamens 6. Fruit a 3-sided capsule, many-seeded. Plants are poisonous.

How to Grow
Grow outdoors only in Zones 9 and 10. Elsewhere pot in well-drained, compost-rich soil in mid-summer. Keep soil moist but not wet. Flowering stalk arises in autumn, followed by a rosette of leaves that lasts through winter. When leaves die down, keep soil barely moist until flowering spikes appear and growth recommences. Propagate by offsets. Handle bulbs carefully, since the juice can cause blistering.

maritima p. 185
Sea Onion; Sea Squill. Bulbs 4–6 in. (10–15 cm) thick. Flowering stalk to 5 ft. (1.5 m) high, leafless. Leaves to 18 in. (45 cm) long, 4 in. (10 cm) wide, lance-shaped, fleshy, shiny-green. Flowers numerous, whitish, ½ in. (13 mm) long, in racemes to 18 in. (45 cm) long. Canary Islands to Syria and South Africa. Autumn. Zone 9.

Vallota
Amaryllis family
Amaryllidaceae

Val-low'ta. South African bulbous herbs of only one species. (Named for Pierre Vallot, a French botanist.)

Description
Leaves basal, appearing with the flowering stalk. Flowers funnel-shaped, in terminal umbels.

How to Grow
Should be treated like _Hippeastrum_.

speciosa p. 212
Scarborough Lily. Bulbs large. Flowering stalks leafless, stout, hollow, flattish, to 3 ft. (90 cm) high. Leaves to 2 ft. (60 cm) long, 1 in. (2.5 cm) wide. Flowers scarlet, to 3 in. (7.5 cm) wide. Calyx of 3 colored sepals. Corolla of 3 petals alternating with sepals. Stamens 6. Fruit a 3-celled capsule. Though leaves die down in autumn at end of growing season, do not allow pots to dry out completely. Summer. Zone 10.

Veltheimia
Lily family
Liliaceae

Vel-thym′i-a. A small genus of South African bulbous herbs, suitable only for greenhouse culture, or outdoors in frostless regions. (Named for A. F. von Veltheim, a German patron of botany.)

Description
Leaves chiefly basal, strap-shaped, more or less sheathing the stem. Flowers tubular, 6 lobes of corolla short. Stamens 6. Fruit a 3-chambered capsule.

How to Grow
Hardy outdoors only in Zones 9 and 10. Elsewhere pot up dormant bulbs in early fall. Water only enough to keep pots moist. When growth commences and leaves appear in late winter, increase water. When leaves die down in summer, reduce water to keep soil just barely moist. Do not repot every year. Offsets are sparingly produced, and are the easiest means of propagation.

viridifolia p. 214
Unicorn Root. To 2 ft. (60 cm) high. Leaves shiny green (as though varnished), strap-shaped, 8–12 in. (20–30 cm) long, 3 in. (7.5 cm) wide, wavy-margined. Flowers pinkish or yellowish, green-spotted, 1 in. (2.5 cm) long, in a large, many-flowered raceme 4–6 in. (10–15 cm) long. Needs a cool greenhouse, and a resting period when leaves wither after bloom passes. Early spring. Zone 9.

Watsonia
Iris famiy
Iridaceae

Wat-sow′ni-a. Bugle-Lily. South African gladiolus-like herbs comprising perhaps 60 species, of which 3 are cultivated for ornament, but better known in Calif. than in the East. (Named for Sir William Watson, an English botanist.)

Description
Leaves basal, sword-shaped, sometimes a few on stem. Flowers showy, in terminal racemes, corolla differing from the closely related

Gladiolus in being nearly regular; tube curved. Fruit a 3-celled capsule.

How to Grow
Should be treated like *Gladiolus*.

Beatricis *p. 208*
Evergreen. To 4 ft. (120 cm) high. Flowers coral-red, 3 in. (7.5 cm) long, bracts below flowers, with pink tips. South Africa. Autumn. Zone 8.

pyramidata *p. 183*
3–6 ft. (0.9–1.8 m) high. Flowers 3 in. (7.5 cm) long, rose-red, tube flaring toward top and as long as segments. There is a pure white hybrid. South Africa. Summer. Zone 8.

Zephyranthes
Amaryllis family
Amaryllidaceae

Zeff-i-ran'theez. Zephyr-Flower; Zephyr Lily. A genus of 40 species of New World bulbous herbs, a few grown for ornament. (From the Greek for "west-wind flower," alluding to the plants' being wholly American.) Sometimes known under the genus name *Atamasco*.

Description
Leaves basal, narrow, grasslike, usually appearing with flowers, persistent in some species over the winter. Flower solitary, its stalk hollow, appearing from a tubular spathe notched at tip. Corolla erect, funnel-shaped, segments nearly of equal length, making the flower faintly irregular. Stamens 6. Fruit a nearly round, 3-celled capsule.

How to Grow
Z. Atamasco is the hardiest and will ordinarily survive winters up to Zone 7 if given a site not too wet and slushy in winter. Plant others in spring, allow to flower, and dig up and store over winter. During storage do not allow bulbs to dry out. Keep them in fairly moist sand. South of Zone 7, they can stay in the ground all year; they sometimes survive this treatment northward, but not usually. The half-hardy species can be grown in cool greenhouses. Dry soil out and then moisten to induce flowering.

384

Atamasco p. 177
Atamasco Lily; Fairy Lily. Flowering stalk nearly 12 in. (30 cm) long. Leaves 12 in. (30 cm) long, very narrow. Flowers white or tinged with purple, to 3 in. (7.5 cm) long. Va. to Fla. and Ala. Early spring. Zones 7–8.

candida p. 166
To 12 in. (30 cm) high. Leaves thick, stiffish, 12 in. (30 cm) long. Flowers 2 in. (5 cm) long, white (rarely, rose-tinged). Argentina. Summer to autumn. Zone 9.

citrina p. 198
8–12 in. (20–30 cm) high. Leaves 8–12 in. (20–30 cm) long, 1/5 in. (5 mm) wide, grooved. Flowers yellow, tube green, 1½ in. (4 cm) long. Guyana. Summer to autumn. Sometimes called *Z. sulphurea.* Zone 9.

grandiflora p. 248
Zephyr Lily. To 12 in. (30 cm) high. Leaves flat, narrow, 12 in. (30 cm) long. Flowers 3 in. (7.5 cm) long, pink or red. Tropical America. Late spring to summer. Zone 9.

rosea p. 249
To 12 in. (30 cm) high. Resembling *Z. grandiflora* and sometimes mistaken for it, but with broader, blunter leaves, 12 in. (30 cm) long. Flowers rose-pink, 1 in. (2.5 cm) long. Cuba. The least hardy of the zephyr lilies. Autumn. Zone 10.

Appendices

Calendar

There is no such thing as a totally maintenance-free garden, but once established, bulbs are among the most carefree of plants. Still, if you want to keep them in peak condition, there are certain tasks that must be performed. Think of these as guidelines rather than as hard-and-fast rules; your own enthusiasm for gardening and an understanding of local environmental conditions will help to determine how conscientious you need to be.

This calendar is arranged according to the months of the year and is divided into four geographical regions: the North, the Northwest, the South, and the Southwest. A fifth section, Indoors and Greenhouse, outlines tasks for those who grow bulbs indoors.

Use common sense when you determine the area in which you live. If your garden is in Virginia, it lies in what we refer to as the South. If the winter has been very harsh, however, refer to the information given for the North as you plan your gardening activities.

Don't be too rigid planning your monthly gardening tasks either. If you live in the North and the winter has been exceptionally mild, you may be able to step up your gardening activities by as much as six weeks.

Remember, the dates of the first and last frosts in your region are always the best indicators of when winter actually begins and spring ends.

A well-planned calendar for growing bulbs indoors reminds you when to start them so that you can have flowers to brighten your windowsill weeks before their normal blooming period. Knowing the growth cycles of different kinds of bulbs also allows you to plan a continual sequence of blooms. And if you live in a cold region, a greenhouse will enable you to try your hand at growing some of the more exotic bulbs that normally thrive only in warm to tropical climates.

North

Here the North encompasses a large area of the country: the states of the Northeast, south through Maryland, north to Hudson Bay, and west to the Rockies.

January

Check winter mulch, adding more if the wind has blown some away. Old Christmas trees and other evergreen branches help keep loose mulch in place. Look over stored bulbs, corms, and tuberous roots. Do not keep them too moist or too cold, which causes injury, or too warm, which may encourage premature growth. Discard any that show signs of decay.

February

During mild periods in February, look for snowdrops (*Galanthus*) and winter aconite (*Eranthis*), the first of the outdoor bulb flowers.

March

Enjoy the hardy bulbs, notably the first of the daffodils and early tulips, as they come into bloom in the garden. Dust 5-10-10 fertilizer over bulb plantings (1 pound per 100 square feet), but do not remove mulch.

April

Many of the early- and small-flowering bulbs are now in bloom—crocus, Siberian Squill, *Puschkinia,* daffodils, and tulips. As you enjoy them, plan new and enlarged plantings for next year.

May

Tender bulbs and corms such as canna, dahlia, tuberous begonia, and montbretia (*Crocosmia* and *Tritonia*) can be planted outdoors now. Plant gladiolus from early May until the end of June so you will have a succession of flowers during the summer and fall. Allow foliage of daffodils and other early-blooming bulbs to ripen fully before removing it.

June

Remove the spent flowers from spring-flowering bulbs so that seed pods do not develop, but do not remove the foliage until it has yellowed and dried. Foliage is essential for the bulb to manufacture food for next year. You can plant gladiolus and dahlias until the end of the month. Plant some daylilies (*Hemerocallis*) now for summer bloom.

July

Order bulbs to plant in the fall. Make sure summer-flowering bulbs have sufficient water. This is the middle of lily season; *Lilium canadense, L. superbum,* and *L. regale* are in bloom this month, as are the daylilies (*Hemerocallis*), Summer Hyacinth (*Galtonia candicans*), and the first of the gladiolus. Spring-flowering bulbs are dormant now, so you can remove the dead foliage.

August

Madonna Lilies (*Lilium candidum* and its varieties) are now dormant and can be planted or moved in the garden if necessary. Disbud dahlias to encourage larger blooms. Order spring-blooming bulbs and work on plans for autumn planting.

September

Prepare areas for fall planting, adding organic matter and fertilizer to the soil. Plant spring-flowering bulbs as soon as possible. In addition to plants with large blooms, include some of the small-flowering kinds like crocus, grape-hyacinth, and squill, which look best in masses. Plant lilies this month as soon as they are available. After the first frost, dig up dahlias, gladiolus, and other non-hardy plants.

Place the bulbs in shallow boxes to dry for several days before winter storage.

October
Add leaves, old plants, and garden litter to the compost pile. To hasten decomposition, sprinkle some complete fertilizer over the materials as they are stacked. There is still time to prepare areas for fall planting. Dig up cannas, dahlias, gladiolus, tuberous begonias, and other bulbs that are not winter-hardy. Dry them in an airy, shady place and then store for the winter. Continue to plant spring-flowering bulbs. Lower-growing bulbs such as crocus, snowdrops, and squills do well under deciduous trees. They grow and flower before the shade of the trees can interfere with their life cycle.

November
Collect leaves, foliage from annuals and perennials, and other garden refuse and add to the compost pile or use for winter mulching and protection on late-planted bulbs. Burn any disease- or insect-infested plants. This is the last chance to plant spring-flowering bulbs outdoors. Mulch the soil to prevent or delay freezing so that bulbs can make root growth before the weather gets too cold. Label or mark planting areas.

December
Finish cleaning up flower beds and make sure all are well mulched. Clean, sharpen, and oil garden tools, shears, mowers, and hoes.

Northwest
The Northwest extends from the Rocky Mountain states west to the Pacific.

January
Begin to peruse the garden catalogues and work on some new ideas for what to plant where. Start a new garden journal; review last year's notes and transcribe any important dates or other information that will apply to this year's plantings.

February
Plant some lilies and other bulbs outdoors as soon as frost danger is past.

March
After early-blooming bulbs such as hyacinths and narcissus have flowered, remove the old flowers and seed pods but leave the foliage so that the plants can manufacture food for next year.

April
Although exact planting times may vary according to elevation, location, and seasonal conditions, you can begin to plant dahlias, gladiolus, and other tender summer-flowering bulbs and corms. Plant gladiolus at 1- to 2-week intervals from now until about July to ensure flowers throughout the summer and early fall. Start dahlias and tuberous begonias indoors in moist sphagnum or other well-drained medium. When roots form and active growth starts, pot them up; once they are established, you can plant them outdoors after all danger of frost is past. Repot and divide tender winter-flowering bulbs such as Dutch amaryllis (*Hippeastrum*), *Clivia,* and *Crinum* as they finish blooming. Also repot forced bulbs as they finish blooming so they will be ready to set in the garden later.

May
Spring-flowering bulbs still need their foliage. Do not remove it until it begins to turn yellow, but do remove any spent flowers of the early bloomers. Continue to plant gladiolus and dahlias. Set stakes at the same time you plant dahlias so that there will be no damage later to the plants' roots. You can also plant montbretia (*Crocosmia* and *Tritonia*), canna, and *Tigridia* this month. Tuberous begonias add color to the garden; use them in containers or plant in sheltered, lightly shaded areas.

June
Mulch plants to reduce maintenance and water loss, as well as to make the garden attractive. Plant annuals in, among, or over the early spring bulbs such as tulips and narcissus. Let the bulb foliage mature naturally before removing it. If you must transplant spring-flowering bulbs, do it as the foliage turns yellow. If necessary, you can dig and replant them before the foliage is mature, but keep the foliage intact. There is still time to plant gladiolus and dahlias this month.

July
Water and fertilize plants regularly to ensure continued growth. You can continue to plant dahlias and gladiolus until about the middle of the month. Stake tall-growing plants. Any spring-blooming bulbs that are now dormant can be lifted and stored for replanting in autumn.

August
Plant *Colchicum* and fall-blooming crocus bulbs this month for flowers in September and October.

September
Begin fall cleanup, adding leaves and other garden refuse to the

compost heap. Plant lilies and fall-blooming bulbs. Dig up dahlias, gladiolus, and other non-hardy bulbs or tuberous roots and prepare them for winter storage.

October
Plant spring-blooming bulbs this month. Dig and store any non-hardy plants that remain in the garden such as cannas and tuberous begonias. If you wish, you can leave gladiolus and dahlias outdoors until the tops are killed by frost.

November
Clean up the garden and put old plants, leaves, and garden rubbish on the compost pile. Continue to dig up bulbs and tuberous roots that are not winter-hardy; allow them to dry for a few days, then store them in dry peat or vermiculite. Finish planting winter-hardy bulbs this month.

December
Finish general garden cleanup for the year. Clean, repair, oil, and sharpen garden tools and mowers. Clean and gather stakes into bundles for storage. Dig up any remaining dahlias; clean and dry the roots, dust with sulphur, and store in a cool, dry place in peat, sand, or vermiculite. Plant the last of the spring-flowering bulbs and protect with a winter mulch.

South
The South here includes all states from Virginia south to the Gulf of Mexico and west to the Louisiana-Texas border.

January
In warmer areas, particularly in Zone 10, it is time to start planting gladiolus, tuberous begonias, and early lilies such as *Lilium regale, L. speciosum* and its varieties, and *L. auratum.*

February
Continue to plant the bulbs mentioned above. Be sure that bulb plantings do not become dry. In the upper South crocus is now in bloom; *Crocus Tomasinianus* naturalizes easily in this region and would be a good choice when you start planning next year's garden.

March
Continue planting gladiolus at 10- to 14-day intervals until late June so that you can have flowers in constant supply from June to September. Start tuberous begonias indoors in moist peat. Once they form roots you can plant them outdoors if weather permits, or pot them up and plant them outdoors later.

April
Now is the time to plant most kinds of summer-flowering tender bulbs and corms, including canna, *Crinum,* dahlias, spider-lilies (*Hymenocallis*), montbretia (*Crocosmia* and *Tritonia*), and *Tigridia.* Plant tuberous begonias outdoors in a shaded spot for summer flowering. Keep planting gladiolus at intervals until July; continue planting dahlias until June.

May
Mulch plants to conserve moisture. Plant summer-flowering bulbs—canna, dahlia, gladiolus, and tuberous begonia.

June
Finish mulching to prevent water loss, and examine plants for diseases that thrive on humidity. Dahlias and gladiolus can still be planted until the end of the month.

July
Disbud dahlias to encourage larger blooms, and keep them staked so that they will be at their best at flowering time.

August
Fertilize fall-blooming plants such as dahlias and water them regularly. After daylilies (*Hemerocallis*) have finished flowering, they can be divided and transplanted if necessary. Early-flowering bulbs such as *Colchicum,* Madonna Lily (*L. candidum*), *Lycoris,* and oxalis become available for planting this month.

September
Prepare the garden for fall planting, adding organic matter and fertilizer to the soil. In more southern parts of this area, you can plant tender to half-hardy bulbs such as 'Paper-white' narcissus. You can also plant poppy anemones (*Anemone coronaria*), bulbous iris, *Lycoris,* ranunculus, and spring-flowering bulbs.

October
Plant spring-flowering bulbs. Dig and store dahlias, gladiolus, and other non-hardy bulbs.

November
Dig and store tender bulbs and tuberous roots for winter, including dahlias, gladiolus, spider-lilies (*Hymenocallis*), and tuberose. In the lower South plant refrigerated tulip bulbs late this month or in early December for spring bloom.

December
Finish garden cleanup. Remove dead foliage of dormant plants. Plant amaryllis and tuberous begonia.

Calendar

Southwest
The Southwest extends from Texas through Arizona, New Mexico, and all of California.

January
You can start to plant gladiolus this month to have flowers that will bloom in May.

February
Now is the time to plant summer-blooming bulbs.

March
Plant lily bulbs outdoors. Plant tuberous begonias in cool, shaded areas for summer bloom. Keep growing plants well watered and mulch them to retain moisture.

April
Plant dahlias outside; stake as you plant them so there will be no damage to the roots later. Low-growing or dwarf types do not need staking if the plants are well branched.

May
Pinch dahlias and annuals to encourage branching. Large-flowering dahlias, which should be individually staked, are usually trained so that each plant has 4 main stems.

June
Water conservation is very important. Check mulch and add more if needed; protect young plants from extreme heat. When cutting gladiolus flowers, be sure to remove only a minimum of foliage with the flower spike. Tuberous begonias are now at their best; provide plenty of water and light shade.

July
When their foliage has yellowed, spring-flowering bulbs such as hyacinths, narcissus, and tulips can be dug up and stored for replanting in the fall. Narcissus do well if left in the ground undisturbed, but tulips fare better if they are dug and replanted each year. Remove yellowed foliage of any bulbs that are to remain in the garden.

August
Plant Dutch iris (*I. Xiphium*), freesia, *Lycoris,* Madonna Lily (*L. candidum*), *Tritonia,* and *Watsonia.*

September
Dig up dahlias when blooms are past their prime, and gladiolus when the leaves begin to yellow. Dry the tuberous roots and corms and then store. Order spring-flowering bulbs to plant in October.

October
Plant late-flowering kinds of tulips and narcissus. Dig up and store any dahlias, gladiolus, or other tuberous roots or bulbs that may remain in the garden.

November
During cleanup add leaves, old plants, and other garden debris to the compost pile. Bulb planting should be well underway. Plant tulips, amaryllis, montbretia, and *Tigridia*. Plant gladiolus at intervals beginning now for a succession of bloom next spring. Plant lily bulbs as soon as you receive them so that they do not dry out.

December
Be prepared to protect tender plants against unusual frosts. Replant early-dug gladiolus corms at intervals to have a continuous supply of flowers.

Indoors and Greenhouse
Bulbs can be grown indoors if you provide the temperature, soil, and light conditions they would otherwise require in their native outdoor environments.

January
This is the month to begin to bring in the bulbs that were potted for forcing last fall, such as tulips, hyacinths, narcissus, and crocus. Make sure they have a well-developed root system. Start them at a temperature of 60–65° F. Watch for growth of those in storage. When there are signs of new leaves or buds, bring the pots into bright light for flowering. Start tuberous begonias in moist, not wet, sphagnum moss or peat, and when roots begin to appear, pot them in a soil rich in organic matter. Pot up Dutch amaryllis (*Hippeastrum*) in a container at least 2 inches wider than the diameter of the bulb, with the top half of the bulb extending above the soil level. Keep the soil moist but not wet, and at 65° F or above. Bulbs from previous years that are dormant can be transplanted but should be kept in relatively small pots.

February
Bring potted spring-flowering bulbs out of storage and place at a window or in the greenhouse. A temperature of 60–65° F is best at the start, but it can be raised once new top growth begins. Lilies being forced for Easter need a temperature of 62–65° F at night.

March
As the sun grows more intense, watch rising greenhouse temperatures closely; lightly shade the glass. To save hyacinth, narcissus, or other spring bulbs that have flowered, allow the foliage

to remain on the plant and grow. Plant them outdoors early in spring as soon as danger of frost is past. Start tuberous begonias in moist sphagnum moss or peat; pot up when active growth starts.

April
Ventilate the greenhouse freely as temperatures increase with the strengthening sun. Shade the glass to reduce light intensity. Do not let plants dry out. Start dahlia roots in moist sphagnum or a similar medium. Once established in pots the plants can be planted outdoors after frost danger is past.

May
This is the month to transfer plants to the garden for the summer or to a cold frame for a few days and then outdoors when frost no longer threatens. Protect plants against garden pests and diseases.

June
Put outdoors as many plants as possible from the house and greenhouse. Cyclamen sown from seed now will flower in about 18 months. Give the greenhouse a general cleanup. Replace dirty gravel or sand on the benches. Clean beneath benches and make plans to replace glass and repaint.

July
If there are still plants in the greenhouse, shade is essential. Fertilize all plants regularly—those in the house and greenhouse, and those outside that are to be brought back indoors in the fall. Apply a completely soluble fertilizer at watering, or a slow-release fertilizer.

August
Finish any painting or repairs to the greenhouse. Fumigate before bringing plants in for the winter. Make any necessary repairs to the heating system now. Order some spring-blooming bulbs now to pot in the fall for forcing.

September
Prepare plants that have been outside for their return to indoors; check especially for insects and other pests. Be ready to bring plants inside as night temperatures become cooler. Do not let them be exposed to frost. Prepare potting soil for winter use. Repot any plants that need it. Pot freesias or plant them in benches from now until November. Order bulbs now for winter forcing—hyacinths, narcissus, tulips, and crocus, as well as tender kinds like anemones, ranunculus, Dutch amaryllis (*Hippeastrum*), *Brodiaea*, *Veltheimia*, and *Lachenalia*.

October
Pot hardy bulbs for winter forcing this month and store in a cool place to encourage root growth. Protect them from freezing. Plunge pots in a well-drained area outdoors or in a cold frame. Cover with 1 inch of sand, then with about 2 inches of soil, followed by 6 inches of mulch. Such outdoor storage is practical only for winter-hardy bulbs. Store tender bulbs such as freesia and 'Paper-white' narcissus in places not subject to cold. Pot *Gloriosa Rothschildiana* now for spring bloom; plant one tuber to an 8-inch pot and grow at 60° F or warmer.

November
Maintain normal temperatures in the greenhouse at night; cool temperatures may check plant growth. Plant *Hippeastrum, Veltheimia,* and other tender bulbs when you get them, in pots at least 2 inches larger in diameter than the bulb. Water sparingly until growth starts. Begin fertilization after flowering. Bring in sand, soil, compost, and other materials for winter use. Water houseplants carefully and place gravel or other material under pots for drainage. November is also the time to pot 'Paper-white' narcissus and Chinese sacred lilies (cultivars or varieties of *Narcissus Tazetta*). They will flower in about 6 weeks. Keep dormant bulbs in a cool, dry place and make several plantings for continuous bloom. Sow seed of tuberous begonias now to have plants that will flower next spring and summer.

December
Grow houseplants in a warm window with as much light as possible. Keep cyclamens cool and moist. Pot Easter lilies (*L. longiflorum* varieties) late this month for April flowering.

Flower Chart

	Page Number	Zone
Acidanthera bicolor	274	7
Agapanthus africanus	275	9
Allium caeruleum	277	4
Allium Christophii	277	4
Allium giganteum	277	5
Allium karataviense	278	4
Allium Moly	278	4
Allium neapolitanum	278	6–9
Amaryllis Belladonna	282	9
Anemone blanda	284	6
Anemone coronaria	284	5
Begonia grandis	286	6
Begonia × tuberhybrida	287	10
Brimeura amethystina	288	6
Brodiaea coronaria	289	7–8
Calochortus albus	290	5
Camassia Quamash	292	4–5
Canna × generalis	293	8
Chionodoxa Luciliae	295	4
Clivia miniata	296	9
Colchicum autumnale	297	5
Crinum Moorei	299	9
Crocosmia × crocosmiiflora	299	7
Crocus biflorus	300	5
Crocus chrysanthus	301	4
Crocus Goulimyi	301	8
Crocus longiflorus	301	5
Crocus Tomasinianus	302	4–5
Crocus vernus	302	4
Cyclamen coum	304	7
Cyclamen persicum	305	9
Dahlia pinnata hybrids	308	9
Dichelostemma pulchellum	309	5–7
Eranthis hyemalis	310	4–5

Spring	Summer	Autumn	Under 12 in.	12–24 in.	Over 24 in.	Sun	Partial Shade
■	▨	□	■	▨	□	■	▨
	▨			▨		■	
	▨			▨	□	■	
■					□	■	
■				▨	□	■	
■	▨				□	■	▨
■			■			■	
■				▨		■	
■				▨		■	
	▨			▨		■	
■			■				▨
■			■	▨			▨
	▨			▨			▨
	▨			▨			▨
■			■			■	
	▨			▨		■	
■				▨		■	
■				▨		■	
	▨				□	■	
■			■			■	
■				▨		■	▨
		□	■			■	
	▨				□		▨
	▨	□			□	■	
■			■			■	
■			■			■	
		□	■			■	▨
		□	■			■	▨
■			■			■	▨
■			■			■	▨
■			■				▨
■			■				▨
	▨	□	■	▨	□	■	
■				▨		■	
■			■			■	▨

Flower Chart

	Page Number	Zone
Erythronium americanum	311	4
Erythronium Dens-canis	311	4
Eucharis grandiflora	312	10
Eucomis comosa	313	7
Freesia × *hybrida*	315	9
Fritillaria imperialis	316	5
Fritillaria Meleagris	316	4
Galanthus Elwesii	317	4–5
Galtonia candicans	318	6
Gladiolus byzantinus	321	5
Gladiolus × *Colvillei*	321	7
Gladiolus × *hortulanus*	321	9
Gladiolus tristis	322	7
Gloriosa Rothschildiana	323	10
Habranthus Andersonii	324	9
Haemanthus albiflos	325	9
Haemanthus coccineus	325	9
Hemerocallis fulva	327	3–4
Hemerocallis hybrids	327	3–4
Hippeastrum hybrids	329	9
Homeria Breyniana	330	9
Hyacinthoides hispanicus	330	5
Hyacinthus orientalis	330	5
Hymenocallis narcissiflora	333	8
Ipheion uniflorum	334	6
Iris Danfordiae	334	5
Iris reticulata	335	5
Iris Xiphium	335	6–7
Ixia maculata	336	7
Lachenalia aloides	337	9
Lapeirousia laxa	338	7
Leucojum autumnale	340	6
Leucojum vernum	340	4
Lilium auratum	342	5

Spring	Summer	Autumn	Under 12 in.	12–24 in.	Over 24 in.	Sun	Partial Shade
■	■	□	■	■	□	■	■
■			■				■
■			■				■
■	■			■			■
	■			■		■	
	■	□		■		■	
■					□	■	
■				■		■	■
■			■			■	
	■				□	■	
	■				□	■	
■	■			■		■	
	■				□	■	
	■			■		■	
■	■				□	■	
■			■			■	
	■		■			■	
	■			■		■	
	■				□	■	■
■	■			■	□	■	
■				■		■	
■				■		■	
■				■		■	■
■				■		■	
	■			■		■	
■			■			■	
■			■			■	
■			■	□		■	
■				□		■	
■	■		■			■	
■			■			■	
	■		■			■	
	■	□	■			■	
■			■	■		■	
	■				□	■	■

Flower Chart

	Page Number	Zone
Lilium canadense	342	4
Lilium lancifolium	343	4
Lilium longiflorum var. *eximium*	344	8
Lilium Martagon	344	4
Lilium philadelphicum	345	5
Lilium regale	345	4
Lilium speciosum	345	5
Lilium superbum	345	5
Lilium Hybrid Classes		
American hybrids	346	4–8
Asiatic hybrids	346	4–7
Aurelian hybrids	346	4–7
Candidum hybrids	347	5
Oriental hybrids	347	5
Lycoris radiata	348	7
Lycoris squamigera	348	5
Milla biflora	349	9
Moraea ramosissima	349	9
Muscari armeniacum	350	5
Narcissus Bulbocodium	352	6–7
Narcissus minor	353	5
Narcissus Pseudonarcissus	354	5
Narcissus Hybrid Classes		
Cyclamineus Narcissus	356	4–7
Double Narcissus	355	4–7
Jonquilla Narcissus	356	4–7
Large-cupped Narcissus	355	4–7
Poeticus Narcissus	356	5
Small-cupped Narcissus	355	4–7
Split-corona Narcissus	356	4–7
Tazetta Narcissus	356	7
Triandrus Narcissus	357	4–7
Trumpet Narcissus	356	4–7
Nerine sarniensis	358	9

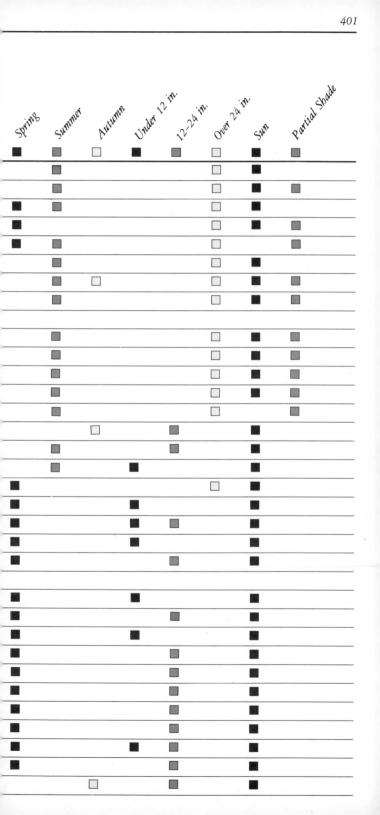

Spring	Summer	Autumn	Under 12 in.	12–24 in.	Over 24 in.	Sun	Partial Shade
■	▩	□	■	▩	□	■	▩
	▩				□	■	
	▩				□	■	▩
■	▩				□	■	
■					□	■	▩
■	▩				□		▩
	▩				□	■	
	▩	□			□	■	▩
	▩				□	■	▩
	▩				□	■	▩
	▩				□	■	▩
	▩				□	■	▩
	▩				□	■	▩
	▩				□		▩
		□		▩		■	
	▩			▩		■	
	▩		■			■	
■					□	■	
■			■			■	
■			■	▩		■	
■			■			■	
■				▩		■	
■			■			■	
■				▩		■	
■			■			■	
■				▩		■	
■				▩		■	
■				▩		■	
■				▩		■	
■				▩		■	
■		■		▩		■	
■				▩		■	
		□		▩		■	

Flower Chart

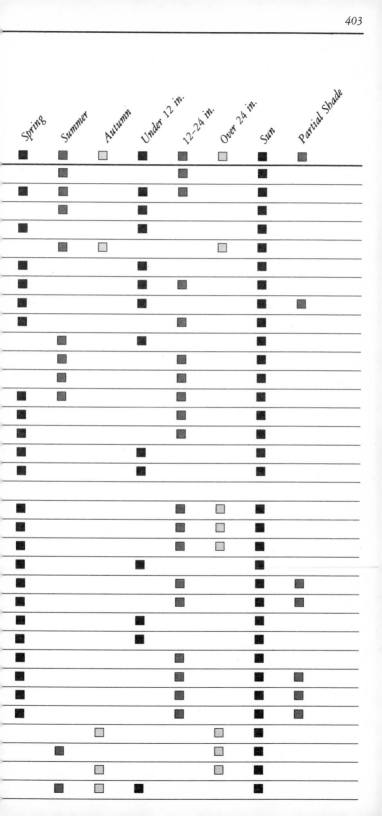

Spring | *Summer* | *Autumn* | *Under 12 in.* | *12–24 in.* | *Over 24 in.* | *Sun* | *Partial Shade*

Garden Design

There is something especially joyous about gardening with bulbs. Planting them is an easy task, performed at a time when there are fewer outdoor chores than there are in the rush of spring. Then, after months of long, cold winter, when you have almost forgotten about them, they send up their blooms in bright profusion all over your barren yard. For many people these flowers are always the first real sign of spring.

Most bulb plantings are permanent. Once they are in, they remain to be enjoyed year after year. And many bulbs are undaunted by cold climates—they depend on them, in fact, for a long, slow growth period during winter before they bloom. In short, bulbs are easy to grow, and even gardeners with minimal know-how can expect success.

Design Traditions

When planting bulbs, few people think about garden design, yet there is an eclectic tradition to draw on, from the tulip-filled courtyards of ancient Persia to the tidy raised beds of Renaissance Europe. In the United States, design inspiration comes largely from the dooryard gardens of our Colonial ancestors, where Crown Imperials, red tulips, yellow jonquils, and many other bulbs flourished in plantings grouped close to the house. In other early American gardens, bulbs were arranged in parterres, geometrical patterns with tidy paths between them. Today our public bulb displays are apt to follow the formal bedding style of Victorian times—tulips of a single color may be massed within a geometrical edging, or cannas planted in long borders. But in private gardens most people plant bulbs informally with little more purpose than that they be able to see the flowers as soon as they bloom in a spot where their early color can be most appreciated. Many bulbs do look best in free-form drifts along the side of a lawn or at the edge of a group of trees. Nonetheless there is just as much room for creativity in bulb gardening as there is with any kind of landscape design, once you consider the possibilities.

Basic Planning

Most of the basic principles of garden planning apply to any kind of garden. Choose colors that go well together, either closely related shades such as pink, red, and purple, or contrasting ones such as purple and yellow. Your own eye and color preferences will tell you when you have a good blend. You'll appreciate the effect the flowers create all the more in spring when the trees have few or no leaves and the colors really stand out. Keep foliage color and form in mind, too. Many bulbs, for example, have long, grasslike or swordlike leaves that you can emphasize by combining them with non-bulbous plants that have similar foliage, such as ornamental grasses or lily turf. Conversely, you might prefer to soften the linear effect by mixing the bulbs with plants that have totally different foliage, such as that of Jacob's ladder or lacy maidenhair fern. Whether you want a naturalized bulb planting or a formal bed, your composition should be harmonious and have a sense of balance. You also need to pay close attention to the heights and blooming times of the plants you choose. At times you may want a tall plant to come up and hide the foliage of another that has blossomed earlier. If both plants are to bloom together, however, make sure you have planted the taller one behind the shorter one. The only way to do this is to become familiar with the habits and needs of the plants you grow, and then plan the garden accordingly. Start with a quick sketch to get oriented before you go to work.

The following questions will help you decide which kind of garden is best for you.

Should Your Garden Be Formal or Informal?

This usually depends on the gardener's taste and the needs of the setting. One person might like tidy regularity and a dressed-up look; to another, this might be anathema. You may want the style of your garden to echo the style of your home. For a Victorian house in town you might prefer formal, stylized beds; for a country retreat, random drifts of casually planted bulbs might be better. But not necessarily—deliberate contrast can also be effective. For instance, you might want to soften the lines of the Victorian home with naturalized daffodils or add a touch of formality to the rustic Colonial house by planting some small, jewel-like, geometrical beds. Bulbs lend themselves well to either extreme. Tulips, for example, are often used in formal settings because of their uniformity. Nodding in the breeze *en masse,* they make a bold regiment of a planting. Other bulbs, especially daffodils, work well in natural plantings because they can stay in the ground from year to year, multiplying readily and requiring little maintenance. And planted deeply, many of the larger bulbs grow well in grassy or weedy areas without suffering.

Should It Be a One-Season or an All-Season Garden?

Most people think of bulb gardens as spring gardens. The most common, popular bulbs, such as narcissus, tulips, crocus, hyacinths, squills, and snowdrops, are all spring flowers. Planting a number of them together is a gorgeous way to start the blooming season.

But there are many bulbs for other seasons as well. You can plant a summer garden composed of gladiolus, alliums, cannas, and lilies. Or you can have color that lasts all season if you make successive plantings of gladiolus and use several varieties of lilies and alliums that bloom at different times. You can also plant colchicums, fall crocus, sternbergias, dahlias, and cyclamens and have a bulb garden that blooms in autumn.

A one-season garden is useful because it yields a very concentrated mass of color all at once. After it has finished blooming, you can

Garden Design

focus your attention on another part of your property. The spring bulb garden can be mowed over in midsummer once the foliage has completed its growth. A summer garden is especially appropriate for areas that receive only summer use, such as pools, patios, or vacation cottages. And a fall garden can be a bright spot after the summer garden has begun to peter out.

Do You Want to Mix Bulbs with Other Plants?

One advantage to growing bulbs by themselves is that you can choose from a wide variety that all have the same growth habits and needs. The summer terrace garden with non-hardy gladiolus and dahlias can be dug up all at once just before frost and the bulbs stored together in the cellar. If isolated from perennials and other plants that need to be dug up, replaced, or divided from time to time, bulb clumps can be left in the ground to mature and multiply undisturbed for an almost maintenance-free garden. But these are sometimes minor considerations. There is no reason why bulbs must always be kept by themselves. Mixed with other kinds of plants, they can work very well.

A blend of spring bulbs looks lovely planted alongside spring-blooming perennials such as Jacob's ladder and mertensia, or low-growing phloxes or violets. A ground cover such as myrtle or sweet woodruff can be overplanted on top of spring bulbs. It not only ties the garden together visually, it also provides interest after the bulb flowers fade, and often covers the withering foliage. Don't use a very dense, deep-rooted ground cover such as pachysandra, however; it will inhibit the growth of the bulbs. Sparser ground covers let the sun in to warm the soil in spring, helping the bulbs bloom earlier.

In perennial borders, taller bulbs work best when planted toward the back; there you will be able to see them bloom before most of the other plants have grown to their full height. Clumps of narcissus foliage at the rear can be hidden by asters, for instance, as the season progresses. Bulbs can thus be the first stage of a border's long-season bloom, with iris, oriental poppies, peonies, columbines, and early yellow daylilies starting to blossom just as the bulbs begin to fade. You can also plant bulbs in overlapping drifts throughout a perennial bed, or plant a few here and a few there between large clumps of perennial flowers. Both lilies and gladiolus are good choices for these situations because they are tall and showy but don't take up much space horizontally. Bulbs can also be grown in rock gardens or combined in other ways with annual and perennial flowers.

Do You Want Exotic Bulbs or Regular Standbys?

In addition to the half dozen or so tried and true bulbs that have been mentioned thus far, try growing others that are slightly less familiar. Good choices include snowflake, Greek anemone, windflower, glory-of-the-snow, colchicum, tuberous begonia, bulbous iris, and ranunculus. Beyond these, there are many other bulbs that might be considered exotic but that are well worth growing. Some can be grown in cold areas. Camassia, some alliums, trout lily, and calochortus are hardy to Zone 5. Montbretia, tigridia, and zephyranthes grow to Zone 7, Peruvian lilies to Zone 5 or 6, and the brodiaeas to Zone 5, 6, or 7, depending on the species. Others such as *Clivia miniata,* crinum lilies, Peruvian daffodil, and African corn lily are slightly more tropical. In colder zones, grow these plants in pots.

It is fun to find out about unusual bulbs and experiment with them. Don't relegate them to a spot far away from the house; plant them nearby, perhaps in containers on a terrace or deck where you can enjoy them at close range. Close at hand, it will be easier to remember to bring them indoors if frost threatens. Your favorite discoveries may become regular accent plants in years to come.

Where Should Bulbs Be Planted?

Choosing a site is important, especially if it is to be a permanent one. Planting several hundred bulbs takes time—you don't want to dig them up and replant them if you find that the site you have chosen isn't visible from the house. Pick a spot where the bulbs will make the most welcome show at the time you most want to enjoy them.

Most bulbs like sunny locations, but there are a number that tolerate or prefer light shade. Few if any like really deep shade. Bulbs will grow if they get sun for only part of the day, or if they receive high or dappled shade. (High shade is created by branches that are far off the ground and let in light but not direct sun.) Remember that even though the plants may flower before the trees leaf out, they usually need sun in the early summer for foliage growth.

Good drainage is particularly important for bulbs, because in wet soil they can rot. In some sites, animal damage can also be a problem. Using trial and error you will soon discover which bulbs can coexist with local wildlife. If you insist on growing bulbs that animals favor, put the bulbs in mesh cages, then bury them in the ground; the mesh will keep animals out and let stems sprout at the same time.

What Kind of Overall Plan Should You Choose?

Ideally the garden you plant is an expression of yourself, full of the flowers that you like the best. Deciding what to plant can be difficult if you are not aware of all the possibilities available. The following list of twenty gardens is a sample of the garden pictures you can assemble solely with bulbs, or with bulbs and other plants. Adjust these garden plans to your own needs. The first two are basic designs that include a number of common favorites and a few unusual bulbs. One is for sun, the other for partial shade.

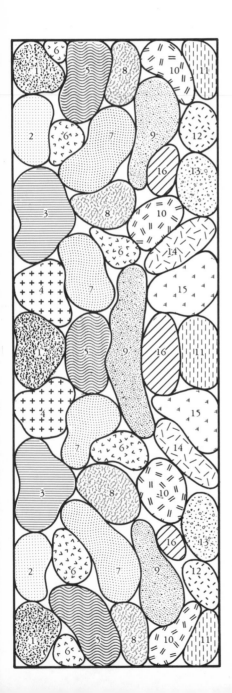

Key to Sunny Bulb Border

 1. Crown Imperial *Fritillaria imperialis*
 2. Speciosum Lily *Lilium speciosum*
 3. Giant Onion *Allium giganteum*
    Plant *A. Christophii* north of Zone 5
 4. Regal Lily *Lilium regale*
 5. Enchantment Lily *Lilium* 'Enchantment'
 6. Camassia *Camassia Quamash*
 7. Tall dahlia hybrids
 8. Tulip hybrids
 9. Narcissus hybrids
10. Hyacinth *Hyacinthus orientalis*
11. Crocus hybrids (spring)
12. Fall crocus *Crocus medius*
13. Glory-of-the-Snow *Chionodoxa Luciliae*
14. Dwarf dahlia hybrids
15. Dutch iris hybrids
16. Colchicum *Colchicum autumnale*

Garden Design

A Sunny Bulb Border

This 25-foot bed, made up entirely of bulbs, is designed to be colorful all season, from spring to fall. There will be weeks here and there when not much happens in the garden, when it hardly seems a blaze of color viewed from across the lawn. To make it brighter, add some showy annuals such as marigolds, zinnias, or cosmos. Even without these annual flowers, though, the bulb garden will be a pleasure to watch as it changes. And with the exception of the tulips and dahlias, the planting is a permanent one that will reward you year after year. It is an almost maintenance-free flower border.

The bed is six feet deep, allowing for some tall plants in the back—the spring-blooming Crown Imperials, with their spectacular heads of red and yellow flowers; white midsummer regal lilies; giant purple alliums; and late summer speciosum lilies, with their elegantly recurved red and white petals. In the middle ground are narcissus and tulips. Since this is a specimen border, choose special narcissus varieties; good choices include the pink 'Mrs. R. O. Backhouse', the double, fragrant 'Cheerfulness', or the big yellow 'King Alfred.' Select interesting tulips as well—pink cottage tulips, striped bizarres, flamboyant parrots, varieties that are almost black, and some plain red Darwins.

Also in the middle ground is spring-blooming camassia, an easily grown plant that bears loose spikes of blue flowers; the spikes will be visible above the narcissus and the tulip foliage. The red-orange 'Enchantment' lilies, a very easy and vigorous variety, bloom after the spring bulbs. Dahlia tubers are set in after the danger of frost has passed; place them between other bulb clumps in the middle and front of the border for a steady supply of summer color. Try combining colors and dahlia forms—collarettes, spoons, pompons, and so forth.

The earliest color in the garden comes from the bulbous iris, which is planted in front overlapping with crocus and glory-of-the-snow. Plant several kinds of bulbous iris for longer bloom. A combination of bright yellow crocus, blue glory-of-the-snow, and blue-purple iris would be beautiful. Hyacinth follows these in shades that will blend well with the narcissus, fritillarias, and tulips. Autumn crocus and colchicums will add later color to the dahlias and to the speciosum lily display.

Note that in planting a succession of bloom like this one, you need to distribute your color for any one time period across the length of the bed so that there is always something happening. For example, the speciosum lilies would still be visible if you planted them behind the dahlias, but you need their late color more at the ends of the bed, where most of the plants blossom early. If you want the bed to be completely permanent, omit the dahlias and plant more varieties of lilies, ones that will bloom the entire season. Plant only the new perennial tulips; although they are not as varied, they remain strong every year.

A Semi-Shaded Planting Under a Tree

This garden is composed of low-growing bulbs, all of which bloom in spring, and all of which tolerate some degree of shade. Most are small-flowered and subtle, rather than showy, and are best appreciated close up. Charming in a number of settings, they are planted here in an oval under an apple tree. Those nearest to the tree trunk receive the most shade and, because of the tree's roots, must tolerate the shallowest soil. Those at the far left have more sun and deeper soil. Those in between have dappled shade and some direct sun for a short time every day.

In contrast to the sunny bulb border, this is a naturalized planting. Its outline is free-form, and the bulbs are planted in intermingling patches. Most are varieties that are close to the original species, so that the garden looks like a collection of somewhat domesticated spring wildflowers.

Ringing the tree trunk are blue scilla. They tolerate real shade and are very easy to naturalize—if they begin to spread, let them. To the left are trout, or fawn, lilies. The Kaufmanniana tulips are one of several kinds of small early tulips. They are short, often marked in several bright colors, and bloom in a classic lily-flowered tulip shape, then open like water lilies. Choose a bright shade with red and orange to contrast with the blue scilla, grape-hyacinth, and yellow narcissus.

There are several dwarf narcissus you can choose from; these are angel's tears, which will grow from Zone 4 to Zone 10. Choose the yellow kind for this garden. Since narcissus appreciate some sun, they belong at the outer edge of the oval. Blue grape-hyacinths and white snowdrops are both old favorites that will take light shade. Also included are Guinea-Hen flowers, or checkered fritillarias, which have purple and white bell-like flowers on stems a foot tall, and Greek anemones (*Anemone blanda*), which make a flat carpet of pink, purple, blue, and white daisy-like blooms.

These plants need little or no care. The bed will give you color for at least six weeks in spring, beginning with the snowdrops and scilla and ending with the fritillarias and trout lilies. You can add other shade-tolerant bulbs as time goes by, or shade-tolerant perennials such as columbines and astilbe. Shade-loving annuals such as impatiens and wax begonias could also follow the bulbs without disturbing their growth.

A Rock Garden

Many bulbs make good additions to a rock garden. In fact, you could build one around bulbs exclusively, using species tulips, crocus, cyclamen, and almost any of the smaller bulbs. Create the illusion of a rocky hillside strewn with wildflowers by planting blue glory-of-the-snow and grape-hyacinth along with wild columbine, johnny-jump-ups, and other naturalized early perennials.

Garden Design

Key to Semi-Shaded Planting
1. Scilla *Scilla siberica*
2. Trout lily *Erythronium*
3. Guinea-Hen Flower *Fritillaria Meleagris*
4. Angel's Tears *Narcissus triandrus*
5. Snowdrop *Galanthus*
6. Kaufmanniana Tulip
7. Greek Anemone *Anemone blanda*
8. Grape-hyacinth *Muscari botryoides*

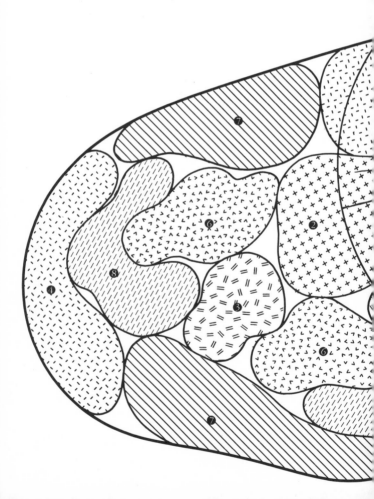

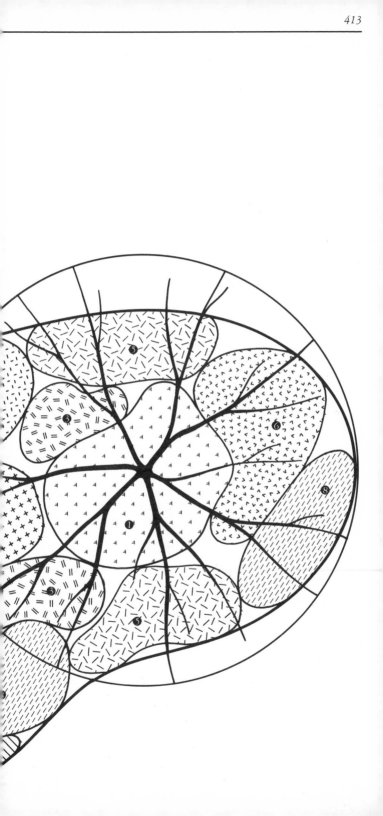

Garden Design

A Terrace Garden
Exotic specimen bulbs that might seem lost in a massed planting are ideal for a terrace. Close at hand, you will be able to give them the attention they require. Although you can grow common favorites there as well, it is fun to plant some tropical varieties either in a bed or in containers, then dig them up and store them over the winter if you live in a cool climate. Summer-blooming bulbs make a grand show just when you are using the terrace the most. Try combining tuberous begonias, spider lilies, Guernsey lilies, ranunculus, and agapanthus. For all-season color, precede these with spring bulbs in pots. When autumn arrives, replace the summer plants with potted chrysanthemums.

Bulbs in the Lawn
Scilla is the ultimate lawn flower—it spreads quickly and pervasively if it likes the site and it doesn't mind if you mow over it after it blooms. Winter aconites are flowers whose foliage withers early; once the foliage is gone, you can mow over them. Narcissus, crocus, and other bulbs can be grown in drifts in the lawn if you are willing to mow around them until midsummer so that the foliage can have its necessary seasonal growth. To create a natural look with narcissus, pick up handfuls of the bulbs and toss them in a random way. Plant the bulbs wherever they fall.

A Summer Pool Garden
Bulbs could be the foundation of a poolside garden, producing tidy, easy-care flowers to enjoy during summer, a leisurely time of year. Group them in pots, in small beds, or even in a long border in front of the fence that surrounds the pool. Use the same bulbs recommended for a terrace garden, or plant gladiolus, tigridias, and a succession of summer lilies.

A Perennial Border with Bulbs
You can easily incorporate bulbs into perennial borders. Mass narcissus toward the back of the border and drop in tulips and lilies here and there. Smaller spring bulbs also make a good edging along with low-growing perennials.

Formal Bulb Beds
To create a formal, geometric look, plant bulbs in concentric circles with the tallest in the center. Or choose a single flower—yellow tulips, for example—and plant it in a long border, edging it with early-blooming flowers such as pansies.

Bulbs Naturalized on a Bank
Grassy banks that are too steep to mow are ideal spots for naturalized narcissus, hyacinths, crocus, colchicums, and almost any

other vigorous, winter-hardy bulb. They not only lend color to the bank, but help prevent erosion.

Bulbs Along a Fence or Wall

For a formal effect, group gladiolus in front of a stone wall. For a more casual feeling, plant a drift of alliums just behind a split-rail fence at the edge of a meadow. Small, very early bulbs such as winter aconite benefit from being grown next to the wall of a house (preferably a wall that faces south), since the warmth from the building's foundation helps them to bloom early.

Bulbs in a Shady Spring Perennial Garden

Shade-tolerant bulbs complement a bed of primroses, mertensia, Jacob's ladder, dwarf bleeding heart, and violets. Keep color combinations in mind while you plant. Try grouping white pansies with purple *Iris reticulata,* blue periwinkles with bright yellow tulips, a pink-to-purple garden of bleeding heart, violets, columbines, and assorted pink to purple tulips.

A Dooryard Garden

Spring bulbs are especially welcome near the entrance to a home. They are the first sign of spring, greeting both those who live in the home and those who visit it. Even with established foundation plantings, you can usually find room for crocuses, hyacinths, or other bulbs in front of the shrubbery. One of the narcissus collections made up of many different varieties would be especially beautiful here where you can really see each one.

A Shrub Border with Bulbs

Mass bulbs against shrubs for a showy effect, planting those that complement the greenery. Gladiolus are a poor choice because they are spiky; it's better to use tulips, tuberous begonias, and a mass of colchicums. Plant enough of them so they don't look spotty.

A Cutting Garden

Bulbs make good cut flowers, so grow them in quantity and you will be able to cut as many as you like without depleting the outdoor display. You might even plant a garden just for bouquets in a secluded part of your property. Fill it with masses of tulips, hyacinths, lilies, and gladiolus.

An Herb Garden

Small spring bulbs make good precursors to herbs. They bloom before the tender annual herbs such as basil are sown and before perennial herbs such as tarragon and sage have become the large, sprawling plants of midsummer. If you grow your herbs in raised beds, the bulbs will bloom especially early, since soil will warm up quickly there.

Woodland Paths
Bulbs that tolerate some shade can be naturalized beautifully along an informal woodland path—they will come up despite the presence of some grass and weeds. Common hybrids are bright and cheerful, but also consider using the wilder looking species such as erythroniums and the summer-blooming wood lily.

A Lily Border
The true lilies (*Liliums*) are so varied and they bloom at such different times that it is possible to have them in continuous bloom for several months. Make sure that the tallest ones such as Canada lilies or tiger lilies are in the background and the smaller ones in the foreground. Overplant them with a ground cover such as myrtle, or with epimedium, a good choice if you are planting the bulbs in the dappled light that lilies enjoy.

An All-Tulip Garden
A tulip garden will not bloom as long as a lily garden will, but you can still plan on up to six weeks of color if you grow early, middle, and late varieties. Vary the shapes and colors, too; use some tulips that are cup-shaped, others that are lily-flowered, and some parrots. Plant the smallest in front and the tallest in the rear.

An All-Iris Garden
Combine the early bulbous iris with the later bearded, Siberian, and Japanese irises. Your garden will bloom from early spring to early summer. It is a delightful experience to see the basic iris in so many different forms and colors.

An Indoor Windowsill Garden
There are many different ways to display forced bulbs indoors because you can control the time they bloom. Start them at intervals and you can have a succession of pots in bloom through the winter and early spring. Or try instead to create one massed display on a given date to celebrate a holiday, a family wedding, or a visit from someone special. Use bulbs that would not normally bloom together. A window with bright light but no direct sun is ideal for this garden, which is, perhaps, the cheeriest one of all.

Forcing Bulbs

To have beautiful spring flowers blooming for you in the dead of winter is surely a luxury—but with bulbs, it is a luxury within anyone's reach. Narcissus, tulips, and hyacinth will bloom for you indoors if you apply a little patience, skill, and dedication.

The principle behind forcing is to trick the bulbs into blooming by putting them through a series of climatic conditions that mimic the plants' normal seasonal cycle. Given a certain number of weeks at cold temperatures, followed by a warming period, bulbs will bloom even though spring may still be many weeks away.

The easiest bulbs to force are tulips, narcissus, hyacinth, and crocus. Dutch Amaryllis are also easy to force, but are grown differently. There are cultivars produced specifically for indoor forcing; most nurseries will have these for sale in the fall. These varieties are also offered and recommended in catalogues.

Medium

The growing medium you choose for forcing will determine how much damage the bulb will incur. All bulbs will bloom best in soil rather than water alone or water and pebbles. If you force a bulb in water, it will use up all of its food resources to bloom, and will have to be thrown away afterward. Bulbs forced in soil and soil mixes can be transplanted into the garden, but it may be two years before they have a normal bloom.

Dormancy

A bulb goes through three stages before it blossoms. Although the period of time for each stage is shortened in forcing, success is achieved only when the bulb completes each of these stages.

The first stage is dormancy, which for outdoor spring bulbs normally takes place in summer weather. Bulbs that you purchase in late summer or fall for forcing will be dormant when you get them.

Root Development

Stage two is the root development of the bulb. To ensure healthy roots, keep bulbs at this stage for a minimum of 12 weeks for the early spring-flowering bulbs (crocus, daffodils, and hyacinth), and a minimum of 15 weeks for later spring-flowering bulbs like tulips. Without sufficient root development bulbs may sprout, but the blooms will usually fall off before they open.

To promote root development, a growing medium should have excellent drainage and yet retain moisture consistently. Plant the bulbs in ordinary garden soil or in a mixture of one part potting soil, one part peat moss, and one part perlite or vermiculite. The pot you use should be only slightly larger than the bulb itself; if you are planting three bulbs to a pot, you will need a container about eight to ten inches in diameter. (Special bulb pans are available for this purpose. They are half as tall as they are wide and designed to hold up tall plants by lessening the risks of tipping over.) Bulbs should

Forcing Bulbs

be placed about half an inch to an inch below the surface of the soil. If there is a neck or sprout, it should be visible on the surface.

When potted, the bulbs should be kept at a temperature of around 50° F for three to four weeks, and then at a colder temperature of 35 to 43° F for an additional eight to 12 weeks, depending on the bulbs you are growing.

If you start early enough in the fall, you can bury your pots outdoors in a shaded, protected spot; as the days grow cooler, the ground temperature will decrease and keep the bulbs on schedule. Cover the pots with three to four inches of soil and a thick layer of insulating mulch. You can also put the pots in a cold frame and cover them on the sides and top with three to four inches of perlite or any material that offers good insulation. The pots will not need watering until you bring them out, after the prescribed 12 to 15 weeks. Other solutions are unheated garages or cellars; or, if you have room for pots in your refrigerator, your bulbs will do very well there.

Sprout Development
The third stage in a bulb's life is sprout development, which occurs after you bring the bulbs into a warmer environment. Bring indoors only those bulbs that you want to have bloom right away; you can prolong your indoor blooming season by staggering the time at which you bring in the pots.

When you dig up the pots from outdoor locations, remove the soil and insulation gently; there may be tender sprouts already coming up that can be injured. Place the pots in good indirect light in a place where temperatures reach between 55 and 66° F. (Hyacinths can take temperatures up to 73° F and crocus prefer temperatures that do not exceed 60° F.) From this point until they bloom, the plants must be well watered. After about two weeks, the sprouts should be close to six inches tall and ready to bloom.

Blooming
Move the pots to the coolest sunny windowsill you have, and leave them there until you start to see color in the flower buds. When this color appears, move the pots back to a cool spot with indirect light. Doing this will help the flowers last longer once they bloom.

Dormancy Again
After the flowers die, cut off the stems but retain the basal leaves. Put the pots in a cool, sunny spot outdoors and gradually decrease the amount of water you give them until the leaves die. The bulbs will go into dormancy, and you can store them in a dry, well-ventilated place with temperatures between 60 and 70° F. In fall, at the normal planting time, you can transplant them into the garden. Remember that they will not produce good blooms for a couple of

seasons, so you may want to let them recuperate in an out-of-the-way spot.

Special Methods for Forcing Crocus and Hyacinth

Crocus and hyacinth can be grown in water alone, although they will not bloom again. There are special jars designed for forcing these bulbs that hold the bulb above the water and let the roots grow in the water. To help prevent algal growth, you should place a piece of natural charcoal in the water.

Keep the jars in a cool, dark place until the roots are fully developed. Bring crocus into light when the sprouts are about two inches tall; bring hyacinth out when the sprouts are four inches tall and the flower buds are visible between leaf sheaths.

Different varieties of *Narcissus Tazetta* are well adapted for forcing in water with pebbles and a piece of charcoal. The plants wrap their roots around the pebbles to support their tall stems. As soon as the sprouts emerge, move the plants to the light, or they will stretch until they can no longer support themselves. If you force the narcissus in water, discard it after it blooms.

Dutch Amaryllis are sold for forcing, usually pre-potted and ready to grow. Keep watering more and more frequently as the bulbs grow, and rotate the pot to keep the stems from leaning toward the light. If you live in a warm area, you can plant these bulbs in the garden after they bloom. In colder climates, water and fertilize the bulbs until the leaves die. Then let the bulbs alone through the dormant stage—until late November—and then begin watering them again for a holiday bloom several weeks later.

Cut Flowers

Part of the fun of growing bulbs is bringing some of that good cheer indoors to brighten a dark corner or adorn the center of a table. Even a few daffodils in a jar on the kitchen counter can be a daily reminder that spring has arrived. Fortunately, many bulbs make very good cut flowers. Most have long, straight stems that hold water well and are easy to arrange, and there's little or no foliage that you need to remove.

Grow enough bulbs so that you can pick bouquets without depleting your outdoor display. Cutting flowers is good for the plants—it channels their energy away from seed production and into bulb growth instead. If your supply of blooms is limited, pick those whose stems are bent over or face the wrong way or those positioned in back of the bed where they can't be seen. If possible, cut them just as they are starting to open, then immediately put them in a generous amount of warm water. The kind of cut you make is not very important, and just plain tap water will do.

My favorite way to arrange bulb flowers is in a wide, fairly shallow bowl. I use a frog in the center to hold the flowers, since the sides of a low bowl will not hold them in place the way those of a tall vase would. If it is a glass bowl, I use a glass frog in the shape of a half-sphere, with holes cut in it to receive the stems. If the bowl is opaque, a frog made of a metal grid will do just as well.

Starting with some tall, upright stems I place them in the center of the frog, then gradually work downward with the shorter ones, letting the lowest stems lean over the edges of the bowl a little. I try to create a big ball of color that is very open and airy, where each blossom seems suspended alone, not leaning on anything around it. A frog, or florist's clay, is the best way to achieve this effect. When you are arranging flowers other than bulbs that have plenty of leaves, you can use the foliage to separate the flowers. With bulbs, however, the foliage is left in the ground, so a frog is helpful.

There are few bouquets quite as lovely as a mixture of daffodils and tulips in different shapes and colors. Grape-hyacinths are a good addition because they add a blue component to the warm red-yellow-orange-pink scheme, and because their dainty sprays are a good contrast to all those globes and trumpets. If picked correctly, grape-hyacinth stems are just long enough to be worked in at the middle or lower parts of the arrangement. After grape-hyacinths have stopped blooming in the garden, true hyacinths are also attractive and they are fragrant, too. It is wonderful to watch the tulips open—as the days go by the arrangement actually gets fuller and more beautiful.

There are many other ways to arrange cut bulbs. A tall vertical vase filled with red or yellow tulips is a beautiful accent in a room. Or fill a very wide and shallow bowl with the flowers of many small bulbs such as scilla, puschkinia, anemone, lily of the valley, grape-hyacinth, and star-of-Bethlehem. For bouquets later in the season, summer bulbs make good cut flowers—allium, gladiolus, agapanthus, and many of the lilies. These large, long-stemmed flowers make grand bouquets and are effective either alone or mixed with non-bulbous flowers such as campanulas, shasta daisies, phlox, roses, and asters. Try using frothy flowers such as Lady's mantle or baby's breath as a foil for the larger, heavier bulb blossoms.

A few cautionary words about lilies: Some have stamens with a pollen that smears and stains everything it touches. These can be snipped off. And some, such as regal lilies, have such a strong, overpowering scent that you may want to keep the bouquet at a distance.

Not all bouquets need to be lavish mixtures. You can make artful arrangements using a few unusual bulbs—several mariposa tulips, for example, or tritonias, or parrot tulips. Here the idea is "less is more"—studied simplicity. Keep in mind the spirit of Japanese flower arranging, even if you are not versed in that art. But don't fuss too much or the results can be stilted and your bouquets overworked. The best way to create a flower arrangement is the way you would create a watercolor painting—concentrating intensely for a brief period of time and knowing intuitively when to stop.

Use your own eye and sense of beauty to make balanced displays. Some design principles are obvious—echo red blossoms on the left with some on the right, and so forth. And use your imagination. What would you add to a stark daffodil display when you want some softness, but not much foliage has leafed out yet? A few twigs of fresh, green barberry might work, or some laurel. Try using pussy willows, too. Although they are normally placed alone in dry vases to keep them from blooming, they are actually pretty when they are placed in water and lose their "fur," sprouting fuzzy yellow flowers. After all, a bouquet is really constantly changing; it's not a fixed tableau. Watch it every day, discarding flowers that have faded, changing the water in the bowl often, adding fresh flowers to fill in holes, and snipping the ends of the long-blooming blossoms with scissors.

Finally, don't forget fragrance. If you always include a few hyacinths, double daffodils, freesias, or other scented blooms, your bouquet will be a delight even in the dark.

Cut Flowers

When you arrange flowers, the vase you use is almost as important as the flowers you select. Try a frog for small flowers like grape-hyacinths and anemones.

*Low, rounded vases are
a good choice for large,
full arrangements.*

Cut Flowers

Spikes of colorful gladiolus in a round glass bowl create a relaxed yet sophisticated arrangement.

A Japanese-inspired
arrangement might
consist of just a few
bulbous iris in a low,
flat vase.

Cut Flowers

The long, straight stems of many bulb flowers make them ideal for simple, elegant arrangements; a single stem or two of freesia in a tall glass cylinder is very graceful.

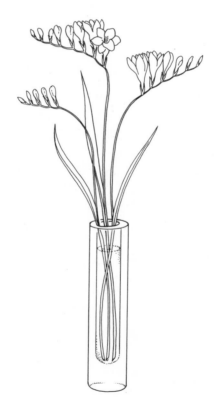

*A full bouquet of
handsome, exotic lilies
shows to best advantage
in a large crystal vase.*

Garden Diary

Gardeners are probably no more forgetful than anyone else. But when so much of your product is ephemeral, or spends most of the year hidden away underground, it's almost impossible to keep track of a garden without making notes. In April you may see a spot that cries out for a handful of *Puschkinia,* but by the time the bulb catalogues arrive in August, that spot will be filled with late-blooming flowers and you'll be hard pressed to remember your April inspiration. Nor will it do you any good to remember it in the middle of winter—garden opportunities, once lost, are often lost for a whole year.

Thus some sort of record keeping is a great boon to gardeners. It doesn't really matter what form your notes take—whether you make them on an engagement calendar, an ordinary notebook, or on scraps of paper that you throw into an envelope. But the best system by far is to keep a garden diary, or journal. Ideally, the journal should be attractive, so you'll enjoy using it, and have a water-resistant cover, so you can take it with you into the garden. Graph paper is useful for keeping an accurate diagram of your land and your planting beds; doing this will save you from plunging a spade right through your choicest daffodil bulbs.

Unless you are a compulsive record keeper or going into the plant business, there is really no need to make daily entries. But just about anything is grist for a personal garden journal; here are suggestions of some subjects you should cover:

Weather
Record the last frost of spring and the first frost of fall; unusually warm or cold weather; heavy snowfalls, or the absence of snow; and any very unusual weather phenomena. Although the weather has less impact on bulb culture than it does on other plants, it is unlikely that you will grow bulbs exclusively.

Bulb Orders
Keep a record of what you order, when you ordered it, when it arrived, and the name of the supplier. When your bulbs arrive, inspect them for quality and health. Were they as large as promised? Once bulbs are planted, you have no recourse if they don't grow satisfactorily, but bulbs that arrive in poor condition should be returned to the supplier.

Planting Records
Supplement these notes with marks on your plot diagrams, writing down the variety and number of bulbs in each spot. Doing this will help you estimate the success of each type, and to calculate the effects of weather. Imagine, for example, that you put nine tulips in at a certain spot, and only three survived; checking your weather notes, you see that the fall was unseasonably warm and humid. You might then conclude that the bulbs rotted.

A Flowering Record

This is the place to record what bulbs and plants bloom together, and which bulbs sent up fewer flowering stalks this year than last. If you suspect that a planting may be in need of division, count this year's flowers. Then next year, if there are fewer, dig up the bulbs after they bloom and give them more room. If your flowering record shows that your earliest bulbs aren't as early as you would like, consider changing or improving their site or buying earlier varieties.

Photographs

In some ways, photographs make the best records of all. Be sure to date your pictures and list the names of the cultivars. This information will prove valuable when it is time to order more bulbs.

Soil Amendments

Record the kind and amount of fertilizer, lime, and other soil amendments you use; be sure to include the dates and rate of application.

Animal and Insect Problems

Insects rarely attack bulbs, but larger creatures can cause significant damage. If none of the lily bulbs you put in last fall has come up at all, you may have rodents. If a flower stalk is bitten off, you may have rabbits or deer. Keep a record of which repellents and insecticides you use, the rate of application, and whether or not they did the job.

Propagation Records

Here's the place to be compulsively precise. You will want to note exactly when you plant an offset or sow seed, if and when it germinates, and the temperature, humidity, and soil conditions.

Bulb Forcing Timetable

Like your propagation records, this needs to be precise. Make a note of the date you pot bulbs and how long they need to be kept cold. Note when you should take them into warmth and light, and finally, the date on which they first flower. You can then modify this schedule for a slightly different time of bloom next year.

Other People's Ideas

With a paper clip or staples, you can attach significant articles or newspaper clippings, or even the instructions that sometimes come with bulbs, to the pages of your journal.

The more use you make of your diary, the more valuable it will be. Once you begin to keep careful records, you will no doubt find many ways in which your garden diary will help you to avoid mistakes—and, best of all, to repeat and improve on the successes of your garden.

Pests & Disease

Because plant pests and diseases are a fact of life for a gardener, it is helpful to become familiar with common pests and diseases in your area and to learn how to control them.

Symptoms of Plant Problems

Because the same general symptoms are associated with many diseases and pests, some experience is needed to determine their causes.

Diseases

Both fungi and bacteria are responsible for a variety of diseases ranging from leafspots and wilts to root rot, but bacterial diseases usually make the affected plant tissues appear wetter than fungi do. Diseases caused by viruses and mycoplasma, often transmitted by aphids and leafhoppers, display such symptoms as mottled yellow or deformed leaves and stunted growth.

Insect Pests

Numerous insects attack plants. Sap-sucking insects—including aphids, leafhoppers, and scale insects—suck plant juices. The affected plant becomes yellow, stunted, and misshapen. Aphids and scale insects produce honeydew, a sticky substance that attracts ants and sooty mold fungus growth. Other pests with rasping-sucking mouthparts, such as thrips and spider mites, scrape plant tissue and then suck the juices that well up in the injured areas.

Leaf-chewers, namely beetles, consume plant leaves, whole or in part. Borers tunnel into shoots and stems, and their young larvae consume plant tissue, weakening the plant. Some insects, such as various grubs and maggots, feed on roots, weakening or killing the plant.

Nematodes

Microscopic roundworms called nematodes are other pests that attack roots and cause stunting and poor plant growth. Some nematodes produce galls on roots and others produce them on leaves.

Environmental Stresses

Some types of plant illness result from environment-related stress, such as severe wind, drought, flooding, or extreme cold. Other problems are caused by salt toxicity, rodents, birds, nutritional deficiencies or excesses, pesticides, or damage from lawnmowers. Many of these injuries are avoidable if you take proper precautions.

Controlling Plant Problems

Purchase bulbs that are firm and robust, not shriveled and spongy, then make sure you store them properly once you get them home. If you are buying plants, check the leaves and stems for dead areas or off-color and stunted tissue. If possible, buy disease-resistant varieties. Before you plant your bulbs, prepare the soil properly.

Routine Preventives
By cultivating the soil routinely you will expose insects and disease-causing organisms to the sun and thus lessen their chances of surviving in your garden. In the fall be sure to destroy infested or diseased plants, remove dead leaves and flowers, and clean up plant debris. Do not add diseased or infested material to the compost pile. Spray plants with water from time to time to dislodge insect pests and remove suffocating dust. Pick off the larger insects by hand. To discourage fungal leafspots and blights, always water plants in the morning and allow the leaves to dry off before nightfall. For the same reason, provide adequate air circulation around leaves and stems by spacing plants properly.
Weeds provide a home for insects and diseases, so pull them up or use herbicides. But do not apply herbicides, including "weed-and-feed" lawn preparations, too close to flower beds. Herbicide injury may cause elongated, straplike, or downward-cupping leaves. Spray weed-killers when there is little air movement, but not on a very hot, dry day.

Insecticides and Fungicides
To protect plant tissue from injury due to insects and diseases, a number of insecticides and fungicides are available. However, few products control diseases due to bacteria, viruses, and mycoplasma. Pesticides are usually either "protectant" or "systemic" in nature. Protectants protect uninfected foliage from insects or disease organisms, while systemics move through the plant and provide some therapeutic or eradicant action as well as protection. Botanical insecticides such as pyrethrum and rotenone have a shorter residual effect on pests, but are considered less toxic and generally safer for the user and the environment than inorganic chemical insecticides. Biological control through the use of organisms like *Bacillus thuringiensis* (a bacterium toxic to moth and butterfly larvae) is effective and safe.
Recommended pesticides may vary to some extent from region to region. Consult your local Cooperative Extension Service or plant professional regarding the appropriate material to use. Always check the pesticide label to be sure that it is registered for use on the pest and plant with which you are dealing. Follow the label concerning safety precautions, dosage, and frequency of application.

Recognizing Pests and Diseases
Learning to recognize the insects and diseases that plague garden plants is a first step toward controlling them. The chart on the following pages describes the most common pests and diseases that attack bulbs, the damage they cause, and control measures to take.

Garden Pest or Disease

Aphids

Borers

Botrytis Blight

Bulb Maggots

Bulb Mites

Description	Damage	Controls
Tiny green, brown, or reddish, pear-shaped, soft-bodied insects in clusters on buds, shoots, and undersides of leaves.	Suck plant juices, causing stunted or deformed blooms and leaves. Some transmit plant viruses. Secretions attract ants.	Spray with malathion or rotenone late in the day in order not to kill bees. Encourage natural predators such as ladybugs.
Wormlike larvae feed on leaves and move down to bulbs or rhizomes. Bacterial soft rot may follow.	Spotted, water-soaked and ragged leaves. Leaves and bulbs or rhizomes may rot due to bacteria.	Clean up foliage and stalks in fall. Spray malathion or carbaryl when fans start to grow in spring.
Gray-brown spots on plant parts. Woolly fungal growth from spots. Common in humid or wet weather. Also called gray mold.	Buds fail to open and are covered with gray fungal growth. Leaves may wither or fall.	Remove and destroy infected plant parts. Improve air circulation around plants. Spray with Botran or zineb.
White or yellow fly larvae, feeding on bulbs.	Feed on bulbs, causing soft, spongy rot. Leaves become yellow and twisted. Plant stops growing.	Discard soft or spongy bulbs. Soak firm bulbs in hot water at 110° F for 2½ hours.
Tiny white arachnids found on both rotting and healthy bulbs.	Feed on bulbs, causing injury; rots may follow.	Discard infested bulbs. Soak healthy bulbs in hot water at 110° F for 1 hour.

Garden Pest or Disease

Bulb Rots

Leaf-feeding Beetles

Leafspots

Nematodes

Powdery Mildew

Description	Damage	Controls
Fungal or bacterial rots of bulbs in soil or storage. Mold may cover bulbs.	Plants turn yellow, wilt, and die, or do not come up. Bulbs become soft and mushy or smaller and hard.	Discard affected bulbs. Plant healthy bulbs in clean soil. Store bulbs in cool, dry conditions.
Hard-shelled, oval to oblong insects on leaves, stems, and flowers. Common beetles include Japanese, cucumber, and rose chafer.	Chew plant parts leaving holes. Larvae of some feed on roots.	Handpick and destroy. Spray with Sevin or rotenone.
Spots on leaves or flowers caused by fungi encouraged by humid or wet weather.	Tan, brown, or black spots on leaves or flowers. If serious, leaves may drop from plant.	Increase air circulation around plant. Remove badly diseased leaves and flowers. Spray with zineb or benomyl if serious.
Microscopic roundworms, usually associated with roots. Cause various diseases.	Stunted, off-color plants that do not respond to water or fertilizer. Minute galls may be present on roots.	Remove and destroy badly afflicted plants. Nematocides are available for use around valuable plants.
White, powdery fungal disease on aerial plant parts.	Reddish spots and powdery fungal growth. Leaves may be distorted and drop. Stems, buds, and flowers are also affected.	Remove badly infected leaves. Increase air circulation. Spray with Karathane, benomyl, or sulfur.

Garden Pest or Disease

Slugs

Thrips

Viruses

Wilts

Wireworms

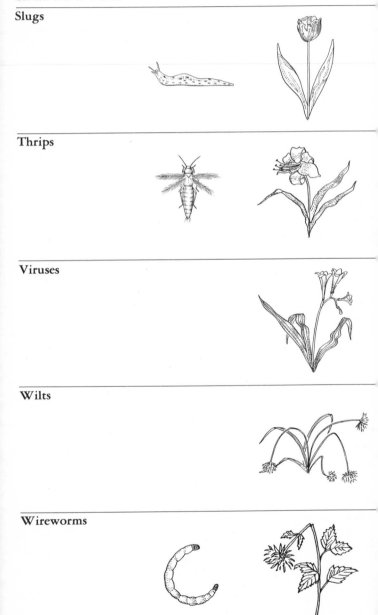

Description	Damage	Controls
Gray, slimy, soft-bodied mollusks without a hard outer shell. Leave slime trails on leaves; found in damp places.	Feed at night, rasping holes in leaves.	Trap slugs using stale beer in pie pans. Eliminate trash and hiding places around garden. Use bait containing metaldehyde. Pick off.
Very small, slender, brown, yellow, or black insects with narrow fringed wings. Rasping-sucking mouthparts.	Scrape and suck plant tissue. Cause browning, white flecking, and gumminess. Sometimes deform flowers, buds, and leaves.	Remove infested flowers and buds. Spray with malathion, or dust with sulfur or diatomaceous earth.
Various diseases, including mosaics, that cause off-color, stunted plants. May be transmitted by aphids.	Crinkled, mottled, deformed leaves, stunted plants, poor growth.	Remove and destroy infected plants. Control the insect vector (aphids) if present. Buy only healthy plants.
Soil-borne fungal diseases that cause wilting, stunting, and eventual death of plants.	Leaves turn yellow and entire plant may wilt and die. Roots may rot.	Remove infected plants. Practice crop rotation. Use resistant varieties.
Wiry, brown, wormlike beetle larvae, feeding on bulbs and stems in the soil.	May attack bulbs, roots, and stems, resulting in plant injury and death.	Treat soil or bulbs with diazinon before planting. Practice crop rotation.

Buying Bulbs

It is possible, by making a careful choice of species and varieties, to have a succession of bulbs in flower in the garden from earliest spring till winter sets in. From the first snowdrops of the season to the last autumn colchicums, bulbs are available in garden centers or by mail near the time it is appropriate to plant them.

Planting Bulbs by the Season
Spring-flowering bulbs are the most popular and are usually sold in late summer and autumn. As a rule, the earlier in spring a bulb blooms, the earlier in the fall you should plant it. To be sure of having your first choice, place your order as soon as the catalogue arrives, or buy bulbs in the garden center as soon as they are on display. They can be kept in a cool, dry place until planting time; but it is best to get them into the ground as soon as possible in September or October, especially in coldest climates. In less frigid areas, a delay until November is not harmful, as bulbs will continue to make root growth until soil temperatures fall to 40° F.
Late-flowering lily bulbs do not arrive at suppliers until November because the bulbs are slow to ripen and cannot be dug from the fields earlier. For this reason, it is advisable to wait until spring to order and plant lilies if you live in a very cold area.
Summer-flowering bulbs can be planted in spring. Many of these are frost-tender and should be kept under cover until late May, except in the warmest parts of the country.
Bulbs for the autumn garden, such as *Sternbergia* and *Colchicum,* should be planted as soon as they are available in August and September. The time between planting and flowering is very short for these autumn bloomers, so give them as much time as possible to develop good roots in the soil.
Bulbs can also be grown from seed. This method is slow, however, and it can take several years for plants to reach flowering size.
No matter what types of bulbs you choose, buy a substantial number of each kind. Individually they make a small statement in the garden, but their visual impact is greatly increased if they are planted in masses. For the most part bulbs are an inexpensive, long-term investment in your garden, and you get good value for your money.

Buying from Garden Centers
Garden centers generally stock the less unusual kinds of bulbs, and buying them in person gives you the advantage of handpicking the largest, healthiest-looking ones. Some large bulbs are also heavy, and by buying locally you will avoid shipping charges, which can be substantial.
Choose bulbs that appear smooth and firm and feel heavy for their size. A lightweight bulb is probably dried out and not viable; one that feels soft to the touch has rot.
The exceptions to this rule are anemone and winter aconite bulbs,

which will appear shriveled when bought; they will benefit from an overnight soaking in water before planting. They are a bit more difficult than some other bulbs to reestablish, so you may expect a slightly higher loss rate.

Avoid Sprouted Bulbs

It is best to avoid bulbs that are already showing signs of green tip growth, unless you are buying them pre-potted. Typically bulbs are planted when fully dormant, and the presence of green stems or leaves indicates the bulb has started into active top growth before it has established a root system that is adequate to support that growth.

Diseased Bulbs

Check bulbs for signs of disease or insect damage and discard any that are questionable. Diseased or insect-ridden bulbs will not perform well in your garden, and they can introduce problems to other plants already present. As a general rule, you should throw away bulbs that are soft to the touch or show signs of rot or other disease; but if a rare or expensive bulb is in questionable condition, it may be worth the effort to salvage it. Cut away the affected part with a sharp knife, then dust the cut surface with powdered sulfur or dip the bulb in a solution of fungicide, such as Benlate. Let the bulb dry before planting.

Buying by Mail

Many mail-order specialists offer a wider selection of bulbs— including rare species and varieties—than do garden centers. Mail-order specialists usually issue descriptive catalogues to help you plan your purchase in advance. A listing of some of these suppliers appears on page 441 of this book.

Do not be influenced too much by low prices, as bulbs offered at very inexpensive rates may be small and take an additional year to bloom. Most bulbs are inexpensive enough to justify buying the largest size.

What to Do About Faulty Bulbs

Occasionally one or two bulbs in a mail-order batch will be dried out or have evidence of bruises, and these can just be discarded. If, however, there is large-scale damage or many of the bulbs appear diseased, notify the supplier at once. Most mail-order firms are reliable sources, and they want repeat business from their customers. They should offer replacement bulbs or a refund, but it would be well to determine in advance the firm's policy concerning refunds.

A more difficult problem is one that usually doesn't reveal itself for some months—that is, if the bulbs supplied were not true to name. Nevertheless, and despite the time lag involved, misidentification is a valid complaint and should be pursued with the supplier.

Buying Bulbs

If your bulbs do not come up in due course, it does not necessarily mean they were "bad." Dig up a few to see if you can determine the cause. If the bulbs appear soft, they have probably rotted because of poor soil drainage. If you can't even find the bulbs, a hungry rodent was probably the culprit.

Plant Societies
Uncommon species are frequently not available through regular retail sources, but bulbs and seeds of rarities can sometimes be located through plant societies (such as the American Daffodil Society, the American Dahlia Society, and the American Rock Garden Society). If you have an interest in a particular plant group, consider joining a plant society; membership may include newsletters, notice of meetings, and exchanges of seeds and information. Addresses for these special interest groups can be found in the classified section of most gardening magazines.

Importing Your Own Bulbs
Travelers returning from abroad, especially from Holland, are often tempted to bring home bulbs but are unsure if doing so is permitted by the U.S. Department of Agriculture. The brightly colored little packages at the airport do make enticing souvenirs. According to the USDA Animal and Plant Health Inspection Service, a plant import permit is not required for the importation of bulbs. Imported bulbs must, however, be declared on your landing card and are subject to inspection at the point of entry. For purchases abroad, the usual caveats, concerning general appearance of the bulbs and freedom from insects and diseases, still apply. An additional consideration is that you are likely to pay top dollar for purchases in specialty gift shops, whose bulbs may not be any fresher than the ones you can buy at home.

Buying Unusual Bulbs
A variety of bulbs can make an exciting addition to the garden. Be adventuresome and take time to seek out some of the less well known ones. The cost is relatively small, and the rewards will be great.

Bulb Sources

Breck's
6523 N. Galena Road, Peoria, IL 61632

W. Atlee Burpee Company
Warminster, PA 18974

Chiltern Seeds
Bortree Stile, Ulverston, Cumbria LA12 7PB, England

Connell's
10216 40th Avenue East, Tacoma, WA 98446

Cooley's Gardens
P.O. Box 126, Silverton, OR 97381

DeGroot, Inc.
P.O. Box 575, Coloma, MI 49038

DeJaeger Bulbs, Inc.
188 Ashbury Street, South Hamilton, MA 01982

Dutch Gardens, Inc.
P.O. Box 400, Montvale, NJ 07645

Gladside Gardens
61 Main Street, Northfield, MA 01360

International Grower's Exchange
P.O. Box 52248, Livonia, MI 48152

J. W. Jung Seed Company
Randolph, WI 53956

Legg Dahlia Gardens
Hastings Road, Geneva, NY 14456

John D. Lyon, Inc.
143 Alewife Brook Parkway, Cambridge, MA 02140

Maver Rare Perennials
P.O. Box 18754, Seattle, WA 98118

Earl May Seed & Nursery Company
Shenandoah, IA 51603

McClure & Zimmerman
1422 West Thorndale, Chicago, IL 60660

Grant E. Mitsch Novelty Daffodils
P.O. Box 218, Hubbard, OR 97032

Nerine Nurseries
Welland, Worcestershire, WR13, 6LN, England

Oregon Bulb Farms
39391 S.E. Lusted Road, Sandy, OR 97055

Park Seed Company
Highway 254 N., Greenwood, SC 29647

Powell's Gardens
Route 2, Highway 70, Princeton, NC 27569

Quality Dutch Bulbs
52 Lake Drive, Hillsdale, NJ 07642

Rex Lilies
P.O. Box 774, Port Townsend, WA 98368

John Scheepers
63 Wall Street, New York, NY 10005

Schreiner's Irises
3624 Quinaby Road N.E., Salem, OR 97303

Strahm's Lilies
P.O. Box 2216, Harbor, OR 97415-0307

Thompson & Morgan
P.O. Box 1308, Jackson, NJ 08527

Van Bourgondien Bros.
P.O. Box A, 245 Farmingdale Road, Rte. 109, Babylon, NY 11702

Mary Mattison Van Schaik
Cavendish, VT 01542

Wayside Gardens
Hodges, SC 29695

White Flower Farm
Litchfield, CT 06759-0050

Gilbert H. Wild & Son, Inc.
Sarcoxie, MO 64862

Glossary

Achene
A small, dry, seedlike fruit with a thin wall that does not split open.

Acid soil
Soil with a pH value of less than 7.

Alkaline soil
Soil with a pH value of more than 7.

Alternate
Of leaves, arranged singly along a twig or shoot, and not in whorls or opposite pairs.

Annual
A plant whose entire life span, from sprouting to flowering and producing seeds, is encompassed in a single growing season. Annuals survive cold or dry seasons as dormant seeds. See also Biennial and Perennial.

Anther
The terminal part of a stamen, containing pollen in one or more pollen sacs.

Axil
The angle formed by a petiole and the stem from which it grows.

Axis
The central stalk of a compound leaf or flower cluster; also, the main stem of a plant.

Basal leaf
A leaf at the base of a stem.

Berry
A fleshy fruit containing one or more seeds, developed from a single ovary.

Biennial
A plant whose life span extends to two growing seasons; a biennial plant sprouts in the first growing season; in the second, it flowers, produces seeds or fruit, and dies. See also Annual and Perennial.

Bisexual flower
A flower with both stamens and pistils.

Blade
The broad, flat part of a leaf.

Glossary

Bract
A modified and often scalelike leaf, usually located at the base of a flower, a fruit, or a cluster of flowers or fruits.

Bristle
A stiff, short hair on a stem or leaf.

Bud
A young and undeveloped shoot, usually covered tightly with scales, that may develop into a leafy shoot or a flower.

Bulb
A short, vertical, underground stem, with a swollen portion consisting mostly of fleshy, food-storing leaf bases.

Bulbil
A small bulblike structure, usually borne among the flowers or in the axil of a leaf, never at ground level like a true bulb.

Bulblet
A small bulb produced at the periphery of a larger bulb.

Calyx
Collectively, the sepals of a flower.

Capsule
A dry fruit containing more than one cell, splitting along more than one groove.

Clasping
Surrounding or partly surrounding the stem, as in the base of the leaves of certain plants.

Claw
In certain plants, the narrowed basal portion of a petal.

Cleft leaf
A leaf divided at least halfway to the midrib.

Clone
A population of plants all originating by vegetative propagation from a single plant, and therefore genetically identical to it and to one another.

Compound leaf
A leaf made up of two or more leaflets.

Corm
A solid, vertical, underground stem, resembling a bulb, with a bud on top and often with a membranous coat of dried leaf bases.

Cormel
A small corm that is produced by and develops alongside of its parent corm. Also called a "cormlet."

Corolla
Collectively, the petals of a flower.

Corona
A crownlike structure borne at the center of the corolla of some flowers, such as daffodils.

Corymb
A flat-topped flower cluster with individual pedicels emerging at different points along the axis (rather than at the same point, as in an umbel), and blooming from the edges toward the center.

Crest
A ridge or appendage on petals, flower clusters, or leaves.

Cross-pollination
The transfer of pollen from the flower of one plant to the pistil of another plant.

Crown
The base of a plant stem, just above the roots and usually at soil level. In herbaceous perennials, overwintering buds are located in the crown.

Cultivar
An unvarying plant variety, maintained by vegetative propagation or by inbred seed.

Cutting
A piece of plant without roots; set in a rooting medium, a cutting develops roots and can then be potted as a new plant.

Cyme
A branching flower cluster that blooms from the center toward the edges, and in which the tip of the axis always bears a flower.

Dead-heading
The process of removing spent blooms.

Deciduous
Of leaves, falling off at the end of the growing season; not evergreen.

Disbudding
The pinching off of selected buds to benefit those left to grow.

Disk flower
The small tubular flowers in the central part of a floral head, as in most members of the Daisy family. Also called a disk floret.

Dissected leaf
A deeply cut leaf with clefts that do not reach the midrib; also called a divided leaf.

Division
Propagation of a plant by separating it into 2 or more pieces, each of which has at least 1 bud and some roots.

Double-flowered
Having more than the usual number of petals; these extra petals are usually arranged in extra rows.

Drooping
Pendant or hanging, as in the branches of a weeping willow.

Escape
An exotic plant that has spread from cultivation and grows successfully in the wild.

Evergreen
Retaining green leaves on one year's growth until after the new leaves for the subsequent year have been formed.

Eye
A bud on a cutting, tuber, or tuberous root.

Fall
One of the sepals of an iris flower, usually drooping.

Fertile
Capable of producing flowers with functional pistils and capable of sexual reproduction.

Filament
The threadlike lower portion of a stamen, bearing the anther.

Floret
One of many very small flowers in a dense flower cluster, especially in the flower heads of the Daisy family.

Follicle
A dry fruit with a single cavity.

Fruit
The mature, fully developed ovary of a flower, and anything that matures with it, usually one or more seeds.

Genus
A group of closely related species; plural, genera.

Germinate
To sprout (applied to seeds).

Glaucous
Covered with a waxy bloom or fine, pale powder that rubs off easily.

Herb
A plant that lacks a permanent, woody stem, and that usually dies back to ground level during cold weather. May be annual or perennial.

Herbaceous perennial
A plant that dies back to ground level each fall, and that sends out new shoots and flowers for several successive years.

Horticulture
The cultivation of plants for ornament or food.

Humus
Partly or wholly decomposed vegetable matter; an important constituent of garden soil.

Hybrid
The offspring of 2 parent plants that belong to different clones, species, subspecies, or genera.

Inferior ovary
An ovary located below the place where sepals, petals, and stamens are attached; in such cases, these appendages seem to grow from the top of the ovary.

Inflorescence
A flower cluster.

Invasive
Spreading aggressively from the original site of planting.

Irregular flower
A flower with petals that are not uniform in size or shape; such flowers are generally bilaterally symmetrical.

Keel
A ridge on the underside of the leaves or petals in certain plants.

Lanceolate
Shaped like a lance; several times longer than wide, pointed at the tip and broadest near the base.

Lateral bud
A bud borne in the axil of a leaf or branch, but not at the tip.

Leaf
A structure borne laterally on a stem, and having a bud in its axil.

Leaflet
One of the subdivisions of a compound leaf, resembling a leaf but not having a bud in its axil.

Leaf margin
The edge of a leaf.

Loam
A humus-rich soil containing up to 25 percent clay, up to 50 percent silt, and less than 50 percent sand.

Lobe
A segment of a cleft leaf or petal.

Lobed leaf
A leaf whose margin is shallowly divided.

Midrib
The mid-vein of a leaf or leaflet; the continuation of the petiole.

Mulch
A protective covering spread over the soil around the base of plants to retard evaporation, control temperature, or enrich the soil.

Multiple fruit
A fused cluster of several fruits, each one derived from a separate flower.

Naturalized
Having become established in the local flora. Also, of a planting, tended in such a way as to produce the appearance of spontaneous or "wild" growth.

Neck
A thin extension at the apex of some bulbs or tuberous roots.

Neutral soil
Soil that is neither acid nor alkaline, having a pH value of 7.

Node
The place on a stem where a leaf, bud, or branch is attached.

Offset
A short, lateral shoot, ending in an erect bud, and arising at or near the base of a plant; an offset readily produces new roots.

Opposite
Of leaves, arranged along a twig or shoot in pairs, with one on each side, and not alternate or in whorls.

Ovary
The swollen base of a pistil, within which seeds develop.

Ovate
Irregularly oval, with a broader end at the base.

Palmate
Having veins or leaflets arranged like the fingers on a hand, arising from a single point. See also Pinnate.

Panicle
An open flower cluster that blooms from bottom to top and never terminates in a flower; a branching raceme.

Peat moss
Partly decomposed sphagnum moss, with a high water retention capacity, used as a component of artificial soil mixtures, as a soil amendment, and sometimes as a mulch.

Pedicel
The stalk of an individual flower.

Perennial
A plant whose life span extends over several growing seasons and that produces seeds in several growing seasons, rather than only one. See also Annual and Biennial.

Glossary

Perianth
The calyx and corolla; also, any structure that surrounds the stamens and/or pistils of a flower.

Petal
One of a series of flower parts lying within the sepals and outside the stamens or pistils; often large and brightly colored.

Petiole
The stalk of a leaf.

pH
A symbol for the hydrogen ion content of soil, and thus a means of expressing the acidity or alkalinity of the soil.

Pinnate
Having leaflets arranged in 2 rows along an axis; pinnately compound.

Pistil
The female reproductive organ of a flower, consisting of an ovary, style, and stigma.

Pod
A dry, one-celled fruit, such as a bean or pea, that splits along 2 grooved lines and has thicker walls than a capsule.

Pollen
Minute grains containing the male germ cells and produced by the stamens.

Propagate
To produce new plants, either by vegetative means involving the rooting of pieces of a plant, or by sowing seeds.

Raceme
A long flower cluster with a central stalk bearing several smaller individual stalks, each of which produces a flower.

Ray flower
In the Daisy family, a flower at the edge of a flowerhead, usually bearing a conspicuous, straplike ray.

Regular flower
A flower with petals and sepals arranged evenly around the center, like the spokes of a wheel; always radially symmetrical.

Rhizomatous
Having rhizomes.

Rhizome
A horizontal stem at or just below the surface of the ground, distinguished from a true root by the presence of nodes, and often enlarged by food storage.

Rootstock
A rhizome.

Rosette
A crowded cluster of leaves; usually basal, circular, and at ground level.

Runner
A prostrate shoot, rooting at its nodes.

Scale
A small, modified leaf, usually covering a bud or at the base of a pedicel. In true bulbs, the scales are leaf bases, swollen with stored food.

Seed
A fertilized, ripened ovule, almost always covered with a protective coating and contained in a fruit.

Sepal
One of the outermost series of flower parts, arranged in a ring outside the petals, and usually green and leaflike.

Simple leaf
A leaf with an undivided blade; not compound or composed of leaflets.

Solitary
Borne single or alone; not in clusters.

Spathe
A bract or pair of bracts, often large, that encloses the flowers in certain plants, such as members of the Amaryllis family.

Species
A population of plants or animals whose members are potentially able to breed with each other, and which is reproductively isolated from other populations.

Glossary

Spike
An elongated flower cluster bearing individual flowers that lack stalks.

Spine
A strong, sharp, usually woody projection that takes the place of a leaf on a stem, and which has a bud in its axil.

Spur
A tubular elongation at the base of petals or sepals of certain flowers, usually containing nectar.

Stamen
The male reproductive organ of a flower, consisting of a filament and a pollen-containing anther.

Standard
An iris petal, usually erect. See also Fall.

Sterile
Lacking functional stamens or pistils, and therefore not capable of sexual reproduction.

Stipule
A small appendage, often leaflike, on either side of the base of some petioles.

Stolon
An unthickened rhizome.

Style
The elongated part of a pistil between the stigma and the ovary.

Subspecies
A naturally occurring geographical variant of a species.

Superior ovary
An ovary in the center of a flower, with the sepals, petals, and stamens attached near its base.

Tap root
The main, central vertical root of a plant.

Terminal bud
A bud borne at the tip of a stem or shoot, rather than in a leaf axil.

Terminal raceme
A raceme borne at the tip of the main stem of a plant.

Terminal spike
A spike borne at the tip of the main stem of a plant.

Throat
The opening between the bases of the corolla lobes of a flower, leading into the corolla tube.

Toothed
Having the margin shallowly divided into small, toothlike segments.

Tuber
A swollen, horizontal, mostly underground stem that bears buds and serves as a storage site for food.

Tuberous root
A swollen root used for food storage.

Two-lipped
Having 2 lips, like certain irregular flowers.

Umbel
A flower cluster in which the individual flower stalks grow from the same point, like the ribs of an umbrella.

Unisexual flower
A flower bearing either stamens or pistils, but not both.

Valve
One of the separable parts of the wall of a pod.

Variety
A population of plants that differ consistently from the typical form of the species, occurring naturally in a geographical area. The term is also applied, incorrectly but popularly, to forms produced in cultivation.

Vegetative propagation
Propagation by means other than seed.

Whorl
A group of 3 or more leaves or shoots that all emerge from a stem at a single node.

Wing
A thin, flat extension found at the margins of a seed or leafstalk or along the stem.

Photo Credits

Kenneth W. Lewis, Jr.
118A

Lee Lockwood
69B, 91A, 100A, 101A, 103B, 106B, 109B, 117A, 121A

Malak Photographs Ltd.
110A, 143A, 211A

Edward A. McRae/Oregon Bulb Farms
126A, 128B, 129B, 131A, 133B, 136A, 136B, 140B, 145A

Gary Mottau
56, 59A, 59B, 63A, 95A, 232B, 235B

Joy Spurr
78B, 92B, 113B, 114B, 133A, 156A, 159B, 162B, 177B, 190A, 191B, 193A, 221A, 222A, 225A, 247A, 269B

Alvin E. Staffan
124, 150A, 150B, 151B

Steven M. Still
104A, 112A, 115A, 120A, 152A, 157B, 158A, 159A, 163B, 185A, 205A, 214A, 215A, 235A, 236A, 242A, 243A, 247B, 252A, 267A

David M. Stone, PHOTO/NATS
178A, 188B, 190B

George Taloumis
62A, 66B, 72A, 74A, 81B, 82B, 83A, 90B, 91B, 94A, 94B, 95B, 98A, 98B, 102B, 106A, 119A, 123B, 146B, 187A, 218A

Thomas K. Todsen
139B, 169A, 184A

Herman V. Wall
126B, 129A, 132B, 134A, 142B, 149A

Index

*Numbers in boldface
type refer to pages on
which color plates
appear.*

Chanticleer Staff

Publisher: Paul Steiner
Editor-in-Chief: Gudrun Buettner
Managing Editor: Susan Costello
Series Editor: Mary Beth Brewer
Project Editor: Marian Appellof
Assistant Editors: David Allen,
Leslie Ann Marchal
Production: Helga Lose, Frank Grazioli,
Gina Stead
Art Director: Carol Nehring
Art Associate: Ayn Svoboda
Picture Library: Edward Douglas,
Dana Pomfret
Natural History Editor: John Farrand, Jr.
Drawings: Sarah Pletts, Dolores R.
Santoliquido, Alan D. Singer, Mary Jane
Spring
Zone Map: Paul Singer

Design: Massimo Vignelli